The Grandfather and the Globe

The Grandfather and the Globe

by
DELL B. WILSON

Vignettes by
Donald R. Baker

Banner Elk, N. C.

© LEES-MCRAE COLLEGE, INCORPORATED 1969
MANUFACTURED IN THE UNITED STATES OF AMERICA
HALLIDAY LITHOGRAPH CORP. HANOVER, MASS.
SECOND PRINTING 1970

For

Henry, John and Douglas

*who, like Lees-McRae College,
have always been "in the mountains,
of the mountains, for the mountains."*

THE military and historical facts in this book are as true as my research could make them. No change has been made in the name of persons and places that are our common historical heritage.

The main characters are fictional. Here is how it works: You may say "General Lee, retreating from Gettysburg, crossed the Potomac on July 14, 1863," and that is true. It is recorded history. But if you say "As General Lee retreated across the Potomac on July 14, 1863, he thought thus-&-so," and if such thoughts are not anywhere recorded, you are over into fiction. The main characters in this book, whose names are made up, do a lot of thinking and talking for which no documentation exists. They didn't even always do what *I* wanted them to do, but took to going off on their own, like up on that cliff. *I* don't cuss, but some of them do.

So while I hope they are in their own way true, they are made up—or they made themselves up—and any resemblance to persons living or dead is coincidental.

THE CHARACTERS IN THIS BOOK,
and they do their own talking, are:

PEOPLE IN THE VALLEY

Andrew Lewis and wife, Emily, prosperous descendants of pre-Revolutionary settlers in Globe valley.

James Lewis, their son, Co. F, 26th North Carolina Regiment, Confederate States' Volunteers.

Pendleton Lewis, James's younger brother.

Emeline Angel Lewis, their little sister, ("Angel" intended by her family as descriptive, not a surname as in Garvy's, below.)

Uncle Theophilus Lewis, Andrew's brother. Wife Saphronia.

Pinckney Lewis, their son, Pvt. 58th N. C. Regt. C.S.V. Younger brothers Jade and Billy. Pat Mast, a cousin.

Kiz Lewis, an elderly slave Negress. Her son Wak and wife Nan. Slaves Bob, Doll, &c.

Valley neighbors: Sgt. Henry Coffey, 45, staunch Baptist, one of the oldest men in Co. F, 26th Regiment, N.C.V.

Mason Byrd, bugler for the 26th Regt. N.C.V. nicknamed "Bugles." Member of strong Democratic family in Globe valley.

Sion Hicks, Co. F, 26th Regt. N.C.V.

ON THE FOOTHILLS IN BETWEEN

The Browns, iron makers at the Forge Flats, "Black Will," "Fog'" (for Fogerty) and Fog's son "Little Whang Brown," a school-teacher.

McCautherns, a law unto themselves, ambivalent politically and ethically.

PEOPLE ON THE MOUNTAIN

Four McKamie brothers: Enoch McKamie, the eldest, and wife Mary Garvy McKamie. Margaret, their daughter, about 15 when the story opens. Thomas, Jake and Bennie, young sons.
    Reuben McKamie, Baptist preacher, wife Nannie and three daughters.
    William McKamie, wife Chaney. Their son, Joel, is a private in the 22nd N. C. Regt. N.C.V. serving, when the story opens, on Acquia Creek, northern Virginia, guarding below the Potomac. Thad, a younger brother. 3 other sons.
    Martin McKamie. Wife, Harriett. Son Washington is also serving in 22nd Regt. Acquia Creek.

William Angel Garvy, son of Mary Garvy McKamie and stepson of Enoch. Nickname "Heath," or, diminutive, "Heese," though there's nothing diminutive about him.

Samantha Garvy, Heath's wife.

Their child Sam.

Neighbors on the mountain: McGillicuddy, unwilling recruit to 26th Regt. N.C.V. Woodall twins, "Thee" and "Dee," recruits. Laban Buckhannon, Army of Northern Virginia, and large family.

OTHERS

Sophia Lenoir Smead, girlhood friend and correspondent of Emily Lewis. She lives at "Fair Forks," Roane (later Loudon) County, Tennessee.

Nathan Gibbs, mailman. Route from Lenoir, N. C. *via* Globe P. O., the McKamie Gap and Shulls Mills, connecting with Abingdon, Va.

Daniel Ellis, Union pilot, Carter County, Tennessee. He was a very real person and this is his real name.

- Lt. Col. George W. Kirk, 3rd N. C. Mounted Infantry, U. S. Army. He was a real person and this is his correct name and title.
- Disaffected persons, stragglers, ex-prisoners and escapees over the Grandfather Mountain to East Tennessee and the Union lines.
- *Grandfather Mountain* is a person, too. His great bulk—noble forehead and acquiline nose—pillowed in the north 5964 feet high, runs more than 5 miles down through the beard flowing southwest. People for miles around look up at "the Grandfather" in the morning to see what the weather will be. If his old face is clear, all is well and they gather strength for the day. If a plume of cloud is over it, you can look out for wind and weather.

1862

JAMES LEWIS

Our orders are to bring the recruits off the mountains and down to the Head of the Rail Road by dark. We put them between us, Mr. Henry Coffey in front and me in the rear. Mr. Henry looks back every once in a while to see if everybody is following and as if he is daring Heath Garvy to step on his heels which seems likely owing to the steepness and Garvy's being six feet three and Mr. Henry about five feet four. Giant though Heath Garvy is, folks say he can melt into a rhododendron thicket and you'd not see nor hear him, anyway not today with the March wind roaring. If he did, there'd be nothing to do but shoot at him if you could, but most likely get shot first because of his aim with that old hog rifle of his.

The black-haired boy walking beside him has a long rifle too. His legs aren't as long as Heath's but he walks in step with his big brother, lithe, easy-like. I've seen him somewhere though I never heard of Heath's having a seventeen year old brother, only step-brothers, little fellers, born after his mother married Enoch McKamie, and Margaret is his step-sister. Heath has only his mother's maiden name, but old man Enoch took him in and raised him good and kind, the mother Mary being a fine person, too.

My folks never talk about the ins and outs of things like that but my cousin, Pinckney Lewis, told me all about it the day he told me a whole lot more things but told me not to tell where I learned or he'd cut my trot lines because Pinckney's mother, my Aunt Saphronia, is a member of the Globe Primitive Baptist Church and believes the body is the temple of the Holy Spirit. I know what any sixteen year old boy knows that's been raised on a farm, but there's gaps—Pinckney had gaps too—and for that I blame our folks but I guess they can't help it owing to the way they was raised, and that's the way things go back and back, the same as this war, 'til there's nothing left to blame but the past.

I wonder what Col. Burgwyn would think of this squad. It's good they don't know what he's got in store for them. Mr. Henry, who's been a school teacher and part time preacher, likes everybody to stay in line. Whenever he looks back the March wind whips his brown beard across his nose and he spits it away. I'd like to relieve Mr. Henry of the two Garvys' stepping on his heels, but after all I'm just a corporal, Company F, 26th North Carolina Regiment, and Mr. Henry's a sergeant and over twice my age. If he wants to go slower or faster all he's got to do is give the order. I believe he aims to get to the Forge Flats before he gives anybody time for even a drink of water.

My face burns due to being down at Fort Macon eight months away from mountain air and because yesterday was my week to shave. Margaret did not come with her folks to say goodbye at White Springs.

For a man that's avoided the war for nearly a year, Heath Garvy seems in a mighty hurry to get to it now. "Rake the thickets for 'em with a fine tooth comb," was Captain Rankin's orders to us. We didn't need to. Word had already got back in the mountains that a Conscription law is coming up, and they were there waiting for us at White Springs church.

Funny I never knew Garvy had a brother before, only Thomas and Jake and Margaret is his step-sister. There weren't two base born, I know, because Mrs. McKamie was ne'er that kind of a woman. But he said 'brother' when we were signing up the volunteers back at the church this morning.

"This is my brother Sam," Heath said, his shadow falling across the keg we were using for a table, shutting out the light the way a thunderhead comes over July sun. The black-haired boy wrote his name, then, good and plain,

"Sam Garvy, Age 17, height 5'6", weight 125 pounds."

Heath made his mark then under where his brother wrote—

« 4 »

age, 26, height 6'3", weight, 210 pounds. Then Heath laid the pen back on the keg.

"Him an' me," he said, pointing to his brother, "don't aim to be separated."

EMILY LEWIS

IN THE loom house on clear days I can tell time by the light. Mornings after the sun gets over the ridge, ripples from the creek play in the rafters. After mid-day, light from the rapids in Johns River keeps the shadows moving until about two o'clock when the top of the big poplar gets in the way. It's about two now, the time James said he'd be bringing the Watauga men down from the mountains to go to Kinston. God help us! A Civil War is the worst kind of war. Andrew says he would gladly give up all our thirteen slaves to keep our son at home. Fightin' a foreign country the way Jesse Lewis did the British in the Revolution is bad, but this kind of war gets down to the very roots of livin', sundering kindred, like the McKamie brothers split South from North right across the Blue Ridge, or the family of Sophia Smead, my old school friend in East Tennessee. I brought her letter out here to re-read where it's quiet and I can think.

Weaving jean cloth don't take much mind—four up, one down, four up, one down—and it takes a lot of jean cloth for a family of twenty souls, white and black. Our slave Nan can weave but after she stoked the fireplace I told her to go back to the kitchen and help Kiz fix food for the men when they come down the mountain. Servants don't understand when we sometimes need to do their tasks. Besides, work's all caught up and Wak says it's too wet to plant Irish potatoes. New knapsack and shirts we sewed for James, socks and soldier's candles we made are packed—so much less than he carried when he went in with Captain Rankin last May, but he says he's learnt to carry as little as he can.

Four up, draw the beater, one down. Weaving rests my mind.

My foot slides to the second treadle, worn smooth, cut from chestnut by our son's great grandfather when he brought his wife down from Fluvanna county, Virginia, in 1772, and cleared this valley under the Blue Ridge—cleared it from wilderness, from cane growing solid over the rich bottoms, from otters and beavers, wolves, panthers and snakes and all kinds of critters—from Indians—until one day Jesse Lewis came full circle with his clearing, stopped to look around, and named his valley The Globe.

This is the loom he built for his Virginia wife, Alley Hamilton. 'Tis said her parents opposed her marriage because the Lewises were poor, but Jesse and Alley eloped and started for Georgia. On the way, Reuben White who lived at the forks of Johns River and Mulberry, told them about this rich valley under the Grandfather mountain, so Jesse came, and bought two hundred acres of land from a hunter for one thousand dollars and went to work to clear it. He built this cabin that is the loom house now. It had a dirt floor then.

Rumors reached him now and then that the deed was no good, but he paid no attention since he'd paid an honest price. One day Governor Martin came with some men, talked with him about the title, said the deed wasn't any good and he'd have to pay for it all over again. So Jesse went to work anew. He put out a peach orchard and the earth gave so much fruit he had peaches to burn, so he started making peach brandy. It was good brandy and sold at a dollar a gallon. In a few years he made over a thousand gallons and paid again for his land.

Some of his wife's weaving drafts, patterns for coverlets, are hanging from the wooden peg here by the window, like little long narrow strips of music—"Rose in the Wilderness," and "Morning Star" that the folks back up in the mountains call "Muscadine Hulls." She used peach leaves the brandy came from to make her yellow dyes.

Wind huffs down the short little chimney, raises ashes, and I slide off the bench and set the old stained white plate straight on the indigo pot. Indigo is precious, is hauled all the way from Charleston and what will war do to that? We bank ashes around the smelly old blue pot at night to keep it milk warm for if it ever cools the blue will never be as fresh and clear again.

I go back to the loom and start the shuttle through but it catches in the shed space within the web because the heddle bars have warped. When I tell Andrew the heddle bars need replacing now, he looks at them, handles them, but never does anything about it. My people, the Bolichs, were Catawba county Dutch, and what they couldn't mend, they replaced with something better. From them I get my dumpy figure and light hair but not their knack to fix a hundred year old loom. The heddles are poplar because that was an easy wood to work with crude tools. Now we have better tools, but when I show Andrew how loose they are, he looks at them but I can tell his mind is going 'way back, the way the Scotch Irish do, thinking about his grandmother and how she spun a flax suit for her son and said "Now Jesse, take this suit and go back to Virginia and marry Hannah Stone. She's a smart girl and will make you a good wife," and that was Andrew's mother and she was a good wife. She saw patterns in everything, like the snowy day she looked out the front window and saw the cat hopping between ripples wind had made on snow under the cedars. She laughed, and later came to this loom and tramped out a pattern—the draft's there now on the peg with the rest—"Hannah Stone Lewis, her draft. Cat Tracks." And the coverlet is upstairs on James's bed, gray and white and a little madder red.

I get down and square the web on the heddles, then remember Sophia's letter in my apron pocket. I draw it out and go sit on the weaving bench near the window. As I open it, my thoughts fly across our Blue Ridge to her lovely valley of the Tennessee beyond the Iron mountains, the Great Smokes and the Unakas—you can see all of them, a high blue line in the east, from "Fair Forks," the Smead plantation in that spacious valley where the Little Tennessee runs into the Big Tennessee, warming the waters with Indian names—Oconoluftee, Cataloochee—and the Pidgeon and the French Broad, the Watauga, Holston and Nolechucky.

It is a valley like the Globe, granted to Gideon Smead in 1795 as payment for service at Kings Mountain—but so much bigger, wider and more beautiful than Globe I always stifle a twinge of envy when I visit Soph'.

I have to hold the letter to the light to make out the handwriting like fine engraving, written down the page, then across, checker-board fashion. Most people do it that way now to save paper:

> "Fair Forks"
> Loudon county, Tennessee
> March 16, 1862

My dear Emily,—

It is Sunday and I have to sit down and try to write you a few lines and see if it will have any influence on my nervous system. How often my thoughts travel across our beautiful mountains from our valley here to yours in the Globe where I have known so many happy times! I wish we lived nearer each other rather than writing letters but I am very thankful indeed we still have the privilege of writing! All our old customary laws are suspended and soldiers are permitted to rule and reign over this country. Our guard, a nice homesick boy from up on the Big Laurel, is going to Loudon Monday morning and will find a way to send this to you.

We are still dazed by the disastrous events which have happened in such a short time since the battle of Fort Donelson. Nashville is abandoned, we have a new capital since Governor Harris has moved the government to Memphis. A new military governor, Johnson, is trying to take over Tennessee. Mayor Cheatham refused to take the oath so Johnson put him in the pen, suppressed all newspapers—even our Methodist publishing house. All we know is by hearsay and wild rumor. One bright spot—old Brownlow has been sent beyond the Southern lines.

And now our dreadful news! My dear Abner, husband of my soul, is among the captured at Fort Donelson! One of the Paxton boys from over on Baker's Creek came to see us—he was among the forty or so infantry that escaped with Forrest. Last he heard of Abner's 26th regiment, he said, they had embarked down river for Cairo, Illinois. They had blankets and clothes, and were suffering from nothing worse than frost-bite and fury. They and one Mississippi regiment were holding a battery under Fort Donelson on the south bank of the Cumberland so the Army could retreat up river, so didn't know what was going on, and couldn't escape. All the time it was their *General*, Pillow, escaping and leaving everything up to Buckner who surrendered! Even the weather was against us. From a fair and mild afternoon February 13th, it turned off cold, rainy and near zero at night. Then while snow blanketed the poor wounded who had frozen during the night, the generals vacillated and passed commands from Floyd to Pillow to Buckner. Owen Paxton said one captain of the 30th Tennessee, called to headquarters and thus cut off from his men, cried when he heard how the little white flags went out from Dover on Sunday morning. Only Forrest stood up to 'em, defying defeat, swearing he would 'get out of this place or bust hell wide open!' Emily, my dear, pray for Abner's safety and return, as I shall pray you will never have to know the anxiety I've known these six months of his absence.

So far our bridge across the Tennessee at Loudon is not burned, and one company of Colonel R. B. Vance's North Carolina regiment is guarding it. The command is made up partly of Indians —imagine! But Nat says most of them have only old country rifles and shot guns. At least we're safe from robbers when we are near the pickets. We are baking some to keep them in a good humor and make a little money. Sometimes I wish I could get where I would not see any more brass buttons! I suppose I should be very thankful tho' that I am permitted to remain at home unmolested.

We still have food, but store goods are very high, calico 50 c and very poor, coffee soda pepper is a dollar and fifty cents a pound. Ladies hats quite common ones sell at twelve dollars and hoods at three.

The negroes are doing very well but I am afraid Dolph will become very dissatisfied, being married to Rosezetta, a freed slave. He asked Nat the other day the meaning of 'loyal citizen.'

If the slaves go my lot will be a hard one as Mother is not able to work and it would all devolve on me.

There is some disorder and violence as neighbors stage their own Civil War here. The execution of some of the bridge burners has had a happy effect—outwardly the country seems quieter, but it is filled with Union men who continue to talk sedition and are evidently only waiting for a safe opportunity to act out their rebellious sentiments. At the farm houses few men are to be seen and it is believed nearly the whole population not in the Army are lurking in the hills on account of dissatisfaction and fear. There is a regularly organized underground, and when darkness comes down over the mountains, guides with tread as soft as panthers lead Union sympathizers through steeps impassable except to those whose lives depend on the coolness, strength and daring of the moment. Their place of rendezvous is Camp Dick Robinson in Kentucky.

Between South and North we have the bushwhackers. They have just been around on their circuit again, tried to make old Mr. Wright Gaddy give them money. They reckoned, though, without old Mrs. Gaddy, she just dared them to touch a thing. She keeps an axe by her side and if anyone bothers her, she runs them with it.

Mr. Abel Klein is the bitterest man I ever saw. The military impressed his team and wagon, gave him only a certificate saying he will be paid therefor if his loyalty to the Confederacy justifies it. The Kleins are our only Jewish people around here, fine citizens who have kept to themselves and tried to run their store and not take sides.

Father is very wrestless and suffers from shortness of breath. Mother has another polypus on her face. We got Dilly Gooding to come stay with Mother and Father at night, but Dilly was called to go back in the hills to Duncans so she went - afraid if she didn't go Duncans would set the 'whackers on her. We had a hard time getting Dr. Washburn to come, so overworked. Since poor dear Agnes died he is the most lost widower I ever saw, and then somebody stole his instruments. He finally came and put the instruments in. Lizzie Fiske happened by at the same time—I do not know whether she came to see us or the Doctor! She had got herself a new riding habit and looked very tempting. You should hear how she softens up her Northern accent when she is around us! Jule Lenoir says Lizzie's accent is a kind of barometer of the political uncertainties of East Tennessee. She always wanted to marry a Southern man and now that her husband is so long missing escaping to Kankakee, she may just manage it.

It is getting late and I begin to feel lonely. All are in bed but me.

> 'O thou, my friend, as God might be my friend,
> Thou only hast not trampled on my tears.
> Life scarce can be so hard, 'mid many fears
> When mortal heart can find,
> Somewhere one healing touch, as my sick soul
> Finds thee!'

Do you remember how Miss Em' made us learn passages from Euripides? I can see the black hairs now bristling from that mole on her chin! O I do think of those happy school days, our recitations and recitals on Friday nights, our giggles, and Miss Em' exasperated and amused at the same time. And the lovely old house, Kirkwood! I ache when I see my children growing up in ignorance, especially Nat who is fourteen now and *our man* on the place. I don't know any school Nat could get into unless it would be Miss Luvenia Luttrell's at Sweetwater. Rachel Klein is going there, which might in-cline him to going!

Goodnight, my dear Emily, closer than sister to me!

> "A tremulous sigh, as a gentle night wind
> Through the forest leaves softly is creeping
> May stars up above with their glittering eyes
> Keep guard over you while sleeping."

Hm'mm. Soph' was our best pupil in language. Miss Em' lost patience with me, said 'twas a pity there were no lady brick layers.

I fold the thin tissue sheets back into the envelope, straighten my aching back and look out the window. Nobody coming down the road yet, just Wak and the children trying to put up a little kite of paper laced with sedge grass. Days are getting longer. The little kite is too frail for this March gale.

Dear Lord, take care of James! He is so worthy of every kind of love—his parents', that of a friend, of his brothers and sisters—of a girl—only he wont find any girl at the War, anyway not the kind of girl I want him to marry. 'A thousand shall fall at thy side, and ten thousand at thy right hand, but it shall not come nigh thee . . . neither shall any plague come nigh thy dwelling.' Maybe that's not the way to pray or think, but it's the way every woman does that has a son or husband or brother in this war—those up in the mountains, too. Andrew says loyalties are worse divided up there than here.

I take up the old applewood shuttle and send it through the web again—four up, one down. The heart is too full! To release it with a spoken word would be like floods plunging down Johns River! Something falls on my hand. I'm getting like the Scotch Irish—all full of faith, fears and tears! Four up, one down—like a heart beat. I never thought of it before, but the loom house is like a heart in the middle of this homestead, with time and old wars all mixed up in patterns like "Whig Rose" and "Downfall of Paris," tied up there on a peg and pinned with an old rusty pin. My foot goes back to the first treadle—four up, one down. Weaving rests my mind. It rests my heart.

McGILLICUDDY

A PRETTY kettle o' fish this is, to be sure—me trompin' down this mountain in a direction I don't keer to go, and a musket in my hand to shoot the Yankees.

There was a time when my paytritism ust to bile clean over, 'bout the time I fu'st sniffed the war. I thought I was the greatest paytryot out.

"Go, boys," I said, "my corn crib an' smoke house is open to yer fam'lies." An' I did throw 'em open an' kep' 'em open 'til them Sugar Grove boys was most outa sight.

The truth is me an' Betsy never once thought o' me havin' to do any fightin', myself. I thought if the scrimmage come thar' was plenty to do the fightin' without me. An' they is, sure.

I look down the line at who is here. Ther's that big Garvy—so much beef an' muscle orter alter the course o' the war. Havin' Heath Garvy in front will be better for me than a breas' work, an' I aim to stay right in back of him. Next, behind that brother o' his'n that I ain't heerd tell of before, come the Woodall twins, Thee and Dee, hardly dry behind the ears. They 'panted fer the fray,' as Zeb' Vance says, 'an' sniffed the curséd war while it was fur off.' Behind them is some fellers from over at Bull Scrape, two of 'em drovers, they said, or teamsters. They got in the wrong outfit with not a horse nearer us than five miles an' then not for us. Seems to me what we're gonna need is cobblers an' cooks.

I look at who's here an' then I think who *ain't*. I heerd of a feller over at the Tennesse line got off because he's got a plantation an' fifteen niggers. Another got off by payin'—I don't know eggzackly who—sixty dollars in gold. There's Fog' and Black Will Brown—we'll be down to their place at the Forge Flats in a little bit. The Confederates lets them alone because they're hammerin' iron for the Confederacy. The Union lets 'em alone because Black Will has give two 'wards' to the Union Army. Fog's son, called Little Whang Brown has got off so far because he's teachin' school down at Goldsburr, clost to where the war is. There must be a wheel in a wheel down there at Rawley, and a lot o' secret kernudlin'!

I got no fancy fer this kind o' thing an' I have a mighty hurtin' in my innards when I think about facin' the enemy an' standin' fire.

I can make as much corn as anybody. But you take a man out forty years old, short, inclined to be corpolant, ust to good eatin', wife in a delicate way—a bullet would go through me like a firkin o' lard!

I wonder if what they call local forces offen gets killed. That is the very las' thing I would like! You take those old Romans, now—the way they ust to fix ther'selves—they took some keer o' ther'selves. They had little breas' plates an' sheels—I seen 'em in a big Bible Reuben McKamie showed me. They had some chance if a bullet was to hit 'em.

In case I get kilt, I'll let Betsy know. "Dear Betsy, In case I get kilt I take my pen in hand to inform you we was chargin' the enemy an' a bullet went clean through me makin' a hole as big as a pa'tridge egg. Don't marry right away as I may get well. See them hogs don't waste that corn."

SERGENT HENRY COFFEY

You can get three steps to the beat an' the words keep goin' over an' over in my head,

> "The Lord ha-as promised good to me,
> His word my-y hope see-cures . . . !"

It keeps my mind off my achin' joints an' how Sarah is goin' to make out with nobody to help her but our deaf mute son now me an' Dan'l's both gone in the war. I hoped to save Dan'l by goin' in myself but now it's took us both an' bids fair to take ever' man in Burke county can stand up an' hold a gun.

I'll let 'em stop at the Forge Flats an' get a drink o' water but disarm 'em first, an' keep 'em away from Fog an' Black Will Brown's methiglen for if there's any drinkin' there's sure to be a fight an' since Manassas I got no fancy for private skirmishes.

To this big stallion, Heath Garvy, that's been avalanchin' down on me ever since we left White Springs, fightin' comes like breathin'. His name's not Heath but William Angel Garvy, but soon as he could walk he started fightin', an' folks up in the mountains call him Heath for Heath Adkins, a scrapper from over at Burnsville. Most people think it's his real name.

It's told that a fighter from Madison county, wantin' to test his stren'th as a wrestler, came to Garvy's place on the Grandfather mountain, laid in the shade an' watched Garvy cut trees 'til sundown, then made his business known. Without restin' or eatin', Garvy hitched up his pants an' threw the Madison feller as often as he wished to try conclusions.

God forgive me for leadin' these young men into this war! There's worse things than bein' deaf like Stevie. At least Stevie wont never have to hear horses screamin', an' men. Though the voiceless sometimes says most. It was a long time before Stevie could bear to see us kill a chicken.

Leavin' out the methiglen the Browns make, we got tinder still for a fracas. The Browns have never been exactly peace lovin'. My Pa told me their comin' on Anthony's Creek in the first place was due to a fight that started after a night feast and frolic. Pa was a young man over in Crab Orchard, Tennessee, and it happened after a log-rollin' when Ward Brown tried to take a new flax shirt an' trousers off Wright Moreland and hurt him up some, rousin' his anger an' causin' him to take out a warrant against 'em. They escaped here with a Creek Indian named Duffield that Ward had brought back from the battle of Horseshoe Bend, an' they all supported themselves diggin' sang. While they was searchin' for yarbs, they happened to come on this ledge of iron ore in the steep face of the clift here just above Anthony's Creek falls. They know'd right off what it was, havin' worked at a forge near Butler, Tennessee. So they built a forge with water trompe, furnace, goose nest, hammer an' all, an' after they'd worked an' made about three thousand pounds of iron, they put in for a grant from the state for three hundred acres of land an' got it.

But they reckoned without John Porter, land agent for the Masons and Pinckneys down in the low country, that was always on the look-out for squatters an' trespassers on what they claimed, though the Browns said the land was theirs under a older or Cathcart Grant 'way back time of the Revolution. That's the way things is split from 'way back. Rich folks with connections at

Raleigh an' ust to havin' everything their own way an' clever lawyers come in an' took over land and improvements the first old settlers give their life's blood to build. Same as Fort Donelson itself that Grant's just took with fourteen thousand Southern soldiers.

There's times when a man has a song in his head but doubts the words.

Trouble goes forward, too, because sooner or later Fog' and Black Will Brown will haf' to make their minds up whether to go with the Confederacy an' folks down in the valley, or go back to Tennessee where they come from an' join Grant. We have orders to let 'em alone because they're makin' guns for the Confederacy. Black Will has give two wards to the Union Army but both of 'em's grandsons of Creek Indians.

Hup—two—three! Hup—two—

> "Through ma-a-nee dangers, toils an' snares
> I ha-a-ve all read-ee come—!
> 'Tis gra-aa-ce ha-as brought me sa-afe thus far,
> And gra-ace sha-hall lead me home!"

We come out at the Old House Place—a big clearin'. The Garvys has slowed down some behind me, an' for a little bit the wind lays an' grass an' sweet fern mutes the scuff-scuff of men's boots an' the squinch of straps on packs. I look back an' both the Garvy's has their heads turned, lookin' back at Grandfather mountain. It's the last meadow where you can look up at that rugged old face turned up ag'inst the sky before you go into the woods an' skirt down the ore cliffs above Anthony's Creek falls.

MARY GARVY McKAMIE

I draw the quilt over the child's chest.

"He's sleeping now."

"The fust he's had in three days."

"Leave the quilt loose."

A gust of wind blowing down from the Grandfather loosens one of the cross planks on the roof and a stone holding it rolls down and lands with a thud outside the shuttered window. One of the older girls in the rocking chair coughs an' the cat jumps out of her lap onto the floor, struts sideways when it lands nearly on the nose of the old dog under the foot of the bed.

I touch the little boy's fair hair. "He'll likely sweat. His cheeks are less flushed than when I came." He is a big little boy for four years. Reminds me of the way mine was.

"I'd be pleased to have you stay the night," Serena says.

"Are you a-fear'd?" Laban has been away for seven months guardin' the Potomac river and some strange-named creek Serena can't call.

"No, I'm not a-fear'd of no real thing—no wolf ner wild cat. Brownie wouldn' let no thing like that git us." She waves a hand toward the dog's nose and paws under the bed. His tail thumps twice against the floor.

"I'll have to be goin'." Serena knows I have Enoch and the young 'uns to care for down in the Gap. "That turpentine, vinegar an' brown sugar hardens as it cools. You break it off an' give it to Matterson like liquorice."

The whole family except the sick one goes to the door with me. The path, beaten between dead cornstalks on one side and froze collard patch on the other like little yeller hats melted on the ground, leads down to the fence where my young mule has tangled his knee in the halter rope. Shadrack is mean, not broke to the side saddle yet.

Before I reach the woods I look back at the little family huddled in the cabin doorway. The cat has come out too, an' the dog—him that is to keep the real critters away.

Serena hollers "You tell Samantha if she wants Grantum to come over an' stay ag'in Heese leaves, I'll send him."

Serena and her young 'uns look for all the world like a nest o' little foxes there with the forest risin' up around them. I wave goodbye. I say no more to Serena about Heese's plans. Enoch says the least you tell people these times the better.

Soon as I turn Shadrack on the trail t'ords home, he starts trottin'. Strange how animals feels directions yet people get so lost. The sun is pale above the Grandfather's nose. Must be about four o'clock. The men should be down to the Globe by now.

Three nights ago Heese come to our house to tell us he was goin' to war. His step-father jest set there quiet. Ever'thing has been said a hundred times over by now—how it don't look like a short war any more; how a man the right age that's not on one side or t'other is thought worse than a deserter; how this conscript act is a-comin', yet even them that formed it is divided about it, the State thinkin' one way an' the Confedrit gover'ment another. How a man in the war nearly a year like Laban Buckhannon can't get to come home even if his wife an' children might starve. These things have been said over an' over on county court days, muster days—threshed out in homes like ours or Enoch's brothers' that's both sent their two eldest sons to the Confedrit army.

There's the older things, too, that's been goin' 'round a long time—how slavery is a great cuss, never profitable in the mountains except maybe for sale, but nobody up here would want them even so. Some have seen how it works—teamsters that have driv' cattle an' hogs to South Car'lina say it makes the rich people who own niggers passionate and proud an' ugly, an' it makes the poor white people mean. People that own niggers are always mad at them about something—half their time spent swearing an' yelling at them. Yet most folks up here think that if a man *has* slaves already an' takes them to Nabrasky or Californ'y, he'd ought to have a right to keep 'em if they're his property. That's one thing really works on folks' minds up here in the mountains because most of 'em has ancestors sleepin' on the hills like the McCurry's an' McKamie's that's already fought one time in the Revolution for folks' right to own what they can make honest, an' to think an' vote free, an' let every other man do the same.

So the other evenin' the men didn't talk much. It was more like the time my boy, William Angel Garvy, first come under Enoch's roof, ten years old, an' so wantin' to have a father 'twas like he was par'lyzed with the chance. He'd seen how it was—he seen families together when I'd take him to church—a big thin daddy sittin' in front of him with a baby hangin' slobberin' over his shoulder, stupid content. Children just *knows* things like that. The Lord meant it to be that way an' it's all wrote down in Genesis—"In the beginning—"

Boys had throwed it up to Heath, too, that he didn' have a daddy. Children can be cruel. And at mill. Good men an' bad goes to mill. At nine Heath carried corn.

"Where's your daddy?"

Enoch was there. Long afterwards he told me how the big little boy stood there diggin' his toe into a hole rats had gnawed, the sun slantin' dusty through the mill door across his tow hair. Later Enoch found the child out back of the mill sparrin' at the mill wheel, both hands clinched, fightin' the roll an' splash of the mill wheel. It was a year after that, after I'd nursed Enoch's mother through her last illness, that Enoch asked me to marry him, a bachelor at thirty one, the way it's figured around here. And not in all these sixteen years has he ever asked me who it was or how it was that Heath came, though I wanted to tell him and many could tell him an' no doubt tried. But that's Enoch's way. When he's made up his mind about somep'n it's made up an' you don't talk to him no more about it. Like his conversion. Like his faith in the Union.

So the other evenin' him an' Heese just set there. Margaret had gone to bed, she's taken to stayin' in the loft now she's sixteen—fixed it up for herself with Enoch's mother's old coverlids an' a chist made out of an old box. The boys was asleep too, owin'

« 19 »

to its bein' a rainy night an' them just tuckered out the way little fellers gets from bein' shut in.

Heese comes in, beatin' the rain outa his hat, fillin' the room with his bulk, pulls up a chair to the fire. Him an' his step-father set there smokin' 'til Enoch asked how it was with Samantha. He's asked it off an' on for six years expectin' to hear man to man he's goin' to have a grand-child or maybe to keep 'em in mind of it. Heese just answers they've not decided yet whether she'll stay up at their place or go back to her folks in Mitchell county. Samantha ain't a-fear'd o' nothin', he says, nothin' but loneliness an' *cats*. One o' the Buckhannons can come stay with her.

"I guess you don't know when you'll be goin'."

"Any time now, just whenever that recruitin' squad comes up from Globe."

Heese smokes on a while, then says "One o' the McCurry boys come to Estes's mill last Saturday. He's been down at some island on the seacoast, half a hill an' half a swamp, called Roenoke."

"Is he the McCurry boy got burnt an' scarred in the still-mash when he was little?"

"No! Neil ain't scarred nowhere. He's one han'some buck."

"Go on."

"Neil said the Unions come up from behind an' fit a battle down there. He said about a thousand Confedrit prisoners was took in the least fightin' he ever heerd of. Neil was *in* it. He'd seed it drawed on a map, an' he drawed it for us in some meal that had run out on the mill floor. It was real plain. This Roenoke Island, he said, is shaped like a grievin' woman with her back turned to the sea. The rebels' main guns would be on her shoulders, high ground. Her skirt is swamp. In between is the waist—" Heese puts his big fingers together in a kinda circle, "just a little bitty waist like this. Jes' three little guns guardin' the belt—that's all they was! All the other guns was fixed an' pintin' the other way. Unions come up from below. From the skirt." Heese snaps his fingers an' draps his hands. "Neil told it plain an' drawed it all off in the meal. He said it's like we would dig in on the Grandfather to shoot t'ords East Tennessee, then the Unions come up from the Globe."

Heath's pipe is gone out. He gets up, lights it ag'in with a scrap of bark.

"Neil says the next comp'ny from around here will go to Roenoke to keep the Unions from cuttin' the railroad."

"When's Neil goin' back?"

"He ain't goin' back! He's paroled. The Unions had more pris'ners than they know'd what to do with. First they took all their muskets away from 'em—those that the fellers hadn' already buried. An' all their dirks an' meat cleavers an' things they had to fight with. Neil said his was the worst armed regiment in the war, he knowed. The State hadn' no more arms to give 'em, an' the Confedrit gover'ment was'n givin' any more to twelve months regiments. They had a few ole made-over flint-locks the gov'ner of Virginny had sent 'em 'cause the Virginians wouldn' have no sich thing—old muskets that wouldn' knock a pin open.

"While the muskets was bein' collected to put 'em in the quartermaster's buildin', one gun went off an' hit a Union so'jer right in the arm. Neil said it musta been his Gram-paw McCurry shootin' from Kings Mountain."

Enoch spits in the fire. "Jonas McCurry wouldna been shootin' at the Union. How does it go about this parole?"

"It's somethin' you sign," Neil says, "not to take up arms ag'inst the Union ag'in unless exchanged. Neil said a guard was put over 'em at first, but in a day or two they was around amongst the rest, wrestlin', playin' leap frog an' boxin' same as if they was all on the same side. All but the Virginny so'jers. A bunch they called the Richmond Blues in fine uniforms. They talked hard of the North an' said they would go right back to fightin' as soon as exchanged.

"Neil said he'd been led to think all Northerners was cutthroats an' robbers that would treat pris'ners bad, but Neil's comp'ny was better used than before they was taken. They et the same fare the Unions did, weather was nice an' warm down there an' he was real content."

"Fine'ly the pris'ners was marched to some boats to go to Elizabeth City to get paroled. It tuk the Unions so long, though, to match names to papers, an' with the wounded an' all, some men from around here just wasn't there by the time their names was called. They found a shorter way to git home."

Heese goes over an' pokes the fire a bit, but you can tell his mind ain't on that.

"I figger" he says, "the lines must be close together down there where Neil was. Clost as any place." He comes back, takes up his hat, rubs it off. "It ortent to be hard to git over on the Union side down there."

Enoch looks through his pipe smoke at the shower o' sparks Heese raised pokin' in the embers.

"Would that be desertin'?"

"Nope. Just choosin' the side you'd want to be on." Heese has picked up his gun and walked to the door.

"You haf' to take some kind of a oath, don't you?"

"If you do, I'll take it like one I hear'd of in East Tennessee—from the teeth out. I never got a chance to vote for this war, one way or t'other."

With that he puts on his hat an' goes out into the dark. My heart goes after him.

Shadrack has kep' up his pace 'til we're over to Heese's place. It's such a pretty walk down to the house even on a plaguey March evenin' like this, I always get off an' lead the mule down to the cabin. I hear'd a lady say when I was waitin' on table over at Burnsville that summer, that mountain folks don't appreciate scenery.

"They just take it for granted."

Well, they do an' they don't. It's one thing to scratch a livin' in the mountains an' another to board here a while in summer. It's one thing to scramble an' squeal up a little foothill an' you in long white muslin skirts, an' look off a rock to where you've come from, an' get back for dinner all melted down an' totin' a bunch o' wilted flowers. It's another to ride a mule through a big forest roarin' with wind an' water with sap risin' like today, an' come out top of a clearin' with the whole blue world throwed out under you like a rollin' ocean.

You can see the Globe plain from here—one thing that I think's worked on Heese through the years—those rich farms laid in like carpets amongst the foothills. I strain my eyes thinkin' I might see Heese an' the others marchin' down the valley, an' I could if I had some spy glasses like Mr. Gray that come that time. But it's growin' dark, must be gettin' on t'ords six o'clock.

Wind has laid the way west wind does about dusk, an' it's quiet, not even a cow bell or dog barkin' an' that's what, all at once, I wonder about. Heese's place has always been lively since first he cut down those big chestnuts an' hemlocks with Samantha helpin' him—her that would allers rather work outdoors than in—an' poplars so tall seem like they fell half-way down Rough Ridge. Most folks girdle their trees, cut a ring around 'em an' wait for winter to bring 'em down. Heese an' Samantha is not ones, though, to wait for a deadenin'. Always somep'n goin' on —hog killin's or bear hunts or sugarin' or burnin' off new ground. Sometimes a play party if nothin' else. Or just a dog fight. Now I don't see one o' those old deep-mouthed Plott hounds anywhere about.

I lower the fence bars, pull Shadrack through an' go on down past the wood-pile, all the time studyin' the house chimney for a shimmer o' heat. It's kind of late in the day for a peep day. A peep day is when you're out of everything to eat except corn meal, hoe-cake or a few roasted potatoes, an' if so, everybody lies low an' keeps dark to make 'em think there's no one at home. Only there's never been any children here to play it.

All at once the mule gives a lunge. I stop still, havin' learnt that steed often has more sense than rider an' you better give him the benefit o' the doubt lest you get snake bit or crack your leg in a boomer's warren blowed full of leaves.

So I pause, wroppin' the bride tighter about my hand. Heese has left some old fence rails lyin' like bleached bones across the choppin' block. I yell.

"Samantha!"

From behind me, the Grandfather echoes back "Samantha!" an' the Globe trills away fainter "Samantha! Samantha! Samantha!" There is no human answer.

I look down to see what the mule is sniffin' an' snortin' t'ords —a dark curvy line layin' under the whitened rails. Though I never seen a snake on the Grandfather before April, I pick up a stick o' wood, take a step forward an' fling it at the curvesome dark shadow. Nothin' moves but Shadrack rarin' back on the lines. I calm him down, then reach my hand down cautious. Then *I* jump, for it's hair! woman's soft human hair, cold but alive, risin' like cobweb over my hand! Every old ghost tale, every old wilderness story, every Indian tale told to scare young 'uns around a red winter hearth is in the touch.

Then I say to myself, Mary McKamie, you're too late for Indians, you're a woman forty-three, a nurse an' mid-wife that's saw lots of accidents an' sufferin', an' more yet to see. I take a fresh hitch in Shadrack's bridle, reach back an' pat his old rock-like face, then lean down an' gather up that soft dark curvesome stuff, long as my arm, taperin' an' loose at one end but at the other whacked off short as on a choppin' block. I straighten up an' stand holdin' it, drawin' out a few strands to wrop the thick end like a switch. It's Samantha's hair, all right. I look down at the dusky cabin and at Globe Valley beginnin' to darken to the color of indigo.

Usually when I'm in a predicament I'm with somebody, births an' deaths bein' hardly ever solitary affairs, but now I'm alone unless you'd count Shadrack. His mind, I can tell, is already made up to stay at the woodpile.

There's no sound as I walk down to the house, no moo nor breathin' from the cow stall, no cheepin' from the cedars—just the babble of Haw Branch before it slips under the spring house, same sound it's been makin' for a thousand years goin' down from Grandfather to Globe. Not a dog barks. Samantha wont have a cat around, havin' an unreasonable fear of 'em ever since one was throwed at her when she was a child, though she ain't atall afear'd of mice or bats like most women, or even of the very devil himself. Cats are just the one thing she can't stand.

I pause on the rock door-step, pull the string that lifts the latch inside. The door swings in easy—it's more ust to bein' open than closed.

Since Heese an' Samantha always keep things handy for leavin', it don't take me long to size up the room. Bed's about the way she makes it, most o' their clo'es are hangin' on the wall pegs. Guns are gone from over the fireplace leavin' the deer antlers empty an' starin' at me as questionin' as if on a deer. Strange how a empty house holds its secrets.

Ashes are banked in the fireplace but cold, cook pots swung out and clean. Mantel is empty except for the candle slut, him an' her not bein' much for havin' medicines about since they're never sick, an' there's a branch o' spice wood she uses for snuff sticks. The snuff box is there, though his razor's gone. I'd 'bout as soon expect Samantha to go off without her drawers as her snuff, but that appears to be what she did. They musta left in a hurry.

It's gittin' dark an' I've got to go. At least there's no blood on the floor. Almost without thinkin' I pick up the hand broom an' from habit, brush back ashes that's blowed out in the room. From the floor puncheons I raise somethin' that sweeps into a little dark cloud on the hearth—more hair! When I rub it between my fingers, it's fine an' even like a man's hair, but Heese's hair is fair.

All at once I want to git home. It'll take more minds an' ears than mine to put together what's happened here, an' when I've been two days away from Enoch I'm not more'n half whole anyway. I stand the broom up, go back to the door an' draw it shut behind me, climb back up the hill where Shadrack is still splutterin', tossing' his head up an' down, impatient to git home. I pick up the hair switch an' fold it into my saddle bag before I mount. We clamber an' thump back onto the trail. Three miles to go before I see chinks of light from our home in the Gap.

JAMES LEWIS

So I have to carry their secret.

It was after the Forge Flats fracas that wont ever be in any hist'ry but started when Heath Garvy jumped across the gap in the Brown's cantilever bridge over Anthony's Creek gorge without waitin' for Fog' to lay in his middle plank. The gorge is deep there between cliffs where Browns have weighted down two long split footlogs that don't meet in the middle. Fog calls it his cantilever bridge because he says he can't leave 'er in place, which shows how Fog is, kind of wordy an' clever but foolish, too. For years now they've charged for layin' in that middle plank an' folks pay a few cents rather than go a quarter mile down below the falls, 'specially as Browns usually regard it as a social affair an' throw in a little drink of the methiglen they make out of honey-comb. In a country where cash is hard to come by, they've made a good little thing of it an' Fog an' Black Will are real proud of it.

So when we get down to Forge Flats, we see Black Will standin' on the far side of the bluff that's drippin' with big icicles, an' Fog an' one o' those Creek Indians are on the near side with the bridge plank.

Garvy has been fuming anyway since Sergeant Coffey took their guns away, and more so when he tells everybody there'll be nothin' drunk stronger than water. Heath Garvy squints up his eyes calculatin' the distance between the log ends stickin' out over the gorge, draws back, takes three long kind of springy-like paces an' sails over the chasm true as a bank swallow to the other side. As we take in what has happened, the other Garvy steps out kind of gingerly but determined, takes his bearings and makes his own leap to the far log, hangs teetering a second flailing his arms, then see-saws on over to the opposite bank.

It's not *what* they did so much as the way they did it. Like it was planned beforehand. Or maybe it's just these times when feelin's run high about everything.

Wind is roaring down the glen through the hemlocks above brawling water but nobody needs ears to tell him a fight is making up under the bluff.

Fog throws his hands in the air an' turns to the rest of us while the Indian fellow slides quiet onto the first log, puts the board in place, then pads to the far side as Black Will lays a blow to Garvy's head and gets his arm and chin knocked out of kilter. Will Brown is a big man himself, 'tis said he is seldom seen without a whittling knife in his hand, and to see him dazed and staggering is quite a sight.

The younger Garvy pauses a minute to size things up as the Indian comes off the footlog—then my view is shut off by our squad of recruits double-timing across the logs. But Sergeant Coffey takes his post at the end of the log, ready for them. Maybe it wasn't done exactly the way Colonel Burgwyn or Captain Rankin would have done it, but the same war that raises people's ire gives the righteous spirit when they need it like Mr. Henry said Bee, Bartow and Evans did behind the Robinson house when they first named "Stonewall" Jackson. Mr. Henry is not any Jackson, but with the butt end of his rifle he puts up a mighty correction that touches somethin' trainable in that mob an' gives me time to get across an' keep 'em down the trail.

"Right—face! Forward—*march!*"

Mr. Henry turns and lays into Garvy who is now in a tussle with the Indian while the younger brother gets hold of Black Will's hair and starts kickin' him from behind.

Then the younger Garvy ducks an' staggers back against the cliff and I see he has snagged his arm pretty bad some way. By then Mr. Henry has got his gun barrel between the Browns and Garvys, dividing 'em, and about as soon as it started the fight peters out except for everybody heavin' an' glowerin' at each other.

I see the Garvy boy tryin' to stanch blood on his wrist so I go over where he's standin' with his back against the cliff where three foot icicles are drippin' down. He's taller than I am but when I come toward him he kind of jerks back, measuring me with eyes cold an' gray-green as the cliff behind him.

I take out a little roll of flax cloth Aunt Kiz put in my pocket yesterday along with a hunk of gingerbread, "'cause dey might be warrin' on de mountain." I offer to bandage his arm but Heath Garvy steps over an' shoulders me away. You can still smell ginger on the bandage. The boy is clean shaven but has little smudges of dark down on his upper lip and between his frowning eyebrows. While I'm trying to think where I've seen him, Heath Garvy takes my roll of lint, breaks off the end of one of the icicles and cleans the bloody cut, slowly stanching the blood before he wraps it.

Sergeant Coffey has got the rest of the squad down the trail and now he comes panting back and slaps some coins in Black Will's hand as if this ends forever the matter of cantilever bridges so far as the Confederacy is concerned.

Like a flash it comes to me where I've seen someone like this Sam Garvy, and as Mr. Henry passes back by me I say as much to myself as to him.

"This recruit looks so much like Heath Garvy's wife."

Neither of the Garvys lets on but you can tell something moves inside of the two of them the way you know a trout shoots deep in a pool without your quite seeing it or maybe you think you've seen it after somebody tells you it's there.

We start on down the trail by Anthony's Creek. Walking with a stream makes walking easier. Not in it, though—not this one. I've fished down Anthony's and it's like sliding down roofs—rock roofs! The Garvys hang back in the rear now right in front of me. Except for a mumbled word or two between 'em that's lost in the roar and hiss of water, they keep up with the others. Yet it's like their backs need to say something to me. First time we come to a break in the trees I squint up at the sun, figure we still have the five hours we need to get to Head of the Road where the railroad begins below Morganton. Sun looks pale the way it does when it might blow snow.

I trip over Sam Garvy who's stopped to draw the sock up out of his boot. A hand jerks me by the elbow and 'most flips me against bushes the way an ox takes up slack on a log chain. Heath Garvy stands over me.

"What you said back there—this feller looks so much like my wife. Family resemblances ain't no business of yours. But we're gonna tell you somethin' an' if you give it away we'll set your whole damn Globe afire!"

The boy Sam has risen from pulling up his sock and I'm sandwiched in between 'em. I know Sergeant Coffey will be right back if there's any stragglin'. I just nod. I've never minded bullies anyway.

"Speak out!" Garvy's eyes are like blue milk in a face that's lived more days under sky than roof. The odd-familiar boy presses against me with his elbow.

"I'll hold your secret," I say more curious than anything else.

"This is my wife Samantha. We're a-goin' to the war together. Don't you tell *no*body! If she cain't go, I ain't a-goin' either!"

"All right. I wont!" We can't afford to lose a man of this squad just one of 'em's being a woman.

For a split second longer they stand looking at me, then hitch up their shoulder rolls an' turn down the path.

I say "I just hope Sam will pass the medical inspection down at Morganton."

We head on down by the big rock.

MARGARET McKAMIE

M<small>A</small> <small>TAUGHT</small> me a charm to use against times I get hurt or disappointed or have to do hard things I don't want to do.

"Rub your nose in it," she says. "Meet it half way! Be as hard as it is! And don't be afraid!"

So when I couldn't go to White Springs this mornin' to see the men go off on account Ma had to go to Buckhannons when Matterson got fever, I played like the very thing I craved was to fly in an' milk an' churn an' feed the stock Heese brought over yesterday, an' his old Plott hounds. It was soon after Ma left Heese came bringin' his cow an' ox, an' him an' Pa stood out back o' the barn an' talked an' I listened from Beulah's stall. First came the wind sayin' "Don't listen! Sh-hh-hh! Don't listen!" Ma has taught us to be straight out with whatever we do.

That was the first I knew my step-brother was leavin' at last for the war, an' that Samantha was goin' with him. That surprised me an' yet it didn't, she havin' always had more men's ways, and no young'uns up there to take care of. Ma says each plant to its own soil, an' nobody thinks hard that her an' Heese thrives best up on the mountainside st'id o' down here in the Gap with us. It's always easier for me when there's a little space between me an' my step-brother, but I hate to see Ma look worried when Samantha goes off fishin' an' huntin' with Heese an' fellers an' no green food on the place, nor weavin' done.

Heese an' Pa penned up the Plott hounds lest they foller him an' her plum to the war, an' because Queenie, our old dog, is opposed to their bein' here in the first place an' hasn't let 'em come nigh the house.

"I brought you what salt we had." Heese says to Pa "It ain't much. Three pounds."

"We'll make out."

"Neil McCurry is comin' to lend you a hand with the potato plantin'."

"It might not be wise. There is some around here is forcin' outlyers."

"You mean your brothers?"

"I ain't got time for dissensions, argyments an' plots."

"Don't let 'em reproach you."

"Seems like they put the new gover'ment ahead of ever'thing else. I'm not a learnéd man but I just don't b'lieve George Washin'ton would a-fit just for South Car'lina or Virginny."

"Hold onto your gun. A better day will come."

I hear the Plott hounds yelpin' to get out, an' Heese nailin' on one last rail. "That's orter hold 'em."

Then there was just the wind sighin' through the stable logs, "Don't listen. Sh-hh-hh!" Or maybe it's more that a woman has no call to overhear when two men is bein' parted, split down the middle, though I'm more blood kin to Pa than Heese is an' Heese hasn't ever forgot that since we were both big enough to size each other up.

All at once I wisht I was the one goin' to the war instead of Samantha. Much as I hate fightin', it seems like Jackaroe in the song,

> "She went down to the tailor's shop
> An' dressed all in men's gray
> An' labored for the captain
> To bear her far away!"

All at once it seemed to me it would be the wonderfulest thing in the world to see James Lewis again an' march along same as we did last Easter but with real drums instead of just a woodpecker, an' with all the flags flyin' an' music, instead o' bein' a girl back up here in a mountain gap, not even gettin' to go to White Springs to see the fellers go down nor him that came to fetch 'em. Even Thomas an' Jake went but I have to stay with Bennie not five years old, an' Queenie to keep her from lightin' into the Plott hounds.

So I use my charm.

"Make up a song about it when you get hurt," Ma says. "Prettify your pain. It may ease it."

So while I fly around sweepin an' sandin' off the table that she keeps as smooth as a plate, I make up my song,

> "O tell me, O tell me
>   my father so true
> Did you see a so'jer
>   with true eyes of blue?"

« 31 »

> "Your so'jer came searchin'
>   my daughter so dear
> Among all the faces
>   but yours was not there."

It's not as good as Billy Mahone and some others that Ma sings to us at night, but I'm s'prised it makes up so easy. I start to forget my troubles but a song's not half done 'til it finds a hearer. Thomas n' Jake always run for the barn when I start to sing, but Bennie don't. He's layin' on the skin rug with Queenie in front of the fireplace, playin' with some corn cobs she brought in. She's always fetchin' something. Bennie lines up the cobs in rows like so'jers. I dos-y-dos around him,

> "O make me, O make me
>   my dear little man
> A cob for my musket
>   a sword for my hand!"

Bennie's a real quick little boy an' when I sing that, his black chinquapin eyes lights up an' he reaches right up an' hands me a corn cob. I take it an' stick it in my apern belt an' toss the broom stick over my shoulder.

> "I thank you, I thank you
>   my captain so true
> Wherever the war is,
>   I'll fight there for you."

That tickles Bennie an' he gets up on his knees.

> "Oh give me, O give me
>   my sister so tall
> Your sword for my apern,
> A stone for my ball!"

Bennie stands all the way up, an' I grab his little hands an' we sashay over the floor in a way Pa an' Ma would call sinful if they were here!

> "Be you gone a short time
>   or be you gone long
> The while we are waiting
>   we'll dance to my song!"

Faster and faster we go, Queenie yipping at our heels,

> "O wind be my music,
>   my flag be a flame,
> Red cloak for my sorrow
>   'Til he comes again!"

JAMES LEWIS

To THE right of the trail here, Gragg's Bluffs hangs out over the Johns River gorge a thousand feet below. I shot my first deer here, but I remember it most because this is where I parted from Margaret last Easter after she started walking home from church in the Globe when her step-brother—this same Heath Garvy—got mixed up in a drinking fight outside the church.

    Preacher Reuben McKamie was starting to call up those to be taken in the church by experience when the disturbance began outside in the grove. Margaret was sitting two benches in front of me and I could see two curls back of her neck like little black smoke that had got loose from the put-up part of her hair. Some giggly girls were on that bench but she was listenin' serious to Preacher McKamie, her uncle, and she wasn't part of them, in fact Heath's wife was between her and them. That's the only time

I ever saw Mrs. Heath Garvy but you could tell she was tuned to the commotion outside, an' bein' tall she could see a little piece out the window. Seein' the congregation becoming unmindful, Mr. Reuben says

"All right now, folks! Let us keep our thoughts inside this place of prayer. If it is the work of God out there, our efforts to control it will be vain. If it's the work of the devil, it wont last."

When the thumps and bumps began, though, Mis' Heath Garvy got up and strode out, leavin' Margaret sittin' there like one bead on a broken string. I could tell from my father's back how disapproving he was of the goings-on outside, our church having always been more Regular and not New Light or Primitive, though really the trouble didn't have anything to do with any church anyhow but was all outdoors.

After the new members started going up to the front, men at the rear began slippin' out, including one or two boys in my row.

It was then Margaret got up, throwin' a red cape about her an' I could see tears shinin' an' she was bitin' the prettiest soft mouth in the world. I didn't know then how came me to do it but it was like all at once I wasn't surprised at all to be getting up and going out after her.

In the vestibule I got blocked by Cousin Flora Shinalt scufflin' with her children over goin' to the back house.

"There's *James*!" says Cousin Flora, bright-like, her scowl changin' to a smile. She says "There's James!" the way I point Pinckney to a rabbit when I'm goin' to paste him one with a snowball in the neck. The off young'un was pullin' her to the left, an' the lead young'un was pullin' her to the right.

"Good day, Cousin Flora," I mumble, steppin' around 'em, not knowin' which I feel sorriest for, but glad I'm grown up and don't have to be jerked around any more. All at once I feel I can look after myself.

In the grove there's a solid circle of men's backs around whatever fracas is going on. I look around quick and don't see Margaret anywhere. Then I catch a flash of red 'way off where the path takes off up Anthony's Creek. I light off the church steps and once headed that way, I fly, not wishin' any company nor any teasing later.

The path bends out of sight where it leaves the river, and once on it, I expect to see Margaret, but she has the start of me, and mountan girls are good walkers, so even with some short cuts I know, I run a half mile before I glimpse that red hooded cloak again.

I want to call out to her, "Margaret!" but the name stops in my throat. Callin' her by her first name would sound like I knew her. And I do—the way we know everybody from Globe up over the Grandfather—I mean we know of 'em an' who their gram'paw was, and our kin on over in East Tennessee. But it's not like she is one of the girls that come to see my sisters all the time.

I'm gettin' winded—strange, because I never have got out of breath comin' up here before, not even the time I shot the deer.

"Miss Margaret!" I decide is better.

She ducks her head an' looks back sidewise, then speeds up. She's deer-fleet herself.

All at once I think how foolish I am to be chasin' up the mountain after a girl. But here I am! So there is just two choices—quit and go home, or overtake her. If I give up, all her life she'll wonder what in thunder I meant, an' probably put the worst possible guess on it. Besides, you can't let a girl get the best of you, not if you want her to like you. So I take a runnin' start up a bank over a big rock an' down through some laurels and come out on the path fifteen feet ahead of her when she comes around the cliff. She stops, quick, lookin' like a cardinal just lighted in the path.

"Don't make me head you off like some kind of game," I say reproachful. "Miss Margaret, don't be afraid!"

"I'm not a-fra-aid!" she drags it out slow an' low, like she was talkin' to a small child.

She's even prettier than I thought, dark eyes still the least bit damp, dark hair peepin' from that hood. I have to take my mind clear back and start all over at the church.

"You ran away," I say. "Why did you run away from church all by yourself?"

She lowers her head an' I have the uneasy feelin' she might cry again. Women crying upsets me. When my sisters blubber, I get out of the house. My mother never cries. Neither does this one. She lifts her head and starts forward as if she means to pass right on through me same as if I was a ghost. But I'm not—she can't go through me, nor around me either for the path's not that wide.

"Are you plannin' to walk home? Tell me—Margaret."

"I'll thank you to let me by, Mr. James Lewis."

"I saw you when you came this morning," I say, "on the mule with your sister-in-law." The prettiest thing about her is her mouth. It curves beautiful and is like rose petals, pale pink, though I never in my life remember payin' rose petals any mind before.

"It's a long way from here to McKamie Gap!"

"The more reason to get started," she says, makin' like she will brush by me if she has to climb the bank to do it.

"What are your folks goin' to think when they look around an' can't find you?"

"It'll be some time before they get around to *that*," she says, soundin' like a school teacher again.

I'm short and round-faced like my mother, but I'm a little taller than she is—our heads are just about on the right levels when hers is up.

We both start when a wood-pecker drums on a dead tree trunk not ten feet above us.

"It's a yeller hammer," I say, as much to break the chill as anything.

"So it is," she says calm, glancin' up, though on the down glance she steals one quick look at me.

"There's lots of them up here. Wild turkeys, too. An' grouse. I hunt up here."

There's many a mountain girl, or girl in the valley either for that matter that you wouldn' always want to stand close to. Their teeth or clo'es or somethin' need lookin' after. But if you got close enough to this one I bet she would smell the way mountain flowers do, wild-sweet without bein' too sweet. At least she knows why I came and wasn't chasing her, though to be honest that was part of it. It seems as if I've got about as far as I can go on this fool's errand.

"All right," I say, steppin' aside so she can pass if she wants to. "I think your mammy'll whup you when you get home. I kinda hope she does. A girl's got no business walkin' a trail alone in times like this, 'specially on a Easter Sunday when there's no tellin' how much drinkin' an' meanness is goin' on up at the Forge Flats an' down in McCauthers' holler, too."

"It's not just in the hollers!" Her head goes down again, she talks kind of muffled—I can't see her face all the way inside that hood. Then she starts walkin' on and I let my steps fall in with hers. I know why she left the church. I've heard my father speak of Margaret's father, and of her mother—an herb woman not just like the common run of folks.

"If you don't mind," I say, "I'd like to walk with you 'til we get to Gragg's Bluff. I can show you a short cut there so you wont have to go by the Forge Flats." I can't tell whether she nods or shakes her head but at least we're going along together. When the woodpecker lets loose again, I say "This is kind of like marchin', isn't it? We even got a drummer."

That pretty mouth squinches up somewhere between a smile an' lookin' prim.

"I guess I'll be marchin' soon," I say. "In the Army."

We're about to have to climb over a big boulder in the path. She kinda lifts her skirt and takes the rock in one quick hop remindin' me more than ever of a red bird.

"Why do you want to fight?"

"Oh-h-h-" I start kind of airy. The truth is I haven't given it much thought. It's just what you would do, the way you go to school, or to church, or plough when your father expects you to. They're starting a company of cavalry at Boone. My younger brother, Pendleton, tried to get in it but old Dr. Horace Rivers scratched his name off the list of Volunteers an' gave Pendleton an awful scolding, said he was acting under excitement.

"Oh-h-h- It seems like the Northerners want to tell us down here how to run our business."

"There's ways to settle that without fightin'." She's started walkin' on fast again.

I *hadn't* given it much thought. You sit around listening to older men talk about state's rights and cotton and things like that and after while you get the feeling it's time to go.

"I guess you're sure of bein' on the winnin' side!" We're on a up-hill slant, an' she stomps her boots down hard. "Fight! fight! fight! It's somep'n that's in men. It's in Heese—" she adds, then stops abrupt like she let out somethin' she didn't meant to.

I look over at her. "I bet you're a spit-fire yourself!"

Her mouth twitches same it did back with the woodpecker but I still can't make her smile outright.

"Heath Garvy is goin' to have a fit when he finds you've gone," I say.

"I doubt that," she says prim. "But in that case, you can tell him where I am. I'll be at home!"

At the rate she is going, she will be, too. We're getting closer and closer to Gragg's Bluff, and the shorter the space the less it seems we have to say. Finally we come to a break in the laurels where you can walk out on the Bluff. It makes some people dizzy to go out there an' look over a thousand feet down on tops of trees in the gorge.

"Margaret," I say when we come to the break, "step here, I want to show you somep'n'." I hold out my hand and she takes it. It don't feel like anything I ever touched before. We bend down and step through the laurels and fern and come out on the cliff. Far below us are spread the Walnut Bottoms, a green mist of new leaves over it, and a warm sweetish smell comin' up. A hawk is floating lazy like a brown leaf a hundred feet under us. My foot catches in a root and she raises our clasped hands to steady *me*! Then she draws her hand away. The feeling of it stays.

"Now let me show you." I take her by the shoulders and turn her around towards Grandfather mountain. "See the white spot up there? like somebody's painted on the cliff? It's just a wet slick, the way light falls on it. That's Beacon Heights where the path comes into White Springs Trail. From there you can see back down here. To a hawk, it wouldn't be far atall. I'll wait here. You take the cliff path. If you're not up there by the time the sun gets even with the top of that big tamarack on the Grandfather's chin, I'm comin' after you. Come out on the Heights when you get there. I guess I could see this red cape from anywhere. I'll go back then and tell your folks you're nearly home."

She kinda shrugs herself out from under my hands and turns around to face me.

"Thank you for showin' me, Mister James Lewis!"

She stoops and bends the bushes that close in the path, then looks back. "I've hunted here, too—not grouse, but ginseng, cohosh, spignet, snake-root—my mother has had up all up and down this ridge. Goodbye!"

There's no sound after that but the birds. I take the time of day by the sun and the Grandfather and sit down on the rock. There's things in the mountains sounds alike—rain comin' across a valley or a water fall before you get to it sounds pretty much the same, and both sound like wind. But there's one you can always count on in the mountains if you listen for it—the whisper of a stream far far off down in a gorge. I rest my elbows on my knees and let my hands hang down between them, separate. One feeling at a time is enough.

SAMANTHA

I seen that same big white house here in the Globe last Easter when we had our little trouble down here at the church. I remember the cedar trees down to the gate an' the daffy-dills along the walk from the kitchen garden, and women comin' out with baskets like now, an' nigger slaves comin' with trays only they was puttin' em in carriages then to take to the church for dinner in the grove. This time I believe they aim to feed us. I know Heese is emptier'n a cave, an' I could eat that whole tray of vittles that old nigger woman is carryin'—her in the gray dress with the white t'owl 'round her head. What I miss more'n anything, I believe, is my snuff stick! Seems like this little ole piece o' birch I pulled up on the mountain has got no suption in it. Heese said a week ago I'd better give up snuff before we ever got started, that it would just give me away for bein' a woman an' the best way to break a habit is just not to pamper it. But it's hard to break a fifteen year old habit in a few hours, an' if it wasn't for gettin' left, I'd go right back to Haw branch an' get it.

"That's old Lewis," Heese growls when a tall dark man, kinda stooped, comes out of the yard gate an' shakes hands with Sergeant Coffey an' young James Lewis same as if he hadn't just seen 'em yestiddy or this mornin'. Sergeant Coffey sweeps his hat off to the little dumpy fair-haired woman behind Mr. Lewis. She looks like James Lewis—same round face an' blue eyes, an' James goes over an' kisses her.

A nigger feller draws a bucket of water from the horse trough at the road to pour over our hands for us to wash. Wind blows the splash back fast as he can pour it. The Lewis children are playin' with old cornstalks for guns, an' a older boy, 'most as old as James but dark an' han'some, is ridin' a beautiful fawn-colored mare. Heese is sizin' up the animal an' glowerin'. Bein' connected any way with Globe—even lookin' down on it as we can from our home—always works on him an' the closer he gets the worser he feels, the land so rich an' level, everything plentiful, people polite an' educated and workin' together, too—not always pullin' ag'inst each other the way McKamies do.

The nigger folks are openin' up the basket tops, foldin' back white cloths from the trays, tuckin' 'em in to hold 'em ag'inst the wind. The Lewises are about to lead the Sergeant to the house, an' we're fixin' to set down an' go to eatin' when old Coffey remembers we'd ought to say the Blessin' so we all scramble up ag'in and take off our hats an' he prays quite a spell, "Stop us, O God, for a minute o' prayer, let us all stand at attention before Thee!" an' so on, not forgettin' to bring in the fight at Forge Flats an' straighten ever'body out about that, an' too bad Fog an' Black Will Brown ain't here to hear it!

I see young James Lewis talkin' to the old nigger lady, an' her starin' at me an' noddin' her head slow with her mouth open like she ain't quite takin' in what he's sayin'. We all set down to eat then, an' I don't pay much attention to anything but chicken an' sausage biscuit, all the while thinkin' how long it's been since I et food I didn' fix myself, an' how maybe that's goin' to be one o' the pleasant parts about this trip. I do despise to cook.

The younger Lewis boy has got off his horse an' is talkin' to those Woodall twins about their guns, an' one of 'em offers his to shoot but Lewis shakes his head, so one o' the twins turns his gun north t'ords the big round hill back o' the Lewis house. There's a giant pine tree on it with a few cones in the top, an' Thee, or ever which one 'tis, is aimin' at 'em when the dark Lewis boy says quick

"Not that way!" Woodall lowers the barrel a little.

"That's our family graveyard up there. My father tells us not to shoot over it—bad luck."

So the twin swings the gun a little more to the left an' as luck will have it there's a chicken hawk floatin' against the west. Everybody turns, watchin', so I hardly notice 'til that old colored lady jogs the basket o' gingerbread ag'inst my cut wrist.

Boom! goes the gun. The hawk flutters an' falls.

The old lady is sayin' somethin' right into my ear.

"Privy back o' the hedge!" She points.

I've got a piece of gingerbread halfway to my mouth. It takes me a minute to take in what she says. But longer to think why she says it. An' why she'd pick out just me to say it to! I just sit there dumfounded how it all come about, wonderin' if Jim Lewis has already broke his word to us an' what Heese'll do to him if he has. But even more, all at once it's like I have to go. It's like she put it in my head to go.

Heese's mind is on Dee Woodall who is tampin' another load down into his barrel. The children are racin' off to the pasture to see can they find the hawk. While the rest are watchin' all this, I get up kinda slow, stretch, start off aimless in the direction of the graveyard hill like I'm bent on visitin' a fam'ly grave. But I stop off in the little house behind the hedge.

Strange how simple some things are at home an' how bothersome they can be away from home. Heese an' me have been so set on not bein' parted, on gettin' over to the other side in the war, we've not give much thought to how things might be differ'nt in ways we'd not counted on. At home, we got the whole Grandfather for a back house, nobody nearer'n three mile, so we sure hadn' spent no time considerin' that.

It's dark as hell in the privy, so to see about pullin' my men's clo'es back together, I open the door to get some light an' there right on the doorstep is that ole nigger lady ag'in! She takes one look at me an' says " 'Fore God!"

I jerk my pants closed an' step out on the ground. Then I reach out an' shake her by the shoulder. "Looky here!" I say, "What did James Lewis say to you about me? Why did you choose just *me* to come out here? Why didn' you ask *everybody*?"

She dandles some little cloths at me. "Mr. Jim," she says, "he say young man done cut his wris' back up on de mountain. He say take him out to de privy an' help him splent it up."

HEATH GARVY

It's plum dark when we get to Morganton and there wasn' no doctor there so Samantha didn' have to pass no inspections. There wasn' no railroad, neither, so we haf' to walk 'bout five miles more down some pastures all froze over, to get to what they call Head o' the Road. McGillicuddy is about give out - he quit talkin' 'long about Mulberry. When he finely throws down the croaker sack he's been totin' ever since White Springs, I take pity on him an' pick it up.

"What-all you got in here?" Part of it's soft like clo'es but there's squares maybe like fat-back, an' little knots like apples.

"Oh, Lord, Garvy," he wheezes, "some o' the best apple brandy was ever made on the head of a branch."

I pinch the bag some more. "Why not lighten the load a little?"

"I figured I'd keep that for 'mergencies," he sighs.

"You done reached that time!" I peer at him, his shadder risin' an' fallin' with the lantern lights bobbin' up ahead. It seems he has swunk in spite of all the vittles he et back at Globe.

We set the sack down then an' he fumbles at the rope, his breath raisin' little mists in the cold air. You can see some—a new moon is somewhere behind clouds. Fine'ly from down under vittles an' long underwear an' stuff he's takin' to the war he comes up with a linament bottle corked with a cob. I take it from him, uncork it, smell the cob an' pass it to Sam who smells it an' nods. We pass the bottle around. The rest of the squad has done gone on off—you can hear the rattle of dry ice when their boots shatter the glazin' over the cattle tracks.

Sam sees to it the bottle goes back in the bag careful, we tie it up, an' stumble ahead in the dark. Walkin' is easier now. For Sam an' me to carry Mac's gear is no burden atall. Spring peepers is peepin' through the glass of the cow tracks, an' we can smell alders nearly like spring, meanin' there's water over to the left, maybe a creek.

Then we see camp fires ahead, double, like they was shinin' in water. We've caught up with the others. Word comes back it's Berry's mill pond where Head o' the Road is.

As we get closer we make out so'jers standin' around, a patch o' railroad tracks shinin' in firelight, an' soon we make out the engine with tender an' two flat cars an' two coaches all standin' under a bluff. Some o' the so'jers sittin' around fires is in uniform, Confed gray with buttons shinin', but others got on reg'lar clo'es like us.

"Hi, Dan'l Boone!" one yells at us when we show up outa the dark. The Woodall twins hasn't ever seen a train before, nor did I but once, an' they make a bee line for where it is standin' under a tank where water comes down off the bluff by a kind of trough.

A feller hollers at 'em "Did you bring us some b'ar meat, boys?" Some o' the men is already rolled in blankets, asleep with their feet to the fire. A few are holdin' sticks out over the fire like fish poles with little cans on the end. They are cookin' coffee. One of 'em offers us some but we ain't got nothin' to put it in.

There's a wooden buildin' on the other side o' the tracks with a kind of porch where some so'jers is standin' under a lantern light. Their uniforms are better with more buttons than the ones around the fires. One of 'em is big with a wide fore-head an' spade beard, stars on his collar an' a proud look. Sergeant Coffey an' Lewis go up to him an' salute an' shake hands an' they all stand perlaverin'.

Sam an' me pick one o' the fires where the men has nearly all turned in, so as not to occasion us talkin' much.

"What outfit you in?" I ask one of 'em that's got his eyes open.

"First Bethel."

"Where would the doctor be?" I ask.

He raises his head an' props it from his elbow. "You hurt?"

"Naw, it ain't that. We heer'd there's a doctor around to examine you an' see if you're fitten or unfitten'."

"Where'd you two come from?"

"Watauga."

"You're fitten," he says, turns over an' goes to sleep.

McGillicuddy has got tired waitin' an' gone off around the side o' the buildin'. The men on the porch—I guess they're officers—is listenin' quiet to one that draws lines in the air like he's tellin' about a battle. I take the measure of all of 'em, those aroun' the fires too, an' I don't see one of 'em I couldn' whup, an' hope how soon I get the chanc't.

The crowd on the porch is breakin' up, the Lewis boy still standin' still lookin' down at the floor, droopy shouldered. Old Coffey is shakin' his head. They all go in the buildin' then an' kinda mill around a while an' presen'ly Lewis comes out carryin' a string o' tin cups an' gives us each one an' tells us we're goin' to have to spend the night here at Head o' the Road. He tells us to foller him 'round back o' the shed where there's a kinda lean-to, an' out o' the pushed-back door comes warm air from a cook stove mixed with lantern smoke an' somep'n else I reconnize soon's I see McGillicuddy standin' inside talkin' to a bald-headed man in blue jeans.

James Lewis, like a banty hen cluckin' to a brood o' ducks, leads us in an' after sayin' somethin' to the man in railroad clo'es, he motions us to line up an' the man ladles out some hot pease from a pot on the stove an' spears us up some pieces o' burnt cornbread from a pan. It tastes good. While we're crammin' it down, McGillicuddy edges over an' tells Sam the station agent is a Mason, "a brother Mason, an' the train ain't a-gonna run 'til mornin'." He's learnt there's been a big battle down at New Bern, clost to the ocean, an' the Confedrits got licked, an' that's where we're headed for. So I figger the lines must be gettin' closter down there an' it ortent to be hard for me an' Sam to get over on the Union side.

The station agent comes around with a ole smoked pot an' pours chicory coffee in our bean cups. Then Sergeant Coffey comes in.

"Now boys," he says, "owin' to the fact not enough blankets has been issued we've arranged with Mr. Ingle, the station agent here, to let you sleep in the store as guests of the Western North

Carolina Railroad. There's valuable property here, an' there's to be no smokin', an' it goes without sayin' no stealin'. Nor cursin', either. Foller me."

We start shufflin' out. I feel a pull on my coat tail. It's McGillicuddy. He jerks his head in the direction of a door into the buildin' that the brother Mason is holdin' open. Sam tries to go on like she'd obey orders but Mac says

"Step lively—it's all right! Back here there's hay!" You can smell it, dusty and sweet-like—see it, too, through the door. It looks good an' soft. So we hang back and slip in thataway. Some of the hay is baled an' some loose. Sam puts McGillicuddy's gear down, takes one o' her long legs an' kicks a couple of bales around so it makes a cubby hole for her an' me in the corner. This cuts McGillicuddy off on the other side. The agent closes the door so it's dark an' we lose no time droppin' down, but we can hear the others comin' in at the front, then lantern light so you can look up in the rafters an' see lumber an' iron pipes an' stuff stacked overhead. Sergeant Coffey calls out the names an' when he names us we answer up good an' prompt, an' Mac adds "*In* the rear!" which brings Lewis back around through the kitchen to see what's up. He holds up his lantern an' right then is when I despise him an' his whole finicky way of life, but more because we ever told him about Sam bein' a woman when maybe we didn't haf' to. I will say, though, he don't look as peart as he did before he heard about New Bern.

The Woodall twins is on the south side o' the bales from us, and still talkin' about the train.

"It goes ten miles an hour!"

"The engine here is the 'Catawba.' It's twin of the 'Swannano.' They pass at Catawba station 'bout ten tomorrer mornin'."

Outside we can hear hogs gruntin' that have got stirred up under the shed. It makes things more like home.

Sam mutters "I hope you don't have one o' your nightmares!"

Every once in a while you can hear that locomotive sigh, lettin' off steam.

"They're from the Bethel Regiment," say Dee Woodall—he talks smarter than the other one.

"I wisht we coulda slep' outdoors with them. What's the name of the General?"

"What General?"

"The big 'un with the sharp beard."

"He ain't no General. He's a Colonel."

"What's the difference!"

" 'Bout seventy thousand men!"

On the other side o' the bales next to us, McGillicuddy has got his household goods in order but is restless owin' to whiskey the brother Mason give him on top of the brandy, or maybe like me he's just walked so far the swing of it is still in him. We can hear him figetin' around. Presen'ly, though, he is breathin' in little fits an' starts. The brandy don't wear off easy for me either an' men's clo'es don't cut down no way on Sam's feelin' like a woman. The Catawba keeps on sighin'. I wisht I coud let off steam like it does!

"I couldn' understand the Colonel's talk," says the slow twin.

"Quiet!" somebody yells.

"He's a *Eng*lishman from down on the Yadkin. He's takin' the First Bethel back—it is goin' to be the Eleventh now. That's what they said the Colonel's name was—Eleven Thorpe."

"Quiet!!"

The pigs is hushed. Sam turns t'ords me the way we do on the edge o' sleep, breathin' slower, reg'lar an' deeper. I wisht I could. Seems like gittin' up an' walkin' right on to the ocean now would be the easiest thing I could do. I ain't ust to layin' awake. I try to remember what Anthony's Creek sounds like rushin' down through the gorge. Gradual' this changes to the roll of a train. I dream I'm back again the time my mother took me to Chattanooga. It was a long time ago. I was just a little boy like Bennie. We went to find some man was workin' on a lumber yard, a big fair-haired man. He made her cry. Then she took me an' we walked back a long way to the station an' she kep' wipin' her eyes an' I couldn't do anything about it. After we got on the train, a old man was in the seat across from us, an' he had a little bag o' stones—gems, he said, rubies an' di'monds he got from mountain rock. He showed 'em to Ma an' she didn' cry any more after that. He asked her when my birthday was, an' she said March, an' he give her a dark green stone with red spots in it, an' after me an' her come to live with Pa, he bored a hole through it an' tied it firm on a leather thong so I could carry it on my belt an' not lose it. The old man called it a bloodstone—you rub it with water the red shows more in the green. I feel it on my belt now ag'inst me an' Samantha.

The hogs have hushed, an' from my bed I can see an eye of fire winkin' from the embers behind the firedogs that stand up straight like little bow-legged men, an' that's somethin' I could always know even when the nightmares would begin—even when I felt I was hardenin' into stone, an' know I have to go the whole way through with it before I can turn back to flesh ag'in, I would know the fire was there, an' Pa hilt me, an' Ma, 'til I was flesh ag'in an' not stone! Ma always told Pa it was nothin' but worms.

MAIL MAN

It ain't as cold up here in McKamie Gap as I thought it was goin' to be. Wind has laid since yestiddy an' noontime air up here is spring-soft as it is down in the Globe.

Water my mule Jarvis is drinkin' runs east to the ocean 'way down yonder. Where he'll drink after dinner, it runs west. In between lies Grandfather mountain.

This is the only place above Globe where, on a clear still day like this, you can see smoke from four homesteads.

In my gram'paw's time, there was only one little smoke, an' not much more'n the old Indian trail up here so nobody hardly ever come up here until Washington McKamie tuk up five hundred acres an' built his cabin. Mis' Martin McKamie believes he tuk up more'n that, an' she's had the land office man up here more'n once to see if there ain't a tract still lyin' around unclaimed.

Washington McKamie's four sons heired the land an' Reuben, the youngest, got the last parcel this side o' the mountain—nice for his wife since she come from this side o' the ridge an' when leaves is off the trees wintertime she can look down on her folks' ridge. Some thinks Nannie McKamie is too good-lookin' for a preacher's wife—anyhow, she don't age much an' I always enjoy lookin' at her with that fine head o' hair an them three han'some girl chillern. If Reuben's at home I'll wait for him to look over this copy of the Carolina Watchman I'm takin' to Squire Miller.

Next smoke, right under where that buzzard is floatin' over top of the ridge is his brother William's. Billie's pale little wife, Chaney, don't never have much to say, an' no wonder with all the work there is to do for Billie an' the five boys - just four now with Joel in the war. Her eyes will ask if there's a letter from Joel, an' it's sorry I am today to haf' to say No. I do have a letter from Washin'ton—that's Martin an' Harriett McKamie's son that's with Joel up clost to Washin'ton City somewhere with the 22nd North Carolina, guardin' batteries on the Potomac. If it'd be anybody else's letter, I'd let the fam'ly read it—save 'em bringin' it back over here—the Confedrit members of the fam'ly anyway—but Harriett don't like for anybody to lay a finger on her property—she's never forgive me for puttin' up the mail gourd at Billie's gate instead of at hers an' Martin's, but I figgered Billie's wife wouldn' have neither time nor likin' for delvin' into other people's business. And too, it gives me time to sort out whatever mail's been put in the gourd while Jarvis rests an' drinks after his climb.

From Billie's house I go sharp down the valley to Enoch's. Enoch is oldest of the four McKamie brothers so he got the old original homestead, an' havin' worked hard an' bein' the last to marry, he'd 'cumulated a good deal, done a lot o' good, too, seein' to it his brothers got learnt to read even when he couldn't. He's always helped 'em the way he does anybody that needs it, an' his brothers is the only ones thinks hard of him that he's taken to have Union sentiments lately. I was plum glad to hear Enoch's step-son, that big hulk Heath Garvy, has joined the Confedrit army. It'll make things friendlier up here in the Gap, though there ain't ever to say coolness up here when a family's divided over the war, bad as that is, an' some of 'em is.

I always learn somethin' at Enoch's, his wife bein' a doctor woman an' if I don't have news for her, she does for me—a new baby, or a death or illness, an' I carry the news along. Not gossip—Mary McKamie ain't one to take any stock in hearsay. Just happenin's. Or maybe she'll be speculatin' about trouble she's run into, like the milk-sick that makes so much sufferin' in the mountains. She has a nat'rul interest in diggin' out truth, Mary McKamie has—just the opposite of her sister-in-law Harriett, that's Mis' Martin McKamie, who seems to have a nat'rul bent for confusin' it, if you don't count land squabbles an' things like that. For such as that she's got the sense of a ferret.

"Can you tell these plants apart, Mr. Gibbs?" Mary McKamie as't me one day. I couldn't. Both of 'em looked to me like they was broke off the same bush.

"I got 'em up on Haw Branch above Heese's place. Both of 'em's haws—this one's black haw an' good for rheumatism. This one's shonny haw an' ain't good for anything but birds. Both of 'em's viburnums."

"How come you know things like this?"

"Oh—'course I know about their bein' haws, an' what they're good for—I've found that out for myself. But there was a man come through here one time—a Mister Gray. He told me the public names—names he said would be the same anywh'ur in the world—like everybody spoke the same lang'widge—like you would go to Chiney, f'r instance, a Chineyman would name it that way, or a Frenchman—anywh'ur you'd go. He said a Frenchman *did* come through here about a hundred years ago just to *git* plants an' give 'em names! Some of 'em I thought different anyhow from all the rest o' the world—" she got a little book off the fireboard an' showed me—viburnum—well, I don't recall the last of the name but she's got 'em all wrote down in a little book that Enoch covered for her with a kid's skin.

Another time I had a cough and she fixed me some cherry bark cordial.

"You know, Nathan," she says, stirrin' it up. "I don't b'lieve all grippe is grippe an' all colds is colds, else why do some folks keep runny noses all year 'round, 'specially childern, that wont nothin' cure?"

I study 'bout that as I go 'long my route, an' first thing I know I'm watchin' ever' little snotty nosed child I see, askin' does he have it reg'lar.

The Martin McKamie's will be waitin' for this letter from Wash'. Their house smoke always has the smell of good eatin' in it. I usually git a bite to eat there.

You might say I come away with some'p'n from each house here in McKamie Gap—a purty woman to look at, a brave little one to admire, a smart one to talk to, an' a good cook to eat with. Not every route has that much. If I was ever to find all them things in one girl—well—I guess Enoch's girl Margaret comes as close to it as any—I seen her grow up from a baby—sixteen now to my fifty but I guess it don't hurt anybody to dream so long as he keeps it to hisself. It kinda warms him, gives him some-p'n to think about. Probably more does it than anybody knows. Fifty or not, I can still carry the mail, from habit if nothin' else.

Git up, Jarvis! you ole long-leggéd snail! If Mis' Harriett McKamie don't talk too long an' mud ain't too bad, we might connect with Old Albany at Shull's Mill an' get some stage mail from Abingdon. You an' me got to earn our four dollars a month cancellations.

JAMES LEWIS

THINGS have changed here at the front since I went home to bring back twenty recruits and one of 'em's wife. Not just the camp, drawn back here now nearly to Kinston, but the faces are changed. There's a good many new ones, those that were here look older, and some are gone—two hundred prisoners the Federals took. About the rest missing, nobody talks much—don't have time. If Colonel Burgwyn was strict on our Twenty Sixth before, he's twice as hard now, drilling us from that beautiful motioned horse, or inspecting, with his flashing dark eyes that see every scrap of disorder. The big difference is that now the men are with him. Before the battle of New Bern, hardly any would have voted to reelect him. They all love Vance, of course, but as for Burgywn, some of our company even said if they ever got in a fight what they would do to him. I think he suspected how they felt. But since the battle they see what he's been aiming at—that in being hard he was their friend, not their enemy.

"You shoulda seen him on the retreat at Bryce's creek," Shorty McLauchlin says. We are sitting around the Garvys' tent on April Fool's evening after retreat and supper, the first time we've had to sit around any—I and Shorty who is a little sawed-off Scotchman with a jutting circle of rusty beard, an' tall quiet Sion Hicks, our neighbor at home, and the Garvys and their stout friend McGillicuddy, an' a couple of teamsters. Sion has one shoe off examinin' real tender the blisters he got during the retreat to Trenton. Vance marched 'em fifty miles in thirty six hours! This is one o' these bland misty evenings after thunder storms, breeders for swamp fever, full of this old marshy smell that makes you wish for one deep breath of balsam or snow. Maybe that's what Heath Garvy is thinking about as he sits there twiddlin' some kinda stone on a leather string between his fingers.

His wife Sam is getting along good. Owing to all the confusion of the retreat and setting up new camp, there wasn't any close medical inspection of recruits, and I haven't told anybody she's a woman, only the bugler, Mason Byrd, who is also from Globe. We play chess together, and have been raised the same way—both our families strong Democratic, only the Byrds live close to McCauthern's Gap. McCauthern's are touchous and unaccountable politically, and Squire Byrd is hard put to it to control 'em sometimes.

Mason would like to get in our regimental band—Captain Mickey's band—but buglers don't have much standing with real musicians like these Moravians from Winston-Salem.

Sam drills and does her duties like a man. So does Heath but he is left-handed and don't seem to learn as quick as she does. Not wishin' him to be placed in the awkward squad, I came by after supper to loan 'em my copy of Gilham's Manual of Tactics and Drill. My Uncle Theophilus sent it to me—my family expect me to be not less than a Major just like the Byrds expect Mason to head the Band. Both are 'way wrong. But I wont be needing the book till regimental night classes start again. Heath can't read, but Sam will teach it to him.

Shorty McLauchlin is tellin' on about the retreat from New Bern. "Bryce's creek is too deep to ford, seventy five yards wide, an' only one little boat is there, size for three men. Everybody is milling around—you can hear firing from Yankee skirmishers on our rear and the steady chop-chop of axes comin' closes an' closer. Some plunged in and swam over, an' about half threw their arms in the stream sayin' no Yankee was gonna get their guns. Three men was drowned. Vance cheered us along an' spurred his horse in the creek but it wouldn't swim an' heavy as the Colonel is an' weighted down with all his gear, he come unseated an' woulda sunk plum outa sight in that ole coffee-colored water if Company K hadn' drawed him up an' towed him over. 'Bout that time Colonel Burgwyn galloped up, cool as if he was out for a afternoon ride, rallied every officer he could find, told 'em they were responsible for their men's safety, told 'em to keep order. Then he sent a bunch of us down river to hunt boats. Half mile down we come on a nigger said he belonged Mr. Kit Foy who had a boat would hold eighteen, so we went with him on down the creek a ways, pullin' swamp mud up to our waists some places, an' found the boat an' rowed it back. By that time Colonel Burgwyn and Major Graham had took their stand on opposite sides of the path to the creek and with swords crossed, counted us off eighteen men at a time, no crowdin' at all, till all were safe. Graham come with the last load, swimming his horse alongside. Then the boat went back for Burgwyn an' he come over the same way. It was about sunset. Over towards New Bern we could see the glow where our men had burnt the rosin works an' railroad bridge across the Neuse, an' military supplies to keep the Yanks from gettin' 'em. Burgwyn took command of what companies were left an' held it till we caught up with Colonel Vance at Trenton next day."

Some men in our regiment suffered loss of speech in the battle (from windage from our own artillery) but Shorty McLauchlin is not one of them. What Shorty lacks in facts, he makes up in supposing. He is our sand pile strategist. Give him one strip of white ocean sand and he can win more battles than T. J. Jackson.

Sion Hicks is the opposite—quiet, cautious. I wait around hoping the Scotch-Irish will go off foraging after a while. We had stewed gray beans and johnny cake for supper. I want to get the straight of it from Sion, clear as was ever in any newspaper. I hate I missed that battle!

Heath Garvy's hands are so big they turn in like bear's paws, and look strange flippin' that little dark green stone on a string, whatever it is. He looks off west where a cloud bank is lying. Squinch your eyes an' you can nearly believe it's the mountains. Ten days of camp confinement are beginnin' to tell on Heath. Sam sits next, then Sion. I wonder what Sion would do if he knew he is sittin' by a woman!—run most prob'ly, though that's all Sion would ever run from. He has never been any ladies' man.

The two Macs do get hungry after a while and go off to see if the sutler has come back from Kinston with a fresh load o' pi-zan cakes. Sion is workin' his shoes back on. He fills his pipe, lights it and draws. After he spits where Burgwyn's fatigues wont see it back under the little porch McGillicuddy built, he says

"It was that brick kiln did it."

I know that brick kiln, beside the railroad from Beaufort to New Bern. Our defense, Fort Thompson, comes at a right angle from Neuse river to the kiln. I worked in Fort Thompson before I went home. We didn't have anything to work with—old worn out broken shovels and axes, though General Branch advertised in all the papers an' pleaded for tools and men.

"On the *other* side 'o the track where *we* were," says Sion, "the line was pulled back on account of swamp in front. It's like you'd take a straight stick for the fortifications an' break it in half, pull the right-hand half back t'ords you a little ways. See— that leaves a gap. The brick kiln was in that gap. And the railroad run at a right angle through the brick kiln an' the forts.

"General Branch ordered the kiln to be loop-holed—I guess he figured it would stand. The evenin' before, he'd ordered down two twenty-four pounder guns but they didn't get mounted. All the troops we had in the brick kiln was some green militia from around here that had never done anything but parade an' a little target practice on muster days.

"Beside these boys was the Thirty Fifth North Carolina—you know—little store keepers from Mecklenburg, farmers from Chatham. An' boys from down around Swansboro with long yeller hair down to their shoulders. Few of 'em ever owned slaves. Their colonel was a preacher somebody recommended 'cause he done right good at Bull Run an' Longstreet had give him a sword. Petway was all they had they could be proud of—Burgwyn's friend, you know.

"Colonel Vance put us right of the railroad and on west to Bryce's creek—that would be like the pulled-back part of the stick. A mile and a quarter, facin' the swamp and three hundred an' fifty yards of felled timber. Our left wing was anchored with Major Carmichael at the railroad.

"It rained all night, slow, an' there was fog next mornin' till

7:30 when the battle begun. In the swamp, they had four regiments to our two—five to our three east of the track. We kep' a steady firing for three hours—nearly the whole fight—then our ammunition gave out. The troops ag'inst us was mostly from Massachusetts. They'd slep' all night in the swamp. Burgwyn had to shoot at his old West Point teacher, General Foster. Colonel Campbell knew Burnside too, at West Point. A man from the seventh told me during the fight Burnside signalled to Campbell,

'Reub', quit your foolishness and come back to the Union Army!'

Colonel Campbell messaged back 'Tell General Burnside to go to the devil where he belongs.'

Sion spits ag'in under Mac's tent stoop.

"If we'd just a-had *one* more regiment at the brick kiln instead o' the militia, the 35th woulda stood as firm as the rest of us.

"But we heard a cheer from the Yanks when they charged the ditch an' kiln. The militia broke an' fled, then the Thirty Fifth went to pieces. The Thirty Seventh went to replace the militia and the Thirty Third to support the Thirty Fifth. But with our middle pierced an' fire comin' in on us from the rear, General Branch had to order a retreat.

"Our Twenty Sixth kep' firing 'til all our forces between the river an' the railroad got out. Major Carmichael was on the railroad when he got shot through the mouth. It come out his neck. He was a good target because he was wearin' a little flag stuck on a stick about eight inches above his cap. Some lady in New Bern had give it to him an' told him to wear it in the battle."

When Sion says that about the lady an' the little flag, I look at Sam Garvy, but shadows are settlin' in and it's hard to see each other's faces. The big difference in her an' Heath, I think, is that her thoughts are *here*. His ain't.

Sion stands up, tests his foot on the ground. "The Thirty Fifth felt so *bad*," he says, "the way they done, they wanted to make amends, so when the call come for troops to guard the rear of the retreat, their Company D volunteered to do it. Levi Newbowl told me when Captain Young met that militia he tried to rally 'em. He exhorted 'em to go back an' all that, an' rejoin their comrades fightin' in the kiln. He told 'em they'd be forever disgraced, an' the newspapers would be full of their cowardice. But one of 'em said 'I'd druther fill twenty newspapers than one grave!' A few didn' stop runnin' till they got to New Bern. One dropped dead on the rear platform of the last train crossin' the river, *expired* as he caught the train. He'd run all the way from the brick kiln—five miles!"

It's dark now, a faint glow comin' from a tent here an' there on the comp'ny street, if you call this lane of sand a street. From 'way up near the cook tent you hear a banjo plunk. Some man is singin' "Old Bangem," a old old mountain song,

> "Old Bangem would a-huntin' ride
> Dillem down an' dillem—
> Old bangem would a-huntin' ride
>   Dillem down—"

Heath Garvy speaks from the dark,
"Where would you say the *en*emy is *now?*"
Something in the way he says it turns Sion's forward step into a sort of curbed hop and it is not just from blisters.
"It's not my business to know. There's Yankees at New Bern. Some says little Washin'ton—" he hobbles on off in the dark.
The group breaks up.
"Goodnight, Sam."
"Goodnight, Jim!" She makes her voice coarser than it is like it's a little private joke between us.
"Goodnight, Garvy."
He answers between a grunt an' a grumble. I go off to my tent, close up to the color line. It is the time of day you feel sad, if that is the way you're goin' to feel. My mind is on those two friends, officers on opposite sides of the war, signaling back an' forth at each other with little flags. And on those little yellow haired boys from Onslow, somehow I can't forget them either. Nor Massachusetts soldiers layin' for us all night in the swamps. Strange how descendants of men that fought the Revolution together like

they did and like the folks from McDowell county did, an' the Mecklenbergers did, an' my folks did, should be layin' out in swamps all night to kill each other now. But if I'd been there, I'd have fought hard as the rest. I'm really sorry I missed that battle!

SAMANTHA

The hailstorm was the week after me an' Heath walked to Kinston to get the bucket. We had to pay a dollar for the bucket out o' the little money Pa Enoch give Heath when he left. There's ten thousand men camped around Kinston, an' the well our company was usin' is dryin' up. Heath says the water down here don't taste like water an' the air don't smell like air, an' the first time he tuk a drink of the water he just opened his mouth an' let it run right back out on the ground. Somebody had to find another spring near our company lines an' now it's the rule that any man carryin' a water pail can pass the guards. Some hides their pail an' walks right on into Kinston. There's been an awful run on buckets. It's run the price up. But it is handy for me to have one 'cause now when I feel a call o' nature, as Sergeant Coffey puts it, I can jest take my bucket an' go off by myself an' I don't have to use the men's sink. I would swear Mason Byrd, our bugler, holds off just the least bit in the mornin' 'til he sees me comin' over the sand hill with my pail. Only there wouldn't be no reason for him to know that. Anyway, I don't keep him waitin' none. Mason is from Globe and is friends with McCauthers that's friends to us.

Kinston is a right big town, bigger'n Lenoir or Boon or Elizabethton. Kinston's got three hotels, one of 'em four stories high with a little porch on the roof that nobody can get up there to set on. While me an' Heese was strollin' by it, a big fine carriage with two ladies in it come clatterin' up from the depot, an' who should walk out o' the hotel to meet it but Colonel Burgwyn hisself, ram-rod straight like always, those black eyes fixed on that carriage like it mighta helt the world. I start to come to attention like he drilled us, also I would get to see who he's meetin', but Heese wont wait—just keeps on down the street amongst the soldiers, some of 'em still on crutches from the battle of New Bern, an' a few is drunk. I do get to see the two ladies, though—one of 'em in black silk clo'es, an' the young one that the Colonel kisses, an' it's plain to see it's like them two was alone on a mountain for all they keered about people in town. He takes a lady on each arm an' they walk on into the hotel, the young one slim an' dark—for a minute she puts me in mind of Margaret, Heese's stepsister, but Margaret is younger an' never had a swishy silk dress that the sun makes rainbows in it when she walks.

Heese is cross with me for not comin' on—he's outa humor anyway because his rebel coat binds him across the shoulders, sleeves hit him above the wrists an' they've not been able to get him any pants to fit him atall, so he just wears his old 'uns but they was his best ones at home. We go down the street past the Old Castle, they call it, a prison for Union an' Confedrit, hopin' we might find a tailor shop an' relieve the bindin' but prob'ly we couldn' pay for it. Things is high—sweet potatoes 75 cents a bushel, Irish 25 cents, cheese 25, apples eight dollars a bushel is the way everything is but liquor, you can git plenty of that on any street corner.

It's while we're walkin' past one o' these places at Queen an' Bright that the two ha'nts come by, two women with flour or somep'n all over their faces an' eyes like burnt holes in a blanket, I guess they are women, anyway they wore skirts, one of 'em a tan one caught up on the side with little buttons to show a red petticoat an' high button shoes an' she was kinda half pushin' half pullin' the other one in a red dress a little differ'nt shade o' red from the first one's hair, an' they was laughin' loud an' lookin' at Heese but couldn' walk straight an' mighty near shoved us over in the gutter. Heese's face turned the color of the woman's petticoat.

"In heat," he says to me like that's the quickest way to explain it an' he draws me back on the sidewalk. Well, we got hussies in the mountains but they don't 'pear much differ'nt from other folks only for a little tipsyin' on Muster days or durin' court week. But I never seen nothin' like them ha'nts before, an' I never did see two pairs of women effected me as differ'nt as the Colonel's ladies an' them two.

We been thinkin' about writin' a letter home but paper is higher than anything if you can find any. But finely we found a sheet an' *en*-velope in a general store an' I wrote down what Heese told me an' we bought a stamp at the P. O. an' mailed it to go up on that train the 'Cannon Ball' if it misses the 'Shoo Fly' tonight,

> "Dear Ma & Pa I haf to do a good many things hier that I do not like and for that reason I will not stay hier longer than I Can find som way to get home or som wair els. I said before I left home that I would not be wating boy for no man long at a time. I will keep you informd. Yr. son Wm. Angel Garvy,
> Co F 26 N.C. Reg.
> Camp Ransom
> Kinston, N.C."

Today I told Heese I smelt hail even before the sky rolled up blue-black around noon time so when Sergeant Coffey come by our little tent to say there wouldn't be no more drill 'til after the storm, we had a little time to ourselves. Even McGillicuddy was out in the piney woods somewheres on picket duty with Jim Lewis. We've had a right smart of trouble with Mac. It's not we don't like him—ever'body does, but he likes us so much it seems like he's bent on bein' with us every minute, tenting an' all. He showed us how much better 'twould be if we'd fasten our three oil skins together instead of two and make a bigger shelter, an' besides, he said, most fellers down here is four to one little bitty tent. We got Jim Lewis to thank that Mac's not in here right between us now.

Heese is layin' scowlin' on our bunk we made outa split logs covered with these ole long-leaf pine needles. It's not so differ'nt from times we've slep' out in the mountains huntin' only there's less room. Heese's head pushes out the tent back an' his feet goes out the front. He don't like nothin' about soljerin' an' on top of that have come the mosquitoes. After taps the tent is a reg'lar hive. We flap at 'em with our hats an' pine branches an' try to turn back to sleep but you can hear 'em comin' 'fore they git here—then close up, they light on our hands, bite us through our clo'es. Finely Heese gets up cursin' hard, lights the grease lamp, takes three cartridges, empties the powder out of 'em onto a dry leaf in the center o' the tent, ties some pine needles to the end of his ram-rod, lights the needles, reaches the rod out to the powder on the floor an' Whoosh!! The explosion shook the tent, blew out the light, choked us with smoke. But things cleared after a while an' when Heese lit the light ag'in there wasn't a mosquito in sight! We ain't had none today either though you can still smell gun powder.

Since we're not goin' to have drill, I bring out the little brown book Jim Lewis lent us, Gilham's Manual for Volunteers an' Militia. On the cover is stamped in gold the pitchur of a man loadin' a cannon an' two officers with plumes on their hats ridin' horses that look like they ain't anxious to charge regardless of the feller pointin' the way with his sword. The print's awful fine. I never tried to read any book with such little writin' before.

I skip the Index an' ten whole pages o' things like "Aim—the act of bringing the firearm to its proper line of direction with the object to be struck," or "Gunpowder—a composition of sulphur, nitre (or saltpetre) an' charcoal that burns with an explosion,"— Heese wouldn' have no patience atall with stuff like that so I go on over where Jim Lewis has marked The School of the Soldier. "The men should be without arms," it says. I skip that too. Havin' to drill without a gun riles Heese more than anything. You take a man's gun away from him it's like you taken his manhood—livelihood too, where we come from. So I skip some more.

"Position of the soldier, Number 83. Heels on same line as near each other as the con—" somethin' or other? "of the men will permit." I guess that would be like McGillicuddy. Lieutenant

Hayes was drillin' our comp'ny an' dressin' up the line yestiddy.

"In there on the right!" he hollers. The line wouldn' come straight so he walks up an' punches Mac, "Stick your belly in!"

"It wont go in, Lieutenant," says Mac, "that's nat'rul!"

The Lieutenant turned his back—Some of 'em say it's the first time they seen him smile since New Bern.

"The body erect on the hips," it says here, "*in*-clining a little forward." "Soldiers" it says "are at first disposed to project the belly" (that's Mac,) "an' throw back the shoulders from which result many—many—" I can't make out the word but some kinda troubles in marching. This is a good book, it always says somethin', then tells you "Be*cause*—" an' gives you the reasons why.

"Heels more or less closed, be*cause*" it will say, "men who are knockkneed or who have legs with large calves cannot without—" somep'n—conscrip'—con-s-t-r-a-i-n-t "make their heels touch while standing." I wonder if the book the Yankees use is all wrote out as plain as this one is.

Sudden comes a flash o' lightnin'! Live fire! like Heese mighta exploded for mosquitoes ag'in. But this is everywhere! Then thunder shakes the earth. Some man in the next tent yells out. Storms ain't new to us. Hill country is where they're hatched. I seen times on the Grandfather seemed like heaven was gonna split earth. There's one cliff up Haw Branch that's divided fifty foot deep an' half mile long—happened time o' the crucifixion, old folks say. The rocks was rent.

I pay no 'tention to the storm but kinda broach the book to Heese.

"We got time now to learn the manual of arms, the loadin's an' the firin's," I say.

"Samantha!" he kicks one o' his big legs at the tent flap, "I can load my gun in thirty seconds, runnin'. You seen me do it many time. So just don't bother me with that."

"But we got to learn to do it *with* the others! Ever'thing you do down here is gotta be done *with* the others! Ever'body loads in the nine times at once or gits put in the awkward squad an' me an' you will get separated!"

"You better load like I do then," he says, "same as you always have. If you want to stick with me."

Wind is gettin' up now, suckin' at the sides o' the tent, flappin' the pages of the book.

"Let's take Number 186 then. 'Loadin' in the four times an' at will.'"

He twirls his bloodstone around his finger. "I'll load at will—only I intend to be shootin' *this*away, not *that*away! If we ever get over there to the Union lines."

I see we never will get down to the long marches in the double quick time, or the runs with arms an' knapsacks, though that's part Heese might reely enjoy. Heese has allers said if he can't learn somethin' jist from seein' it with his eyes, he'll just go without learnin' it. He never would study, no time.

'Bout that time somep'n hard strikes the tent like a bullet—then another, then a whole splutter of bullets.

"Hail! I told you I smelt it!"

Heese flops over on his side, props his head from his elbow.

"Samantha," he says "I wanta go *home*! We ain't one bit nearer the Union lines than when we was back up on the Grandfather!"

"*Desert?*" I've heerd tales down here about deserters bein' chained to a twelve pound ball, or have their hair shaved off, or be stood on a bar'l, or *in* a bar'l.

"There must be some better way. Like you could get sick."

"I've not ever been sick."

It's the truth. He ain't. Not even the time Timmy Toaler come to the health rally at Boon an' give ever'body the small pox. Timmy's daddy said Timmy had looked forward to the trip an' he just didn' aim for him to be disappointed.

Hail is splatterin' down now fit to bust our tent, an' Heese is scowlin' up at the fine mist siftin' down through the cloth. "I hope it ain't hailin' like this on Pa's pertaters," he says, "if they've got any made."

I put the book away in my knapsack, lift up the box I'm settin' on an' brace it against the tent post to hold the front flaps together.

"Sion Hicks says there ain't a Yankee in twelve miles o' these swamps," Heese says. "Just our pickets. Yankees have gone plum off to Elizabeth City."

When Heese says 'swamps' I remember somethin'.

"Yes you have been sick! *One* time! Remember when you got the p'izen ivy at school?" He was sixteen years old then, his mother's last try at havin' him learnt to read. He'd do anything for her but that. I always thought 'twas because Pa Enoch couldn' read an' Heese always wanted to be exactly like him. Mary always believed he got in the p'izen ivy a-purpose, rollin' an' fightin' at recess. He had it two whole months, an' it's come on him ever since off an' on.

"Samantha!" Heese's voice is kinda low an' happy like for the first time in three weeks. "I believe you got somep'n! Samantha!" He reaches out an' pulls me down by the arm. "Come here!"

When you been actin' like a man for so long it's hard to get right back into bein' so much of a woman, 'specially in the midst of a hail storm that bids fair to jerk the tent right off the top of us an' us stripped.

"I'm loadin' in the nine times, Samantha!" His voice is low, kind of gaspy but he is laughin', too.

The beat of the hail drums into one long steady rumble that comes close around you like your skin, 'til your feelin's is turned outside in the way you'd roll a warm sock.

After a long time my bare arm drops down between our bunk an' the tent side. I feel lazy an' sleepy. Then I get woke up by a drop of ice water splatterin' up on my wrist from a puddle under the tent side. The storm is over! Up the comp'ny street you can hear men gettin' up an' out in the mud. In a little bit we'll be drillin' ag'in! I open my eyes an' look down. Sun is shinin' full on a ditch full o' hail, pourin' through the tent flap, winkin' on my bucket in the corner.

JAMES LEWIS to PINCKNEY LEWIS

Camp Ransom
Kinston, N. C.
April 30, 1862

Dear Pinckney—

It is with pleasure that I take my pencil in hand to write you. It is nearly sun set we have been down to the river bathing the whole company has been excused from drill this afternoon for that purpose. We have very good times hear only on guard duty when we have to be very strict or drilling which is most of the time.

I went fishing the other night and caught five eels and two cat fish and one bullhead. I caught them on that line you gave me I would like to have you send me a fish hook or two then I will send you something and that something will be a whopper.

Do not think that all we do is go swim & fish Far from it. I can inform you since the elections things are stricter here than ever. Captain Nat Rankin was elected major instead of Carmichael (killed.) There is many that do not like Rankin's hard schoolmaster ways but I have got as good confidence in him as any. You wanted to know what rank I hold I am now Second Sergeant. I did not get it in the elections but I got it by a kind of hapandstance which was all fare & Square but quite unexpected. The other evening the adjutant sent me to Company headquarters with some reports late in the day and when I went in Colonel Zeb Vance was sitting there alone and he was having a toddy. He looked like he was enjoying it and he asked me to join him and I said No sir I do not indulge. He asked me my name then and where I was from and he knew all our family and the Globe and asked me about Uncle Theophilus and Father and Squire Byrd and if there is much disaffection above Globe. I told him I thought some but if he wanted to know more he could ask our bugler, Mason Byrd, the Squire's son. He was very interested in learning about that and I wouldn't be surprised if he dosent call Mason up. Colonel Vance is interested personaly in each man 'specially right now with State elections coming up.

Colonel Vance has keen eyes, a big square head and makes you think of a lion or a bull dog or any animal that is strong and watchful. Lewis, he said, the next opening I have for an appointment I am going to remember you. And he did because when Second Sergeant Gerganus went home to Wilmington on furlow because he lost his speach at the battle of New Bern the Col. told Captain Rankin (maj) to give it to me so I am now Second Sergeant and there is only one above me and that is Orderly Sergeant.

Don't tell my folks about this I will write them but I will leave out about the toddy because you know how high they regard Colonel Vance and how they all feel about total abstnance except Uncle Theoph.

Mason Byrd is inhopes to get in the Band—for one thing they make a *lot* of money giving concerts in Kinston and Goldsboro and even as far away as Greensboro but they are a very hard outfit to break into on account of being Moravians and playing serious music.

You ask me what to do about volunteering now that the Conscript Law is in force. It did not effect our Regt much since ours was a 12 month Regt and most volunteered for the war at the start but they do want a furlow. I do not know how much longer we will be hear. You would stand a better chance to get promoted from the rankes in one of the new Regt than one of the old ones. And one more thing is that if you came hear it would be worse than if you went into Camp somewhere further North for more die hear with fever than bullets. There is four shaken in the tent next to this one. I feel sorry for all that have to come from the mountains it will be so warm and so sickly and they will have to drill anyhow. It is warm here today I wish I could be enjoying the cool dusk on Johns River or better still Anthony's creek. I am satisfyed that you are better off to stay in Globe until your 18 birthday you think the same as I did that they was some fun in being a soldier and they is but you do not call sport to march through rain when it is pouringe down in torents or to stand Picket in hail storms.

I wish some of those lowfers at home would have to come down here and do Picket duty for a while and maybe they will but the old Volunteer Regts do not want any part of them. I am glad to hear about the company drilling at Lenoir for Vance's Legion which gives me pleasure to learn that most of the people are so uniamously united.

I am as fat as a skunk. I have been in a mess (where you eat and and eat with) Sion Hicks and the two Garvys from the Grandfather mountain and the Woodall twins and a fat fellow from Watauga by name of McGillicuddy that likes to cook and he built us an oven from brick out of a deserted smoke house and we draw flour and do our own bakeing Mac made some big biscuits and they were grand. Pinckney I have some thing to tell you that is real interesting that I have not told to but one other person and that is Mason Byrd but I cant put it in a letter besides I have got to go now it is near Four½ inspection retreat and dressparade.

Eubbard Harmon is one of those with the ague but don't tell his folks for he is worse.

Don't forget the fish hooks. You can't get them hear I have tryed.

I remane your cousin Write soon

                        Jim

There is one thing I forgot to mention is I have a very heavy mustash.

ANDREW LEWIS to JAMES LEWIS

                        Riverside
                        Globe P.O. N.C.
                        May 10, 1862

Dear son,—

As I have not answered your last letter I will try to give you some account of my trip to S. Carolina. We went to Asheville, next day to Charles McDowell's for dinner and found all well, then to Hendersonville to Cousin Lena's found her & children well but her Husband quite unwell with asthma and Cousin Lena quite uneasy about him but I think twas more confusion from the house being full of refugees distant cousins from Corinth. Took the stage for Travelers Rest, got to Greenville about dark & remained there next day being the Sabbath. Went to preaching Psalm 64 "They encourage themselves in an evil matter. But God shall shoot at them with an arrow. Suddenly they shall be wounded." Took the cars for Columbia on Monday morning but got off at Frost Mill and staid Monday night at Profitt's & being very *flush* with money gave him $30 for two lambs one Southdown one Cotswold & $100 for a Devon bull calf—tried to buy some cotton but Profitts would not take responsibility for safe keeping. Went on to Columbia and bought 4 pair cotton cards for $24 ($6 pr) all they would let me have, & badly needed here to supply our clothing needs. Next morning went down to Hampton's place and gave his overseer Ephegenius one hundred and fifty dollars for a ram lamb, Bakewell & Southdown, the stock to be delivered next fall & put on the car for Greenville at any time that I may order it done. Everything seems to be very high and money more plenty than I ever knew it—I am afraid provisions especially of the meat kind are going to be very scarce. What will become of the poor who have nothing to buy with. Next came up to C. P. Howard's near Hope Station & also near to Pokatia & in sight of Summers. Made all night at your cousin Mish Howard's & went down with him early next morning to Hope's Station— paid John C. Hope fifteen hundred dollars for cotton at 13¢, arranged for him to store it & took his rect. for the money. It is *good fair* cotton and is to remain in safe distance from the R.R. subject to my order. I thought it would go up & expected to be late for the Market and so it was. But the war has assumed such gigantic proportions that the immense amount of paper currency must make prices advance still more. I also bought a bale for our own use & another for families of Volunteers—for the last I gave

$50 and expect to give it all away. Next day left for Greenville detained five hrs by cars off the tracks. Remained Greenville, it being the Sabbath, with Mrs. Atwood & her folks & very kindly treated by them all, attended Episcopal Church with them, always a little popish to me but fine sermon by the Bishop on Psalm 98 "His right hand and His holy arm hath gotten Him the victory." came to Hendersonville on Monday and to Mills River ten miles Monday night and home next nightfall and found all tolerable well but hands behind in their work generally due to long wet spring and me not being here. Globe valley looks pretty now with red maples fringeing out green willows and fruit trees in bloom above clover.

The Browns passed through Globe from Forge Flats yesterday bringing down another load of iron for the Confederacy, their 6 ox team in much difficulty with the mud. I asked about the roads. They merely said *there ain't any*. Fogerty Brown's son, the school teacher they call Little Whang Brown, may soon be in your camp, Fogerty says, his school having closed up on him. F. very proud and believes son may soon be whanging the Yankees the way he rapped his scholars nuckles. But of course you can't tell how Browns really feel.

The 'striction law' as they call it here is working very badly just now I fear. Those about to enlist resent removal of the Volunteer spirit—a few even gone through the lines to Kentucky rather than take conscription. It may take more men to enforce the act than will be gained in passing it.

Your mother hurrying me as she wants to meet Nath Gibbs with a box of provisions for you as he brings mail down from the mountains. All here are eager for news from Mississippi and Yorktown. No stamps available but we hear George Harper has carved one out of holly wood. Available at store in Lenoir. God preserve and keep you. All send love.

Father

JAMES LEWIS to MARGARET McKAMIE

> Out on picket
> Near Camp Ransom
> Kinston, N. C.
> May 30, 1862

Dear Margaret—

It is with pleasure that I take pencil in hand to write you these few lines. You will be surprised to hear from me but I have not forgoten and if you had any such thoughts you are in earer for I shall never forget and I hope you feel the same. You will have to excuse this writing I am out on picket near Daughertys Branch a few miles from camp and writing on my nap sack. I am at sunrise in a peace of woods amidst the tall pines Oh what a beautiful morning this is the sun sends its rays down thrugh trees on a floor of brown pine needles. It is not like the mountains dens with larel thickets but like a carpit with green ferns in it. People lived hereabouts but they have gone from their homes. Darkies around hear say the Yanks are in heavy force twelve miles from hear. I would like to have a chance to come in contact with a Yank then I would be satisfyed.

Your *brothers* are fine They learn fast or *he* would if he did not get impatent and be mad all the time at somebody or something. He has learnt the way of soljering does he like it No I can tell you that. Wether is very hot and damp but we stand it pretty well and take things as cool as we can. Our camp is about half mile from the Nuese river and the boys go swimming there often and Heath goes in but Sam has not that I know of Ha.

My folks are good about writing but I have not got to write much because somebody is after me all the time to write for them. I guess I have written more than one hundred letters. Margaret I am sorry you dident come with your folks to White Springs to say Goodbye. I have not forgotten about our walk up Anthony's at Easter time a year ago and over. Last night out hear on picket I got to thinking about it again and I could see you with that red cape on like a red bird lighted in the path. Margaret I wish there was some way you could go to Boon or Elizabethton or some where and have your picture made and send it to me in a letter. I would do the same in Kinston but I guess it would not be much specialy as I have a very heavy mustash now Ha. Margaret I hope you will not be to friendly with any of those tall fellows at church until I have got back on a furlow. One of the fellows I wrote a letter for wrote back home to Globe that this is a place of bad morals a regular Soddom and Gommorrer but I can inform you I am still in all things like I am in my Southern Confederacy. There is good people every whear even in Kinston.

I will close now since I have filled the sheet anyway tho I fear I not interest you. The frogs fill the air with thear lonesome songs. But thear is a better time coming when this dark cloud will drop away and leave the future brighter than at present. Always your true friend

Jim

Write to Sgt. James Lewis
    Co F 26th North Carolina Infantry
    Vance's Regiment
    Ransom's Brigade is so they will send it on.
    I do not know if we will be hear much longer
    Kinston, N. C.

HARRIETT McKAMIE

THE clo'es dried early this mornin', even Martin's jeans was arned by the time he was ready to go to Shull's Mill to fetch back meal an' salt. You can still get three pounds of good salt over there for a pound o' bacon. I woulda gone with Martin but he needed the room, he said. Mark my words, he'll pick up somebody, though—

one o' the Moodys at the ford or even old man Eagles. For a man that has little to say at home, Martin can loosen up mightily when he gets with somebody besides me.

It's gonna be warm today. Onions an' potato plants that Heese Garvy's hounds trompled Monday has begun to lay over in the heat. That was the first I suspicioned some change over the ridge —when the Plott hounds come sailin' in an' no Heath ner Samantha after 'em. The bear come first, loose in his winter skin as old widder's weeds, and frummicked off t'ords Huckleberry ridge. Voices of dogs like hoarse gongs a-tollin' come up from the holler —then here they come over the ridge! '*cross* the pasture!—right over my wet garden—cleared the fence same as if it wasn't there, lef' leg holes a foot deep in the loam! Dogs an' children cause more wranglin' in fam'lies than anything, only difference dogs don't know an' children forgets, but grown people don't forget. I finely sent Wash's old hound Princess over to Chaney's Thad to keep 'til Wash' gets back—she was always diggin' up my garden, pissin' on my touch-me-not's.

I was still straightenin' up plants an' weedin' when Nath Gibbs come by with Wash's letter an' news about Heese's goin' away to the war an' Samantha goin' with him which he'd only just learnt about over at Enoch's. I stood there dumfounded thinkin' how Mary's strappin' son that seemin'ly didn't even know how to behave hisself at the house of God had seen the light at last, only not all the pieces fit in with a person like Heese that hadn' never shown no fondness for what property rights stands for no more'n his step-father would

Nath's voice brings me back to my senses. "Ain't you goin' to open Wash's letter?" It lies there between us, small as a leaf—no doubt Nath' would already of read it if he could've. I can read printin' but Nath' knows I can't read writin', anyway not the writin' of this Daughtery feller that pens Wash's letters for him. I've been a little put out with Nathan since he put the mail gourd at Chaney's when anybody knows there's a heap more passin' here in the flats of the Gap than there is over there.

"You'd think" I said "some of 'em woulda come over to tell us about Heese's goin' away to the war! To say nothin' of Samantha!"

But I give Nathan somethin' to eat same as I always do, fried pies an' buttermilk fresh churned an' with his mouth full he told me some big tale about a Confedrit rout he'd heerd of down the country sommers where our boys got chased across a deep creek an' one o' the Luckadoos took off his clo'es an' left 'em for the rest to bring over, an' waded across holdin' up his gun, but the clo'es got misplaced by accident or joke, an' William Luckadoo had to march four miles mother-nekkid right in front of Colonel Vance before the clo'es was finely brought out. It seemed more the kind of story Nathan should be tellin' Martin or Reuben. "Havin' your conversation seemly," says Saint Peter—'specially with me standin' there already took up with unholy thoughts about what Samantha's goin' to do about dressin' an' undressin' that's unhandy for a woman even on a short journey such as camp meetin', to say nothin' of other things like how is she goin' to put on her monthlies skirt when she ain't even wearin' skirts atall! It give me quite a lot to think about after Nathan was gone, an' here I am still standin' in the doorway midway of a fine spring mornin' an' a whole day ahead o' me before Martin gets back.

We turned our stock out to upland pasture yesterday. They did real well through the winter—nobody'd dream how many hogs an' sheep we got up there now—some thirty head nobody even knows about without any taxes on 'em. Folks down in the valley thinks of us up here in the mountains as poor, an' God knows we are, but give me hogs any day that can root for theirselves an' you don't have to clothe the way you do slaves. All we need to do is salt 'em about once a week to gentle 'em an' keep 'em from strayin' too far. The good Lord does the rest. He clothes the sheep an' tempers the wind to the shorn lamb, blessed be His Holy name!

It would be a nice day for visitin'. I could go over to the Chaney's an' lend her a hand an' stop off at Enoch's an' Mary's an' tell 'em I'm glad about Heath Garvy's change o' heart, an' reproach 'em for not tellin' me. Mary wouldn' be there—she's allers gone sommers, 'relievin' sufferin' she would say, but leavin' Margaret an' the children to mind the place an' burn up somethin' for Enoch to eat.

"You can't fatten a McKamie," they told me when I married Martin, but now he would make two of Enoch that always reminds me of a old gaunt turkey.

Three miles across Rough Ridge Mary can go to Buckhannon's or for pi'zen plants down in the gorge, yet she don't have time to darken the door of her kin, married to her own husband's brother!

And that's all right. "That's all right," I say to Chaney. Chaney don't come much either but she's got good reason with all them boys to look after, an' Billie. I can usually guess what Chaney's a-doin'—I know when I churn she churns. On a good wash day like this I can almost smell Chaney's smoke an' suds in the air—anyway I know she's not off diggin' sang to send to heathen, or bilin' snake root and other unholy yarbs.

"It's the same distance," I've said to Chaney, "from Mary's an' Enoch's house to ourn that it is from ourn to their'n! There's no call to wear the path more on one side than t'other." I say that to Chaney! "Hate is sometimes better than love," I say. "It don't ask nothin'."

I've said it to Reuben's wife Nannie, too—her that blousies about the place all day not learnin' her gals to work an' they the daughters of a preacher an' s'posed to set examples to the flock. When our gals was still at home, I'd say to 'em " 'If any would not work, neither should he eat for God shall bring every work into judgment.' " That's what Mama taught me. If our daughters tuk a notion to marry young an' leave here, at least they left knowin' how to tend animals an' poultry an' crops an' to cook an' weave an' sew an' iron. Washington, too. He'll not have to beg fruit while he can plant trees nor borry tools when he can make 'em hisself.

"Bestir your own self then," says Conscience to me, "st'id o' standin' idle in the doorway belittlin' others! Cast the moult out of thine own eye."

But when the visitin's all one way—pride just says you'd haf' to have some good reason to go to their houses—like one o' the mules strayed, or you'd want to put a flower pot on Mama's grave on the hill above Enoch's house, or they'd want to hear Wash's letter that I can read now 'cause I learnt it by heart,

> Co. A Caldwell Rough & Ready Boys
> 22nd North Carolina Infantry
> French's Brigade
> Ivansport, Virginia 26 April 1862

Dear folks—

I take pen in hand to rite you thease few lines. I am well and inhopes you are all well. J. P. Daughtery is ariting this for me. At present the Company has not got stout since they had measels but I keep up and am inhopes to remane so. Labe Buckhannon was sick with informations of the lungs. He is some home sick to. Pa I am inhopes you can make me a pr of bouts you cannot get a pr hear for less than 10$ I will send you my mazure in this and when we get our pay I will send whatever it is for we are agon to pull back from hear soon and Goverment Shoes is not the things for anyones health. I wont them made out of heavy calf skin and double soles the whole lenth and plates and no nails in the toes of the bouts and heal plates.

We have dug enuff diches to come out the other side of the earth it seams like. The Yanks is other side of the river we see them every day. John Mundy has just come in with a hol in his coat the Yanks shot thrugh. He put his coat over a bord and held it above the rifle Pits an when they shot he let it fall over an we could hear them chear across the river. The Company is anxious to get in a battel an they say they cannot go home satisfyed with out a fite I think we will get a fite before we go home.

Give my love to all the folkes in McKamie Gap what has Heath Garvy don about gon in the War. Tell Thad I thank him for looken after Princess an' not let her get up a fox she is to old and heavy. and I will bring him the duble-barl pistol I have hier if nobody jay-hacks it from me. How did the peach buds live that I put out. I am inhopes to hear from you soon I have got only one letter from home in five weeks Your loving son Rote by J. P. Daughtery for Washington McKamie to Martin McKamie and Harriett McKamie.

Wash's learnt a lot since he's been in the army. He says he's in one of the thickes' settle places he ever saw—there's eight fam'lies livin' in hen crow of each other. There ain't any Mc-Kamie can write a better letter than that, not even Margaret, that smart girl o' Mary's. It's better, if you ask me, to know what the names of grains an' vegetables is an' what's good for 'em than all the wild flowers an' plants, or even roses the way Chaney does.

I fold the letter back in its little cover that's got the Confedrit flag drawed on it, red white an' blue, and the words "These Colors Warrented Not to Run."

A jar fly starts chirrin'—a jar fly? More'n likely a cricket or grasshopper complainin' ag'inst the heat. The sound puts you in mind of every summer that ever was!

I reach for the gourd by the water bucket, drink a mouthful, spit it out. I been laz'in around here, forgot to go to the spring. I lay Wash's letter on a stool, come back for the bucket and walk down to the springhouse under the cool hemlocks.

It's not lack of news keeps Nannie from visitin' me. Some preachers may be shut-mouthed an' more credit to 'em since one thing that got 'em into it—the gift for standin' up and havin' folks listen to 'em—is what they'd always haf' to be workin' ag'inst. Anyway, Reuben McKamie is not shut-mouthed. Chaney told me how Reuben gets home in the evenin', comes up from the barn, fetches a chair, takes the measure of Nannie more'n likely still in her wrapper, sets down with his fists on his knees, starts tellin' at the hour he left home an' ends right where he is, puttin' in the right scripture an' all. Chaney says one o' Reuben's home comin's is as good as a camp meetin' an' a fun'ral all rolled in one. Nannie an' the girls just listen. What's aggervatin' to me is how months later somethin' will come out just enough to let you know they'd know'd the facts all the time.

I dip the bucket, wait for it to fill, set it by on the stone. I know why Nannie don't come over here to see me. She'll never git over the time Nelson McCauthern come to take her to the magistrate's meanin' to marry her. And I met 'em on the path an' faced her around an' put a stop to it. It wasn' nothin' but two young folks with spring fever anyway. In due time she married Reuben, good an' proper, an' you'd think she'd be grateful to me she's got a roof over her head with a congregation to look after 'em, an' not livin' down on McCauthern Creek with the quarrelsome an' the lawless—some of 'em gone a year already over the border to East Tennessee to join the bridge burners an' the hiders-out rather than joinin' the Confederacy with respectable people down in the Globe an' up here in the Gap!

I lean over the spring an' suck my fill o' cold clear water. The water skimmers scatter back into the cave.

The snap of a twig brings me up an' to my feet. Somethin' is movin' off in the bushes—too slow for a critter, too light for a man.

TOMMY McKAMIE

The Plott hounds haven't come back. This is the longest they've ever been gone, three whole days. Ma says Heese will have a cryin' duck fit. Queenie started out with 'em but after about an hour she come back winded, tongue a-quiverin' out, gums drawed back like she's laughin'. She flopped down sudden an' slep' a while but uneasy, her paws twitchin'. Even after she waked she set on her haunches an' kep' lookin' at the woods an' ever' once in a while she'd fidget an' whimper.

Neil McCurry says "That dog has seen somethin'." It is the second day Neil is here to help Pa cut rye. The four of us work down the field, Neil an' Pa cradlin', Jake an' me pullin' it on the sledge.

"If it was a animal she'd a-brought it back, even if it's just a rabbit or a boomer, half alive." Wash's old dog, Princess, that

Thad is keepin' will not do that though she is Queenie's pup. Wash has promised to bring Thad a double-barreled pistol just for keepin' Princess for him. Thad talks so much about it Jake an' me are sick o' hearin' it.

"It's got two hammers like my daddy's rifle, an' the barrels have holes as big as my thumb, an' you can shoot a squirrel out of the tallest tree with it."

"You seen one, I guess."

"I seen a pitchur of one in a book down at Patterson when we went to get thread."

Neil McCurry wears Confedrit pants because he has been in the war, but he is not goin' back to that war any more.

"He is a deserter," Thad says.

"He is not! He is paroled!"

With Thad an' Jake an' me, it's always been two against one. Now, with the war, seems like it's worse. Thad's daddy, that's Uncle Billy, ust to bring Thad along when he come to help with the harvestin' an such. Pa an' Uncle Billy would just get on with the work, not talkin' much. But he don't come much any more, an' if he does, or Uncle Martin or Uncle Reuben, it's on Sundays an' they're dressed up an' talk loud an' shake hands a lot like they'd cover up their real feelin's. But they don't work together with Pa nor talk natural any more.

"We ain't goin' to help raise stuff to feed Yankees," Thad says. Me an' Jake was goin' to whup him for sayin' that but Pa come between us. It's gettin' more an' more that way. Seems like even the dogs feels it.

Neil McCurry goes nekkid above his waist. His muscles are big and slide under his skin that is sweating and brown from bein' in the sun where he was at the war. The first day he come, Jake an' me wear our shirts. Next day we leave 'em off. Then Margaret comes to make us put 'em back on an' we scuffle with her about it 'til Neil catches us, twists our wrists 'till we holler. He learnt that grip from a Yankee.

Margaret flounces back in the house and Neil watches her. She don't let on but I can tell when a feller's around just by watchin'

Margaret. Just hearin' about one makes her mettlesome the way sayin' 'squirrel' does Queenie. Like when Pa an' Ma were talkin' last night about the man Ma come upon in the woods. Margaret is sittin' by the candle knittin' a sock. They thought I was asleep.

"On Green mountain branch, 'bout noon," Ma says. "Near the gully."

Pa is finishin' up a shoe, workin' sheep's oil into the uppers. It is a man's shoe. We don't wear any only in the coldest weather.

Ma says "Queenie barked an' bristled. Then the man riz up— just a boy, he was. Musta been bathin' his feet in the branch, then laid over on the warm rock an' feel dead asleep."

"The dog wont hurt you!" The boy staggers back ag'inst the bushes. "I'm Mary McKamie. I live at McKamie Gap—that-away." His eyes is wild watchful. I take a stick to Queenie that has braced herself for a scrap.

Ma says, "I lift the lid o' my bucket, take out a yam. He nearly falls headlong to reach for it. I pin Queenie betwixt my legs, then lower myself to sit on the rock, rub the dog down and quiet her. The boy breaks up the yam, crams some into his mouth, chews it skin an' all. He is wearin' a plaid shirt an' his pants are tore considerable. His poor feet—swelled like half-scalded meat, not ust to goin' unshod, you can tell.

"I reach back t'ords a bear-bark bush, break one of its big leaves to fold into a cup, dip it in the stream.

"This'll help it go down. Sweet 'taters is kind o' bulky by theirselves.' "

He sips the water. "I never tasted anything so good! Thank you, Ma'am!" He is soft-spoken, a nice young feller you can tell.

Margaret draws out a long string o' wool. I'm wide awake now. Earlier in the evenin' when we were havin' prayers, I could hardly hold my eyes open—"Blessed are the poor—" an' all that. Ma's talk is always int*eress*tin' an' I'm not sleepy now atall.

She says, Queenie muscles out, sniffs the boy's feet. He glances up at the sun.

" 'Bout what time is it?"

"Noontime."

"I musta slep' two hours!" He reaches his hand out to Queenie, "Here girl!" She backs off. His eye falls on my lunch bucket ag'in. I raise the lid an' give him the other potato.

"Oh, thank you!" He raises it to bite. "I'm takin' your lunch!"

"Help yourself. Me an' Queenie can eat at home this evenin'."

He seats hisself down on the rock, gives a sigh, "I wisht I could!"

He eats slower this time, breakin' the pulp into little bites like he'd make it last.

"Where mout your home be?"

"Ohio. My name is John Rousie. I've walked all the way from Virginia. Lexington. A man in a place called Wilkes told me yesterday to come this way to get to Tennessee. East Tennessee. He was the last human I've seen 'til I waked and saw you. And your dog."

His light hair falls down in a shock over his nose. He eats dainty now, slow, makin' it last. I still got pork an' corn pone in my pail but, thinks I, I'll find out a little more about him first.

"You got a famb'ly in Ohio, I guess?"

"Yes, my parents, my brother and two sisters. I'm the oldest." His eyes are green like trout water. You'd expect 'em to be blue with that fair hair. He's starin' at the tow sack I dropped when Queenie barked.

"There's nothin' but Seneka Snake root in there," I say, "and hops."

"You an herb woman?"

"Some folks calls me that."

"What's Senaka Snake root good for?"

"For me, it's good for fifty cents a pound at the store in Lenoir. If it's cleaned an' well dried, that is."

"It's good to bring on vomitin'."

"So it is. How'd you know?"

"My uncle's a druggist. In Lexington, Virginia. I lived upstairs over his store and went to school 'til they were about to conscript me. So you might say—I ran." He offers his sticky fingers to Queenie, she eyes 'em, sniffs, gives them one little lick. "I'll volunteer in Ohio. Or maybe join a cavalry comp'ny in Tennessee. After walkin' so far, 'twould be good to ride a while."

"Well—you're among friends here. At least Queenie an' me is."

"Are feelin's divided up here?"

"Summat."

"That's what the man in Wilkes said. Well, I'm glad anyway I met up with you, Mrs. McKamie. I've kept to the woods all the time. If you hadn't come along, I guess I'd a-starved. Do you know where Valley Forge on Doe River is? Or Turkeytown, Tennessee?"

"Yes. But I doubt them feet o' yours will ever get you to Turkeytown. If we can't get shoes for you, you better lay over an' put some grease on 'em 'til they heal." I go in the bucket an' bring out the pork an' bread.

"I can't take that," he says, but looks at 'em, still hungry.

"Aw, g'wan."

"Thank you, Mis' McKamie. The Lord sure sent you to me!"

"Praise His Holy Name."

"Amen."

He eats thoughtful. "There was more to it than that," he says—"I mean, about me leavin' Virginia. The borders are closed—Fremont is in the mountains, Banks in the Valley, and Jackson —nobody knows where Jackson is right now. Whenever I'd go home to Ohio, I'd bring back letters for whoever wanted to send 'em. It didn't make any difference to me what side the senders were on. Mails from Ohio were stopped and I did it for a kindness to neighbors no matter how they believed. Rebs heard about it, threatened to arrest my uncle, conscript me an' send me as far south as they could."

Queenie is plum friendly now, waggin' her tail, beggin' for a bite, givin' away that she an' I ain't et since breakfast six hours ago. John Rousie don't notice, though, he just keeps diggin' in with strong young teeth.

"I tell you what you'd orter do. My son an'—my two grown

sons—ain't at home right now. They got a house up on Grandfather mountain, 'bout four miles from here. You could lay up there a few days 'til you're fitten to travel."

"Where are your sons?"

"They're—well, they're in the Confedrit army right now. They're down at Kinston—"

He stops chewin' a minute, just sits there with the last bite o' cornbread between his fingers.

"But that ain't where they want to be!" I say, all at once kinda desp'rate.

How can you put in words, Ma says, a thing as mixed up as things these days has come to be! You take Heese alone, an' his feelin's! Much less explainin' about Samantha! An' here's this nice young boy—it's easy to guess his folks would love him—an' the saddest thing is he'll go off about dusk, lookin' behind all the time to see who's follerin' an' maybe goin' to shoot him!

Margaret is sittin' up straight, knittin' fast, holdin' her work close to the candle that's burnt down to about an inch.

"Oh!" Ma says. "One o' the last things he as't me was, did I ever know of a Dan Ellis, at Valley Forge, on Doe River, in East Tennessee."

Pa gets up stiff. His long shadder rises up into the rafters.

"Did *you* know a Dan Ellis?" Ma asks him.

Pa walks over an' sets the shoes careful on the mantelpiece. It's as if he hasn't even heard her. He says "You'd ort not to be goin' in the woods any more by yourself, Mary. An' Mar'grit not atall."

Margaret loops an' ties a thread, bites it off, turns the sock an' smooths it hard over her knee.

"Them Plott hounds has not come back," Ma says.

"About huntin' dogs you can't tell. I've know'd 'em to stay gone a week or more."

I wish I was sleepy. Nothin' gets you so wide awake as your dog bein' gone.

Margaret gets up an' crosses over an' lays the socks across the new pair o' shoes, and climbs the ladder up to bed.

SAMANTHA

I seen a somebody today I wisht I didn' see.

It's while some of our comp'ny and the Thirty Seventh is in swimmin' after drill—all but Heese an' some others that's been on outpost five days. I asked to get sent with him but the night before while I was on sentry duty at Post Three the goddam black cat got in the commissary at midnight, fire-eyed, its back curved up like the very devil hisself. I ain't afeard o' much but this ain't fear but more a dread that comes over you like Heese's nightmares from all the time you can remember an' rivets you to the spot 'til screamin' brings help to turn you loose. So that starts a whole round o' yellin' from sentry posts—"Halt!" an' "Who goes there!" an' "Rounds!" an' "Advance Rounds!" it rises an' falls along the whole dam' chain from here to the guard house an' back like echoes in the mountains 'til finely the sergeant of the guard come runnin' up outa breath an' Andrew Biggerstaff is with him. The sergeant holds the lantern up but me bein' a head taller, I can see him better'n he can see me. I'm still a-trimble.

"What's the commotion here, Garvy?"

First thing comes into my head I say, "Some kinda animal," I says, "Sir," I says, not bringin' myself to name it.

This little sergeant is some kinda Quaker from a place called Salem. "I thought I heard a woman scream," he says.

"Santers do scream like that sometimes," I say. I get my voice back down husky.

He holds out the lantern an' circles it around. "Santer?"

"Face like a man but voice like a woman! Oh, it's a animal too, all right!" Anybody raised in the mountains has heard about santers. They come out after dark, jump from tree to tree, don't never come down long as they live, if they ever die.

Andrew's mouth twitches. He's from Bunkem county—Swannano. "I never know'd a santer to come down on the *ground* before," he says curious.

"Was this a—male or female, would you say?"

"Oh, I doubt if anybody ever *sees* a santer. The scream is all you know 'em by. Don't you have 'em at Salem?"

"You saw this one, didn't you?" He's a touchy kind of furriner, likes to show off with the flute in the band. "Private Biggerstaff," he says to Andrew, "you stay here with Private Garvy. You both report to the Guard House after roll call in the mornin'. The rest of us will do a little recon—" whatever the word is, means to prowl, or snoop. I look around for some sign o' the cat, an' shiver. He an' some others that've joined us go off liftin' up tent flaps here an' there with their gun bar'ls, their shadders waverin' in an' out among the tents.

"*Was* it a woman?" Andrew asks interested soon's they're outa ear shot.

"It was a santer," I says. But I know it was the devil in the shape o' that half starved critter, an' it started all my troubles, for that's how I had to take fat-teeg duty next mornin' an' join the mourners which is what they call the squad whose bad luck falls to haf' to bury the horses that dies every once in a while from glanders, an' to keep it from spreadin'. It's common for one or more o' the mourners to puke just from the smell o' the carcasses an' diggin' in the heat an' all, an' that's what I done. For 'bout the second time in my life, I throwed up. But it was part due to Heese bein' sent off an' me an' him bein' separated. Heese ain't so well hisself. The pi'zen ivy he rubbed all over hisself in the swamp finely took, bein' slower than the mountain kind like ever'thing else down here, but when he went on outpost he'd raised a pretty good crop o' blisters 'specially 'round his middle where he ain't exposed to air.

So after we get through buryin' the horses, an' I thought I was through vomitin', I felt like I would give my two months pay what we ain't got yet for one good cold dip in Linville river. So I took my bucket an' went off like I was goin' to the spring but the taste o' that ole oily water just stuck in my mouth an' made me sicker'n ever. I wandered on down to the Neuse thinkin' I'd strip an' get me a bath, an' relieve the smell o' them dead horses an' fergit how one of 'em's leg kep' stickin' up 'til we had to break it off with a shovel.

But before I could get in sight o' the river, I heerd shoutin' an' laughin' an' sure 'nuff some o' the Twenty Sixth boys an' the Thirty Seventh was in there swimmin'. So I find me a seat up on the bank amongst some live oak roots that coil out over the water, an' try not to pay no attention to my dizziness an' watch the boys frolic in that ole tea-colored water.

You can might'n near tell where each is from by how he swims. Mountain fellers ust to narrer streams an' swift water fights this ole slow wide river like fightin' fire, git as far as the middle, gives out an' has't to come pantin' back, while them little Onslow boys gives up to it as natural as air, floatin' under water as much as on top, their long yeller hair lazy above them as water weeds. The ones can't swim atall cuts up the liveliest, stayin' clost to the bank that curves under where I sit in the tree roots. Some with beards look like they forgot to take 'em off, an' you'd wonder that the Lord Almighty that furs each beast suitable even to the flat curl in a heifer's forehead could put hair so ever'whichaway on men—north, south or mossy all over—not one of 'em, though, smooth like my man an' hard like beech bark—even with the pi'zen ivy.

"Enjoyin' yourself?" The voice comes from behind me. I guess I'd know that voice in hell, wheezy an' comin' from no place like a hawk's but you'd know it was around for no good even when you can't spot it.

I look back an' sure 'nuff there he is—Little Whang Brown, his so'jer hat set back on his greasy-waved black hair parted in the middle real prissy. It's always seemed to me like a face that was finished an' set on separate, not resemblin' any o' his folks nor even a Creek Indian but more like one o' the Irish peddlars comes through the mountains, or the chiney-headed doll Nath' give to Margaret.

I turn back an' stare at the bathers an' for the first time my face flames up 'cause they are men and nekkid an' because it's the devil himself settin' there behind me, not just a black critter settin' on a bar'l o' salt pork.

« 85 »

"If you don't mind, Samanthy," he says, "I'll seat myself down here by you." He does, weighin' down the tree roots that swings out like a nest o' sarpints from the bank.

"I thought you was teachin' school at Goldsburr!"

"I was. Until the Confed'ricy got so hard up for recruits it started takin' in wimmen. I thought 'twas time then for me to join up!"

He takes out one o' them little blocks o' no-'count Confedrit matches an' clay pipe the sutler sells for thirty five cents that breaks if you look at 'em an' he lights up.

"I mighta know'd you'd be where there's somep'n goin' on—a hoe down or a fire ballin'—"

That's to bait me with that tongue o' his'n that's not stopped waggin' since his ole daddy Fogerty first took him to camp meetin' at the age o' six an' stood him up on a stump so folks could lis'sen to him preach an' sing.

I raise my hand to hide my face a-burnin'—not for what happened nine years ago come Fourth o' July because that coulda happened with many a boy an' girl goin' on fifteen that's had a little brandy the first time an' gets throwed together at a fire ballin'. But more that it happened with such a blitherin' dwarfish fool as Whang Brown!

"Why ain't you in there with 'em?" he wheezes, short o' breath. He always gets like that when he's around me.

"I figure Heath'll be back in a minute," I says. The namin' of Heese steadies me, though if he was here an' know'd what I ain't ever seen any use in tellin' him, it wouldn' be no use ever to look for a chip o' Whang Brown's chiney head ag'in. Heese scorns him anyway. "Me an' him will go in later, after these gets out. That is if Retreat don't sound first."

The smell o' that clay pipe is makin' me sick, or maybe it's recallin' that night on the bald o' the Yeller mountain when one o' those turpentine soaked balls the girls sewed fell t'ords us an' Whang Brown, runnin' from it, for I know he wouldn' have the guts to play the real game an' catch it an' throw it high, come down on top o' me there in the dark edge o' the woods. Who throwed the fire ball or what feller scooped it up I never know'd, but what flared up between me an' Whang Brown couldn' be squinched 'til it went on an' burnt itself out.

Now he blows some o' his old terbaccer smoke slow ag'inst my neck an' says "You're gonna haf' to wait a good while on Heese."

The swimmers is brayin' over duckin' a feller right under us an' I think I ain't heard him right.

"What did you say?"

"Your *hus*'ban' has been took to the horspittle. In Kinston. I thought I'd come down an' keep you comp—"

My boot slips on the roots so I pur't nigh slide through the hole an' down into the water. This jars my stomach an' I haf' to swaller hard.

"If you ain't lyin'," I say, turnin' to look at his un-movin' doll face, "what's the matter with Heese?"

"He come off picket 'bout the time my relief come to the guard house. He was considerable broke out!" He p'ints to his little stubby hands that I wonder how I could ever a-had the feel of 'em on my flesh, a-pushin' an' a-pullin' an' pawin' like swimmers that can't swim an' the whimperin' like some kinda animal only I was so took up with my own su'prised inside feelin's I never got around to the outside ones. That come later—to know I'd wipe the slate clean of it if I could, and never have nothin' to do with Whang Brown ag'in.

He stretches one o' his banty legs kinda slow across where he knows I'll hafta step over it. Puke or no puke I scramble up, careful to watch where I place my foot, an' I take one good leap off'n that basket o' roots onto solid earth an' I start runnin' across fields 'til I get to the north side o' camp back o' the slaughter pens when I remember I left my bucket back at the river an' I got no pass.

There's considerable movement over amongst the horses an' wagons where they're tied up, like they might be gettin' ready for a battery drill. But I'm bent on findin' Jim Lewis or Bugles or even Sergeant Coffey or somebody can help me find Heese. One o' the Woodall twins, Thee or Dee—I got no time to tell 'em apart—is on Post Nine an' he says "Hi, Sam," an' lets me through tho' it wouldna made no differ'nce if I'd a-had to knock him down to get past, an' he calls somethin' after but I'm bent on findin' Jim Lewis or Bugles an' at the same time I keep swallerin' to hold back the bile. Seems like by now I orter be gittin' over buryin' them horses. Heese's mother an' me never have been close, but right now I'd give my 'leven dollars a month's pay for one dose o' her peppermint or tansy to settle my stummick.

There's a group o' officers by headquarters but I run on past an' down the comp'ny street where ours is the last tent t'ords the color line, an' McGillicuddy is standin' in front there talkin' to Bugles who is rubbin' on his horn with a rag.

"What do you know about Heese?" I am pantin'.

"Nothin'. What's the matter, Sam? You look right green! Seen another santer or somep'n?"

"I hear'd he's been took to the horspittle!"

Mason Byrd, that's Bugles, looks at me kinda odd. "That's so! Your—brother was broke out all over with a rash—an' mosquito bites, too. All the pickets were, but he was really bad. The surgeon didn' know what it was. Sent him in to Kinston. 'Fraid o' smallpox or—" he named some kinda other pest disease.

"Didn' he leave no word?"

"No—Sergeant Lewis saw him—"

"Where's Jim?"

"Up at headquarters. Say, have you heard, Sam? Our regiment's bein' moved out! Ransom's whole brigade! We're bein' sent to Virginia! Some Yankee general has ditched hisself from the ocean plum up to Richmond!"

THE BUGLER

SAM Garvy is absent at Dress Parade and Retreat and is so reported. Sam did not look well while talking to McGillicuddy and me about Heath Garvy's being taken to the hospital, in fact, she clamped her hand over her mouth and dived into her tent as if she was going to throw up. But I could not wait to help because I had to blow Dress Parade and drummers were already gathering for the roll.

It was a special Dress Parade due to reading orders for our departure to Virginia and also announcement of Colonel Zeb' Vance's nomination for governor of North Carolina which was no secret, my father having already written me about it with clippings from the Asheville paper, and Captain Mickey had our Band practicing "The Old North State" a week before the Fayetteville Observer even printed Colonel Vance's letter. The Band are very strong for Vance because he was the one got them into the Twenty Sixth in the first place—just met 'em and asked 'em in a New Bern hotel one day last March. Not every regiment is blessed with such a Band—some don't have any.

It was I who suggested to the 2nd B♭ cornet player, J. O. Hall, that they learn "Cripple Creek" because of Vance's being from the mountains. They didn't think much of the idea at first, the song being below the standards of music they like to play and besides, they said, "Cripple Creek" was a Gold Rush song. So I had to go get Andrew Biggerstaff to prove it to 'em that there was a Cripple Creek in the Smokies long before Forty Niners. They believe Andrew because he drives their instrument wagon for them.

So this gave me a chance to be friendly with J. O. Hall, especially after Andrew told them about our folks being strong Democrats, and we came to find we had other things in common such as chess and he showed me some things about breathing and about interpreting the bugle calls which until now I had not thought of as a thing to be interpreted atall. J. O. also told me there is a rumor that Floegel who plays 1st B♭ cornet in the Band may go to the Cape Fear as there is a Colonel Cantwell down there with the Fifty First who is very anxious to work up a Band that will be the East's answer to the West—that's Vance's and Mickey's. J. O. says if this happens, he would like to take Flocgel's place which would leave 2nd B♭ cornet open and he will speak to Captain Mickey and the adjutant about me getting that place.

There are a great many orders at this Dress Parade. When my name is called along toward the last to report to regimental headquarters after tattoo, I am very surprised. Interested, too. While our camp has a number of un-trained or would-be musicians, I am one of the few outside the Band that has had horn lessons three summers under Mr. Plumley-Piggott who comes to the mountains summers as organist for Saint James's church.

Tattoo is one of the bugle calls I do best. It is quite long, 32 measures to only 13 for Drill. Retreat is longest, 63 measures. The shortest is Watering Call, 2 measures. J. O. says Tattoo gives a musician scope. Here is how I play it: The first three notes are whole notes, c,g,e. I play them very commanding like a warning the men had best stay in their tents. The next eight measures are the same. Then come seven bars that go up to a G, as though you would question whether the men are going to stay in or not. If all is quiet as it usually is, J. O. showed me how you can play the rest of Tattoo softly, nearly like a lullaby, and still more softly, to the last note which returns to a beautiful low C! I don't think even Floegel can play Tattoo now any better than I can play it.

Tonight, though, when I get to the ninth measure, the question whether someone is going to stay in their tent or not is answered immediately. Sam Garvy is not. He is coming up to the color line, striding along on those long legs. I have not seen a finer looking man than Sam Garvy to be a woman. She is on the muster rolls as seventeen years, but I think she is older than that, probably 26, the age of her husband. They just put it that way to explain her soft voice and not shaving. Ever since James Lewis told me he is a she, I have watched her. When you know he is a she you can kind of tell. But it is hard. For instance when I put on women's clothes to be in the regimental entertainment, several men watched me for days after that and one or two came to my tent to tell me how well I played the part of Sweet Evalina, and seemed to enjoy hearing me practice, and telling them about musicians like Daniel Decatur Emmett who travelled with a circus and wrote "Dixie," but after a while they lost interest, which is how people are who do not really love music.

So here comes Sam Garvy breaking into my playing.

"Bugles!" she says, "Come with me to Colonel Vance!"

She cheats me out of enjoying that last long beautiful note!

"What *for*?" I lower my horn, brush my wet lips against my jacket shoulder. It's as if *I* might have done something wrong.

"You'll find out." When you look at Sam close up, you see she has a faint dark smudge of hair over her lip like smut almost like she *could* shave.

"Have you orders?" I ask.

"No."

"Then I can't go with you." I shake out my horn.

"Bugles, I have *got* to see the Colonel!"

"Then go to the captain."

"Captain Ballew is at the Quartermaster's."

"The lieutenant, then."

"He has gone to take a deserter in."

"Go to your corporal, then."

"He's on a post!"

"How about the sergeant?"

"I've not seen Jim Lewis in five days. Bugles—"

"Where is your orderly sergeant?"

"Old Coffey? Messin' with all them papers somewheres. Or off holdin' a prayer meetin'."

"*I* have orders," I say. "You heard my name—where were you at Dress Parade?"

"Sick!"

"And Retreat?"

"Sick-by-God-sick!" she says staccato, then mumbles "Don't bring that up."

"All right," I says, "You can go along when I go. But tell your own tale." She wipes her mouth on *her* shoulder.

We go up the company street. Camp has not got quiet. Not at all. For one thing, it's a very hot night. "Let me go by and put my bugle away." When I come out, Sam is standing by a tent listening to a high-pitched voice.

"McGillicuddy," she says, "sortin' his gear. He's gonna hate to leave all them little conveniences he's built in."

Sam walks on fast then. We skirt around behind Companies E and D. Riders clop in and out. They are strangers from brigade headquarters. Officers' tents are brightly lighted. 'Way out in the dark where wagon trains are, lanterns bob, trace chains clink, and boxes thud on barrels. This brigade is going to move.

"Maybe it will be cooler in Virginia." We slap at mosquitoes. "Do you want to go to Virginia, Sam?"

"I' druther be in a burnin' hell, Bugles!"

It's about fifty paces now to regimental headquarters.

"We don't haf' to go in together," I say. "If we *get* in." Burgwyn and old Nat Rankin have tried to make things strict in camp but not even they can get Colonel Vance to close his tent to any man that wants to see him, 'specially now with the election comin' up. The guards know that anybody gets in he gives the nod to. When we are five paces from the big lantern lighted wall tent, we hear voices.

"You'll begin duties as Sergeant-Major tomorrow, Sergeant Coffey." This is the adjutant's voice. The adjutant is in charge of the Band, and the Sergeant Major is the adjutant's assistant. So this affects the Band because I don't think Sergeant Coffey knows anything about music except hymns.

"Sergeant Lewis will take over as Orderly Sergeant."

James Lewis must be in there, too. James and I are close friends, in fact he is about my best friend down here. He can't carry a tune, but we've been raised the same way—Baptists, Democrats and all that, and we play chess together.

"Reduce baggage to the strictest regulation limit—that is, to each man what he can carry." This is the Colonel's voice.

There is a little pause, then the adjutant says kind of dry, "This will go hard with some of the men. Our regiment is very rich in personal effects, Sir."

"It is a military necessity," says the Colonel.

Sam Garvy, in the meantime, hasn't a bit more paid attention to the guard, but quicker'n lightning can strike a tree she steps out of the dark and is past me and inside the tent door. I show my pass.

"Just a minute!"

Some officers are coming out, a quartermaster looking worried. It falls on him to move these 20,000 men out of here. The guard takes my pass, stares at it—I doubt he can read. I have decided I don't want to miss whatever Sam has on her mind, so as the guard draws himself up kind of slow, I take a long step forward which puts me not exactly *in* the doorway, but not out, either.

Colonel Vance sits at the center of his field table facing me. A big lantern under the roof pole throws its light down on his heavy shoulders and long mane of dark hair and the braided crown of his cap. To his right is the adjutant, and to his left Major Gaither, the regiment's assistant surgeon. Sergeant Henry Coffey and James Lewis are right of the adjutant, kind of back as if they're about to leave. A second lantern wavers their shadows up into the tent roof. The desk is piled with papers. Sam Garvy stands very straight and salutes.

"Private Sam Garvy, sir, Company F."

The Colonel is toying with a pen staff, jabbing it in and out of a little box of sand beside the ink well.

"What can I do for you, sir?"

The Colonel's hands are very fine. He would make a good cornet player.

"I've come to ask you for a furlough, sir!"

"Where is your captain?"

"Captain Ballew is at the quartermaster's, sir!"

Colonel Vance's split bottomed chair squeaks as he shifts his weight toward the shadows at the right. "Sergeant Coffey?"

"Yes, sir!"

"Do you know this man?"

"Yes, sir. He *is* Private Sam Garvy, Company F, of our regiment, sir." Sergeant Coffey is old for this army—fully forty five. He has a sort of hoarse voice.

"How long have you been in service, Private Garvy?"

"Three months, sir."

The adjutant is shifting some big wide ledgers. If you are an adjutant, you have to be ready to come up with quick answers. I have heard that this adjutant is our regiment's best chess player. I should like to have a game with him. James Lewis and I learned to play chess well with Mr. Plumley-Piggott, the organist for Saint James. There are some summers in the mountains when it does not do anything but rain.

The adjutant runs his finger down the page. "Private Garvy has been in Company F two months, twenty three days."

The Colonel leans over to look at the wide book. I think our Colonel would do anything he could to help one of his men even if it is some fool private's request. "I can't give you a furlough, Private Garvy," he says. "There are men in our regiment who have not been home in nearly a year. You have been in only three months."

"Eighty three days," says the adjutant who is pressing his forefinger on a line in the book.

The Colonel leans over to glance at the page again, his thick neck stretching above the three gold stars on his collar.

"You're from Watauga!" He straightens up and tilts back in his chair which brings his stomach up in a double curve of gold buttons. "Watauga!" The word lies in the air before us and seems to give him satisfaction.

James Lewis's face is what you might say is a study. If the lantern was not so orange I would say his face is red.

Then the Colonel sees me.

"Who is that?"

"Corporal Mason Byrd, Sir!" I say, saluting. "Bugler for the Second Battalion, Twenty Sixth Regiment."

"Yes, Oh, yes! From up Mulberry! How are your father and Uncle? And the precincts?"

Well—you never can tell about McCautherns. I say "Safe, sir. We mean to keep 'em so!"

Sam turns to me and grins. She'd forgotten I'm there. I step forward and lay my pass before the adjutant and step back.

He frowns, then nods. "The Band," he says to the Colonel. "Floegel to the Fifty First."

The Colonel nods, turns back to Garvy again. "It must be something very pressing to bring you to headquarters this time of night, Private Garvy—a busy night like this, to seek a furlough."

"It's my brother! he is sick—"

"In Watauga?"

"In Kinston, Colonel. I've got to git to him—"

"In Kinston?"

"He's Private Heath Garvy, sir. Same company, F, the Twenty Sixth!"

The Colonel brings his chair legs down bump on the turf and turns left to Major Gaither.

"You wouldn't need a *furlough* to visit the hospital in *Kinston*," he says. The surgeon is some slower with papers than the adjutant. "Sergeant Coffey, do you know this man's brother?" The Colonel turns to the shadows.

"Yes, Sir! Heath Garvy, the brother, was taken to regimental hospital this morning. He came off picket with a very heavy rash—we feared airysiplas or something."

The surgeon has found the place—six places, in fact. He puts them together and seems to read among them.

"The name is Garvy, William Angel Garvy." Major Gaither has a little square silver beard and wears steel spectacles with square rims. "Private Garvy was taken to regimental hospital suffering from a profuse maculo papular skin rash involving his entire body. Since we have no pest house and Private Garvy was considered well enough to walk, he was granted furlough—"

"Oh my God!" says Sam, throwing her arms together the way a shivering man would hug himself to keep warm, "I got to git to him! Jim—" her voice rises.

The surgeon peers over the rims of his little steel specs. "Private Garvy," he says soothing, "there is no reason to be—" he trails off as if her cry has really just reached him—all woman.

Sam stays hunched a minute, hands clutching elbows.

She leans toward the three men at the desk. They blink back at her. "What I'd orter a-asked for is a *dis*charge! He's my husban'! I'm a woman! I got to get with my husban'! Doctor—"

"Sergeant Coffey, can you throw any light on this?" This is the adjutant.

The lantern splutters, flickering the old man's shadow up the tent walls.

"I don't foller it a-tall," he answers hoarse.

"Sergeant Lewis?" For the adjutant, you can tell he sees a knight fork where the lonely and unwatched knight can take a man on either of the last two moves.

"Jim don't know nothin' about it!" Sam Garvy snaps. She straightens, brings her long hands down behind her back where I plainly see each middle finger cross around the fore-finger next to it. "If I choose to come here to the war with my husban'" she says, "an' if I do the so'jerin' good, it's nobody's business but mine! I guess I've done as much drillin' an' guardin' an' marchin' an'—an' fat-teegs as anybody, not to mention buryin' them horses an' not gittin' paid for any of it!" One of her boots, at attention until now, slides to the At Rest position. "An' now," she says, "I'll thank whichever one o' you writes out the *dis*charges to write me one out, because I aim to git to Kinston an' git with my husban' an' catch that train the Shoo Fly before it runs in the mornin'."

Colonel Vance's face is all strong straight lines, kind keen eyes under straight brows, firm mouth under straight dark mustache.

All at once, a single spasm shakes his big frame the way a dog Woofs in his sleep.

He turns to the surgeon. "Billy," he says, "there's only one way to settle this—" he glances around as if expecting some kind of cloud to descend like over the ark of the cov'nant in the Bible. The Major has his glasses off and is rubbing them hard with a handkerchief. "You will just have to take Private Garvy to medical—"

"Oh-h-h No!!" This is Sam. Her hands, quiet to now as any bound prisoner's, fly to her shirt collar. "Oh-h-h No! There ain't a bit o' use in takin' time for *that!*"

With the nimbleness of one who for eighty three mornings has been to the woods and back and still got in line ahead of half the Company, her fingers fly from buttonhole to buttonhole. She jerks her shirt tails out, baring herself to the waist.

It was the only thing this evening I missed. I mean, being behind her, I could not see her. Her face, that is.

I could see the others, though, and Sir, if you'd held a magnifying glass across that sweltering tent you couldn't have seen each man's character plainer. It's like Doc Rivers showed me once how, by dropping a chemical in a glass, the liquid separates into different powders.

The surgeon clears his throat and rubs harder on his glasses as if preparin' to seveer somebody's arm.

Sergeant Coffey's head is still raised, his black beard jutting toward the tent roof, his eyes squinched tight shut.

James Lewis's round face has taken on the color of the round full harvest moon.

Only the adjutant and the Colonel look at Sam Garvy straight— the adjutant as if gaugeing his last queen or pawn, the Colonel as if he sees nothing in any way contrary to Nature. A little smile twitches the corners of his mouth and he Humphs again like a dog in a happy dream.

"Sergeant Coffey, how does the record say?"

Old Coffey's eyes fly open but he keeps them fixed on the ridge pole.

"She drilled an' done her duties like a man," he says.

Sam, buttoning her shirt, strikes the tails back down into her pants.

"Sergeant Lewis?"

James opens and shuts his mouth before he makes any sound come. "She was particularly good at learning the manual and drill, Sir."

"Well!" The Colonel's voice changes to light and gay, same as my father's would when he accidentally comes in on one of my mother's tea-parties. "Well!" He pushes his chair back as much as the rough turf will let him and heaves himself up. He lifts off his little forward-jutting cap with the gold braid on top and lays it on the table. His head is high as the lantern and a beetle circling around drops buzzing into his thick shoulder length hair. He hits it away.

Major Gaither gets up too. The Colonel's fine hands touch here and there on the table. Something about the whole thing seems to please him the way the little word "Watauga" did but I can't yet put it all together same as I could have if I could have seen Sam's face. "Mrs. William Angel Garvy!" He looks about, fingers an empty toddy glass on the desk. "If we'd known we had a lady in our midst—*How do you say, sir?*" he thunders at the adjutant who rises slowly to his feet.

"There is nothing in our Articles of War, I'm sure, that is relevant to Private Garvy's case," drawls the adjutant, giving a little sideways shrug. "He—or *she*—has done nothing prejudicial to good order and military discipline, of which general or regimental court martial might take cognizance, sir."

Colonel Vance looks down and straightens the papers back against the ink well. "It is not in my authority, Mrs. Garvy, to grant you a discharge. Only General Ransom's office can do that. As for your being paid—neither were those who died at New Bern paid."

Sam has come back to attention and shifts uneasy. "Seems like sayin' that don't do no good for nobody!"

"In the morning, Mrs. Garvy, I will provide you with an escort to General Ransom's headquarters. If you don't mind missing that 'Shoo Fly,' it is possible you may catch the 'Cannon Ball' at night." He holds out his long fine hand. "Goodnight, Mrs. Garvy!" Sam salutes sharply but shakes hands loosely. "As for your husband, I trust he can return to us shortly. When his indisposition is cured. We need him." His shoulders sag. He draws up his chair and sits down heavily. All at once he seems tired.

"And now what was it about the Band?"

James Lewis and I, with passes the adjutant has just scribbled for us, walk back through the steamy night to our Company street. Floegel is going to the Fifty First. Colonel Cantwell needs him. J. O. Hall will take 1st B^b cornet and I will have 2nd B^b cornet. Captain Mickey will have to be under the adjutant and Sergeant Major Coffey too, so things are never just like you'd like them to be.

"Tomorrow is Tuesday," James says. "They ought to be home by Friday."

"I just hope I can come up to what they expect of me."

"They'll be drinkin' the coldest water in the world!"

"You saw Sam's face," I say. "What did she look like?"

"Her *face*?"

"Yes, her face. Was she shamed, or proud, or what? What was she?"

"Well, I'd say she was proud. If I had to say something I would say that."

Most tents are quiet except for restless movements of sleeping men.

"Andrew Biggerstaff says the Moravians make a *lot* of money on these concerts."

"Flowers growin' where nobody sees them. Red birds in the path—"

"*What?!*"

"I'm stopping here."

"G'night!"

"G'night."

I will write Mr. Plumley-Piggott that I am to play 2nd B^b cornet in our regimental band. We might have a good time too in Richmond. Andrew Biggerstaff told me Moravians don't care what they do so long as nobody finds it out.

Whenever you finish taps, you can hear other bugles ending it all up the camp. The vibrations go on sometimes fifteen minutes.

I will blow taps one more time before we rise and move away from here. Twenty thousand men. Less three. That I know of. Heath Garvy, Sam Garvy and Floegel.

SAMANTHA

First it's the train, smellin' o' burnt wood an' stale spit.

"You know what these wheels is a-sayin'?" Heese says, liftin' up his sleeve real careful-like to keep it off the ooze from his pi'zen **ivy,**

" 'Twarn't no use!
'Twarn't no use!

We're further from the Union side now than we was two months ago!

'Twarn't no use.
'Twarn't no use!

An clos'ter to rebels! They've started a camp right near Morganton, at Head o' the Road. They're goin' to call it 'Camp Vance.' So *we're* a-goin' home by way of Lenoir!"

"Well—" I say, thinkin' of Colonel Vance standin' there in the lantern light, pullin' off that little pushed-forward cap, "the Colonel's a pretty good feller."

Then it's the road from Hickory Tavern to Lenoir, dusty and warm with horse dung to make me nauseous again. Shadders of gravel all point west in the mornin' sun.

Heese says "My pants is gallin' me raw."

"Whyn't you jest take 'em off?"

Later it's white noon, no shadders a-tall, an' Heese takes me in the store in Lenoir. It's cool an' dark in there an' smells like leather and sassafras. The lady keepin' the store is little an' she's in a delicate way. Heese calls her Mis' Harper. She is kind an' gives him some brine to put on his pi'zen ivy an' some home made bread an' salt mackerel to eat. Her husban', she says, has gone to Kinston to join Vance's Legion. The bread tastes good though I can't stomach the fish. An idee the size of a turnip seed has took shape inside me.

When we get to Globe Valley it's evenin' and the road is white with river sand an' rocks is fewer—just little round smooth river rocks. Their shadders point back east where we come from.

"You smell that?" Heese says. "Willers along Johns River!"

All I can see is his shirt shoulders where the sores from his pi'zen ivy has weeped through. My insides wince at the sight and I look away t'ords the river, bordered with sycamores, an' Rough Ridge in the west raisin' its bulk, an' above it the Grandfather. And on it is our home.

I stop in the middle o' the road.

"Heese!" I say, "'Fore God. Either from actin' like a man I've turn't into one, or else we're goin' to have a young 'un!"

He stops in his tracks. We face each other in the road with the musky smell of waist high corn from Andrew Lewis's acres all around us.

"Ain't you had it yet?"

"Not in two months!" Just like a man not to think about inquirin'. The last time was—it ought to a-been before that hail storm in April, the way I figgered it. Has the seed laid inside me maybe longer than that—six years? But I never give it much thought after the first year or two.

Heese's face looks kinda helpless. It's caterwampus from the rash.

"I ain't had any use for a monthlies skirt since we lef', much less a third pair o' pants."

"Samantha—"

From a sycamore at the river comes a sound I ain't heard in a year,

"Whip-poor-*will*! Whip-poor-*will*!"

"Samantha, for you to be in a delicate way would be kind of unhandy with the war an' all. We ain't near over on the Union side yet."

"Whip-poor-will!" What a lonesome sound!

I think of somethin'. "He's namin' it. You hear him? Hear him say 'Will'? We'll name the young 'un Will—William Angel Garvy!"

"No!" He takes a stride to me. " 'Sam!' We'll call him Sam!"

Some o' the brine the lady put on his face sticks to my mouth. Light brightens the way it does in the mountains just after sunset. What a sight! Two Confedrit so'jers standin' there kissin' in the middle o' Globe valley!

CHANEY McKAMIE

I TOLD Billie and the boys to go on to church, I'd come if I could, knowin' the hard choice is still ahead o' me whether to come or steal this beautiful summer mornin' to work in my flowers or bake the bowls I shaped with clay the boys brought Friday from the low meadow, but knowin' conscience would win out in the end. An hour after they're gone I'm right on the path to White Springs church with a sigh that everybody in this world has somethin' beyond just livin' that's always beckonin' him. *In this world.* I'm not worried about the next. Plenty of chance there. It's here the thing you long to do is always gettin' pushed away, a hell an' a heaven, outside the endless tasks. Even Thad—takin' the food off his plate to feed Washin'ton's dog because Wash' is goin' to bring him that special pistol for keepin' his hound. For me, it's my hands in clay or at the roots of flowers. For Mary McKamie it's plants more serious, learnin' about medicine. For Reuben it's the church. For him an' Billie an' Martin, it's war and the Confederacy. For

Harriett McKamie it's things she can hold on to, own, touch—land, livestock.

And that's all right. For your thing can't be somebody else's thing. Or if it is, an' you was ever to meet such a one it'd be like you'd know'd 'em always. Like Mary an' that Mr. Gray, the man that come just once but a fine educated man that left her thinkin' new ways an' new things to learn about. I guess heaven is a place of just knowin' early what you'd choose to do an' then havin' a chance to do it.

I draw breaths of this sweet air, bitter with galax, leaf mold an' hemlock all the time prayin' for our boys that's away—for Joel north of Richmond fightin' in a freshet that has swole a stream the Chickahominy an' thirty men hit by lightnin' like the war itself wasn't bad enough. Four of 'em died.

On a June Sunday like this it's hard to believe there is a war anywhere—birds singin', laurel an' honeysuckles bloomin', clouds high overhead to chase shadows down the mountains.

I've hardly been noticin' where I've come when I pass a path to the left down the hill where a spring is, and beside the spring a big beech tree where folks has carved names so long the earliest ones has dimmed and fattened out in the tree's girth. A man's voice low and then a girl's come up through the rhododendrons that are considerably wore and bent from folks goin' down for drinks of one kind or another, or courtin'. I look down and it's Mary's girl, my niece Margaret, standin' with her back against the tree, an' Neil McCurry in front of her. Somethin' in the way he is standin', his arm braced against that beech as if he might be holdin' her against her will from comin' back the path makes me stop an' wait. Neil has been helpin' Enoch work, causin' folks to name 'em both Union sympathizers. It don't set well around here, for boys like Wash' an' Joel to be fightin' in Virginia and then folks see a McCurry flouting parole, heedless of things his great grandfather Jonas fought for. Enoch gets blamed for it too.

I can't hear what they're saying—prob'ly the same old words the beech has heared a hundred years, spillin' its green light down over 'em in ripples where he stands, two heads taller than Margaret, twenty years old to her sixteen but seems even older due to the black beard he's grown. Some people say it's to make it easier for him to pass the militia now it's past time for him to go back to his regiment.

Margaret wears her white flax dress that Mary's let out for her the third an' last time since it shows her ankles now but the goods is strong, not a hole in it. Her hips and shoulders press the tree, her straight young back arches out bringin' her body an' breasts up in a way she may or may not be aware of. Reuben's girls call Margaret a flirt, say she has a letter from Andrew Lewis's boy down in the Globe—the one that came to take the Watauga men to the army. I've seen James Lewis a few times—once or twice with his fam'ly at church—a stocky fair-haired boy Margaret's size, much different from the muscled dark young giant standin' above her now. I wonder that Mary would let her come off alone with Neil. If she must be courted, let it be with a soldier in good standin', even if she later has to learn the parting, the heartache, common lot of women now. Margaret is as near daughter as I'll ever have—closer than any of my other nieces, certainly than those sleepy ones of Nannie's. Seems like Margaret understands better than anybody the things I love to do and never get to do. She tries to help me do 'em. While it's true most girls are married by sixteen, Mary and me have hoped the best for Margaret—maybe that she could get to go to school away from here like to that new college Methodists have started in Lenoir. I'd work my fingers to the bone to help her go, as would Enoch and Mary, I've got nothin' against McCurrys, good folks if a little stubborn, but my heart cries,

"Wait, Margaret! Wait! You are pretty and clever! There is so much time! *I* didn't know, because I was the child of my parents' old age, so pale and tow I wonder William ever sought me out. No brother came nor sisters—not even to two foot graves upon the hill, so I could learn how it happens to humans from seein' it about me—the heaviness of mother, whispered tales of older children, the long days and then the long day not like any other runnin' into night, or night to day ag'in when the mother you've always seen toil upright is laid low since that's the way it is when human souls comes in this world or goes out.

"But Margaret!—*you* ought to know! I've seen you when I'd go to Mary. The first time you were sleeping, not bothered by the noise, the moving about, the strains and cry held back because Mary is a woman brave an' one that had her womb opened long since by a ten pound son! *Heath* was the one that waked when you was born—him not old enough to help yet scared to leave. When Thomas was born Heath *did* leave and stayed gone 'til things were straightened out—hid out, we later learned, with hogs denned up under a crag on Grandfather. He always liked Thomas, Heath did, and all the little ones. It's you—*you*, Margaret, he's never been at ease with, a girl whose birth he long forgot yet can't forgive!

"When you were eight, you were a little nurse yourself, carin' for Thomas, for Enoch and for Heath while Mary healed. Dark like your mother but with the curl that lies so soft upon your shoulder now.

"When Jake came, Harriett went to Mary because I was having Thad. And Bennie's birth was almost a daytime joke, a bright fall Sunday he dropped in like a ripe little nut with bright brown chinquepin eyes, before any help could come. Enoch and you did what there was to do. So you know! Will you reach out pledging your youth by look or touch when half a century's still before you—but never enough to do the things that are better than food to bring interest to life—they are food! There's years an' years 'til your fingers so supple on that tree are twisted so you can't raise the spoon to toothless gums, much less feel clay rise smooth about your hands in answer to your touch, an' yours the power to alter it the way your girlhood molds this man now."

Through the screen of gnarled rhododendron limbs I see him arch her in until she is seen no more except her arm along his muscled back, his dark head bent as if bent o'er a gun, the weapon of a passion learned elsewhere and well, but she just learning now!

Oh Margaret! *Wait!* The Neil that went away did not come back—a thing that you might say of any trip, but truest of those who go to war.

Can I stay here? I cannot! It is not in my soul to peek and peer nor toast my drying marrows through the young. If love must come then give it room—a meadow on a mountain top, a crag above a roaring glen—not here beside the common path!

I hurry past the flowering laurels, down the widening trail. Quiet, Lord, my heart for the church, my answer to their kindly words,

"Yes, Joel is well. The place of the battle has a name of trees—Fair Oaks or Seven Pines. Joel is spared but the general was hurt—Joe Johnston. In him they had faith—"

I've hardly had time to think this when I hear her calling—

"Aunt Chaney! *Wait!*"

She has come into the path and runs to me—"Aunt Chaney! Wait!" Her legs fly as if fleeing from school—she is summer running from spring, a bundle of flax and curls, and sweat is under her eyes.

1863

SAMANTHA

A sure way to have somebody come you don't want to see is to be doin' somethin' you wouldn' want 'em to know about.

While I'm waitin' for the men to come outa the woods from the sink an' for the corn pones to cool enough for me to sack 'em to send on their journey I hear a man's steps crunchin' on the path back o' the house. Since the militia an' secessh have been pressin' men into the army, we've been wary, so I crack the shutter an' look out an' see Heese's Uncle Reuben comin', crunchin' down the ice mush that's raised like grass in the night after yestiddy's thaw. I quick close the shutter, jerk one skillet of bread from hearth to shelf, throw a cloth over it, grab the kiver off the bed an' start to the door with it. Reuben might have militia hid, an' it's understood between Heese an' me that if I throw that Irish Chain kiver over the bush by the door, he don't come nigh the house 'til I take it in.

Reuben is workin' the latch up an' down the way kin do that's ust to comin' right on in with no leave only maybe a word of scripture. I left the bar down, open the door an' push my own self out, quilt-first.

"Good mornin', Reuben."

"Good mornin', dar'ter!"

I kick the ice off top the rose-of-sharon bush, shake out the kiver an' throw it over. It's a glass world, sun rainbowin' mist risin' out of the valley, rime casin' every twig.

"You're sunnin' early this mornin', dar'ter—figure the ground hog's goin' to see his shadder?"

"Sun generally shines after rime ice like this. Will you come in?"

He stamps his boots on the door stone, steps inside, draws off his brown toboggin' an' raises his arm. "Peace be to this house!" He looks kind of like a old ground hog hisself. I've not seen any o' the fam'ly since word come Joel was killed up in Virginny 'longside a railroad at a place called Fredericksburg. Heath's mother told me about it the day Sam was born, thinkin' even bad news might keep my mind off the crampin' 'til I told her I'd just rather not talk about nothin'! What a day that was. Calvin' an' lambin' is easier!

Sam is fightin' his fists outa the kivers. He's like Heese, he don't like no kind of confinement, and is not been fed since before daybreak, so I drop down on the stool by his crib, first kickin' the half-packed knapsack under, not having' on no skirt to hide it because I still wear my uniform that's comfortable an' I found I can get more work done wearin' pants than steppin' on skirts to say nothin' of savin' washin' that's bigger now than ever.

I dig Sam up outa the crib an' hold him up for Reuben to look at. He's big an' fair like Heese, a fine lookin' poppet, even mad like he is now, beginnin' to get red in the face but his head white an' downy like a week old biddy.

"I want to git his pitchur made like some I seen down at Kinston in the house they was usin' for the horspittle."

Reuben straightens up an' I'm damned if he don't look like he's goin' to cry. Thinkin' about Joel, I guess. Draws out his han'cher an' wipes his eyes an' nose. Uncle Billie an' Aunt Chaney has had five boys yet they can't do without a one of 'em whereas I ain't fully made up my mind yet how I feel about Sam. Old granny women tell you how te'jious carryin' a baby is, how painful to birth one, yet I don't recall a one of 'em tellin' me how one ties you down after it gets here! With winter weather an' all, I've hardly been farther than the spring in two months.

Reuben goes over to warm at the fire, beats ice off his cap and the flames spit steam, then turns with his back to the fire. He looks more bent than when I saw him last. That was about Christmastime when him an' Browns an' Uncle Martin come by huntin' hogs, they said, but that's what all say that's pressin' outlyers.

I unfasten my uniform jacket an' get Sam pacified. I'm glad Reuben's got hold of hisself. Seein' a man teer up always shames me some way. "There's pones in the skillet an' a little sassfras tea in the kettle."

"It is not meat to take the children's bread," he says raisin' his hand ag'in. "Let the children first be filled!" which is scripture, I guess, but don't make sense to me, we don't give Sam cornbread yet. Reuben leans down, though, an' breaks hisself off a bite an' stands there chewin'. His eyes rove about the room.

"It's a little short o' seasonin'." We got only six pounds o' salt left an' will haf' to share some with the animals.

"I was hopin' to catch Heese home."

"He's out trackin' a weasel killed two of our hens."

He chews an' nods. "I seen a right smart of tracks as I come down the hill."

I just leave those words go by, thinkin' it was about this time yestiddy they come—the boy, Romie Allen, from Wilkes county, an' Tallison Howard, Confedrit so'jer from the war. A feller in Wilkes give 'em our names. Allen says they call Wilkes county 'the old United States' so many down there now don't like this war no more. Lots passin' through from Virginny tryin' to get home like this Tallison Howard wants to get to his uncles', William an' David Howard on Little Doe River in Tennessee.

The boy Allen looked skittish when he first saw me, never havin' seen a woman in a uniform before, I guess, an' fearin' it might be some kind of trap. But after we got 'em warm, dried out an' fed the little we had—squirrels, sweet potatoes an' bread—Allen told us how come he wants to get over to the Union side in Tennessee. Said he was drivin' his waggin' from Elk Creek up to Darby to look up some hogs the wife of a volunteer had up there when he met a squad of militia guided by Henry Shelton, a secessh. Shelton pointed Allen out as a Union sympathizer which Allen said he was not—said him an' his brother had helped many a family of Confedrit volunteers. Last spring him an' his brother put in a crop in partnership an' agreed one or the other of 'em would go on an' volunteer. So the brother joined up to a rebel

« 111 »

comp'ny bein' formed an' went off to Virginny. The militia first tried to make Allen turn his mules around an' drive 'em in the waggin' back to Elkville. When Allen wouldn', they forced him down, took the team an' waggin' sayin' they'd leave 'em for him in Wilkesburr. But when he went to get 'em, they wasn' there, an' right then an' there he swore hell ag'inst any kind o' gover'ment would take a man's mules an' waggin' an' not pay him for 'em.

While Allen was tellin' this, the escaped so'jer, Tallison Howard, was scratchin' his waist like he is itchin' considerable, an' rubbin' his shoulders ag'inst the chair-back, so Heese as't him why didn' he take his clo'es off an' we'd help him skirmish the graybacks outa his clo'es, so we did—throwed a quilt about him an' put some dry deer bones on the fire for a steady light an' set there goin' over the seams an' poppin' lice in the fire so wouldn' none of 'em get on Sam.

Howard told us he joined up to a Tennessee regiment because he was curious to see a army, though never expected to go further than Bristol or at most White Top mountain, but said they didn' stay in Tennessee no time. He said he'd never been so far from home an' so long from home in his life. After the Fredericksburg fight his regiment went in winter quarters an' wasn' doin' nothin' much but picket duty across some rivers, the north Annas. They swapped words an' jokes with the Yankee pickets, sailed tobacco across the river in little bark boats an' got newspapers back or sometimes a little coffee. Howard asked his captain for a furlough, captain said No, so he took it on hisself to come on home anyhow by way of Lynchburg, Flower Gap, Traphill an' Wilkesburr. In Wilkes he was told he better not try to get through the mountains in snow on account of melish trackin' him, but the man whose barn he slep' in give him Pa Enoch's name an' Heath's, so he come on. Camped at a old house place, heard a noise like a whippoor-will, then like a owl. Uncle once told him that was a old Tory signal. Anyhow it wasn't no season for birds, so he taken a chance on answerin' an' sure 'nough there was this Romie Allen from Wilkes county. They spent the night together at the old cabin an' come on here to get Heese to help 'em get through

Watauga gap an' on over where Allen can get with a pilot an' go on through to the Union lines.

I asked about the fight at Fredericksburg an' if he know'd Joel McKamie but he didn'. He know'd the railroad track though. It was in front of some woods where Howard's regiment was in the battle, an' they charged across the railroad an' got in a ditch an' fit 'til their shot give out an' their colonel got killed.

We finished skirmishin' the gray-backs outa Howard's clo'es, then all lay down an' went to sleep, all but Sam who just got waked up good, so I hafta nurse him, an' after that it don't seem like more'n ten minutes 'til Heese is up an' I haf' to get up an' get breakfast. It's while Heese is takin' the men out to the woods that Reuben McKamie comes.

"You an' Heese been gettin' along all right, I guess," he says, his beard movin' up an' down while he chews an' looks thoughtful at nothin' in partic'lar.

" 'Bout like common." We've been home, we have, tendin' our little crops, stayin' outa the way of secessh an' Confedrit so'jers, sometimes helpin' some Union man tryin' to get across the Grandfather. This last month all we've done is try to stay warm an' take keer o' Sam. Heese sets a lot o' store by Sam.

"Well—I been wantin' to see you too, dar'ter. I have agreeable news for you." He rocks back an' forth on the hearth. "We had quarterly meetin' of our Association the fourth Sunday. New Year's snow crushed in the roof o' the buildin', but we met at Brother Harman's at the old fording place in hearin' of the falls. Some twenty souls present heard three sermons, many exhortations an' there was some quickenin'."

Heese an' me always been wary of the church an' plum out of it since the disturbance down at Globe two years ago. We got baptized because seem like nothin' would do Mary an' Enoch but we should. Heese says church folks remind him of bees—useful, but sot in their ways an' a menace when crossed. Like they disfellowshipped Comfort Wade for tellin' Phoebe Eggers a piece of cloth was flax when it was tow an' Brother Whitmore for not givin' full weight at his mill, an' Sary Reece for sayin' it took three to finish one of Uncle Reuben's sermons—Reuben McKamie, Billie McKamie, an' the devil! Comfort's husband got her a hearin' though, an' it was throad out of doors.

"God has manifested His goodness an' power in the hearts of many on the solitary banks an' in the lonely vales," Uncle Reuben sing-songs kind of mournful. "Dar'ter, the Association has depitized me to tell you an' Heese that they've re-heard your case for disturbin' public worship an' are willin' to take you back in full membership, 'specially in view of you an' Heese takin' the oath of allegiance to the Confedricy. *An'* upon proper submission an' repentance, of course!"

I pull Sam away from me an' settle him in to the other tit, all the time keepin' my ears cocked for a sound from above the house. I don't know what Heese is goin' to say to me, keepin' him an' Allen an' Howard back up on the hill watchin' that quilt when all the time it's just Uncle Reuben.

"Repentance for what? For the fight, or for takin' the oath?"

"For the dis-turbance," he snaps, then goes on persuasive, "You would not want this little lamb to be brought up outside the fold, would you? You want him in the full faith an' baptism of the church?"

Sam sucks slow after his first full gulpin'. It's almost like he is listenin'.

"How old would Sam haf' to be, to be baptized?"

"Our church don't hold with infant baptism, dar'ter. He must be ree—" somepn. Some big word. Sam is little to be doused under water.

"How old is that, generally?" Sam starts to grunt an' turn beet red.

"About twelve years."

I put Sam ag'inst my shoulder. Seems like that always helps him. "In that case," I say, "we got plenty of time." I wisht I could hear a dog bark or somebody movin' around but since our Plott hounds got killed, Heese wont have a dog. Somebody found them on the trail down toward Forge Flats with their throats cut, done it just for meanness, a secessh or maybe Browns or one o' them Indians.

The room is gettin' lighter—must be brightenin' outside.

Uncle Reuben reaches down an' breaks off another piece o' bread. It takes a bushel o' corn to make fifty pounds o' meal. We got about five bushels in the crib to do us through spring. "We are as a vapor that appeareth for a little time. Ye know not what shall be the morrow. We are as grass—"

Seem like Reuben don't know what a long spell o' silence is, how comfortin' it can be. I look over at the flax I was gonna lay to bleach on the patch o' snow at the west side o' the house. His voice changes to sociable.

"I guess you've not seen anything of the McCurry boy lately?"

"Which one? There's lots of McCurrys."

"You know the one. Neil. The one helps Enoch. The one was paroled from Roanoke."

"We've not seen nobody. I wisht to the Lord we did. We don't see nobody but each other. The three of us!"

"Uhm-hm-mm," he dusts off his fingers delicate. "Yankees is comin' in on the coast ag'in'. Where you was."

" 'Zat so!"

"They're up to Goldsburr ag'in. Cut the railroad. I got a Carolina Watchman here." He takes the newspaper out, considerable wore at the creases. It drops open limp from bein' read so much. He hands it to me. Down the lef' hand side is a list of killed and wounded at Fredericksburg an' I look to see can I find Joel's name but it's a long list an' Sam keep strainin', so I haf' to hand it back.

"Heese wouldn' be thinkin' o' joinin' up ag'in any time soon?"

"He'll speak for hisself about that." I just hope he don't take a chance an' come on to the house anyway. He's not got much patience an' it must be chilly back up there in the l'arls. I keep pattin' Sam on the back.

"They got lists now," Reuben says. "Absentees. Their regiments, comp'nys, whur they left from an' when, how long they been gone, an' all!"

"You got such a list?"

« 115 »

"No, dar'ter." He rocks back on his heels. "But you took a oath—I mean Heese did—that he would solem'ly swear to yield obedience to the Confedrit State of America, an' serve them ag'inst all enemies *what*-so-ever!"

Sam lets out a big fart. I let him get through, then take him off my shoulder an' hold him in front of me. He's smilin'! The first time! Got his eyes wide open!

"*Look! He's smilin'!*" I cup his chickabiddy head with my hand, and he lays there curlin' his fingers around like posies. Sam would look good in one o' them dresses like I seen in the pitchur in Kinston, white starched, high collar'd an' a yard long.

Uncle Reuben goes on with his preacher talk, "If a soul swear, *what*-so-ever it be, then he is guilty and shall make amends. So says the Lord to Moses after Moses come down from the mount, an' the cloud of the Lord was upon the tabernacle by day an' fire by night, *in sight* o' the house of Israel!"

I seen another baby pitchur at Kinston, it was in a photog'- apher's window right across the street from the bawdy house where twenty seven people got throad out one night by police, twelve of 'em Confedrit so'jers. None of 'em from Company F, though. The baby in that pitchur didn' have on no clo'es atall, was laid on a sheep's skin, belly down to hid his privates. Wasn't no doubt, though, it was a boy same as Sam would look. I could have his pitchur took that way, give me a ex-cuse to slaughter that old Satan blue-eyed ram o' Heese's. But the ewe's hide might work up better.

Reuben's tones has riz' so loud I think surely Heese'll be bound to reconnize it an' come on in.

"If a woman vow unto the Lord then her vows shall stand an' her bonds wherewith she bound her soul shall stand. Numbers— thirty nine."

"You ain't suggestin' *I* go back to the army, are you?"

"No, dar'ter!"

" 'Cause if you are, I gotta discharge. I can show it to you right up there in that knapsack hangin' on the wall."

"No, dar'ter, no! You done enough. You might say you done too much."

I go spit in the fire, carry Sam an' lay him on the bed. I'd like to give Reuben a dis-charge from here. I'm wore out with him. I clean Sam up an' toss his britches in the crate.

"Here, you hold him a minute while I put the canteen in the crib." That bottle's come in handy for a bed warmer.

Reuben takes Sam an' sets down. Outside you can hear twigs snappin' off the way they do when wind rises on ice. I open the shutter an' peer out. Trees are swayin', sky is blue, the quilt's still in place. We're goin' to hafta think up a new meanin' for the quilt like you'd jerk it wrong side out to mean You can come on in now, it ain't nobody but your gabby ole Uncle. Still—if Heese did come, word would git back along the creeks to Confedrits guardin' the passes.

I close the blind an' take Sam who is droppin' off to sleep 'til Reuben blows his nose loud as a revelee, causin' Sam's eyelids to flutter. In a minute, though, he's gone, an' I put him down in the crib.

"If you don't mind, I'll go right on with my work." I fetch Sam's clo'es outa the crate in the corner an' start sortin' 'em, thinkin' I might can stink Reuben out. Two or three months o' bein' shut in all the time is beginnin' to tell on me. My mind keeps goin' over things Reuben's been sayin', like about that oath, an' Sam bein' a lost lamb.

"Heese says there's two kinds of gover'ment now," I says, "the Confedrit gover'ment an' Zeb' Vance's gover'ment. In Zeb' Vance's gover'ment you can't build a army by pressin' the citizens."

"In that case," Reuben snaps, growin' red in the face, "you've not been in touch with the Gov'ner lately." He stands up, pulls his paper out ag'in, shakes it out an' strikes it with his hand. "In this very paper is the Gov'nor's proclamation—ammesty proclamation he called it, or somep'n, to deserters, which is a name I don't keer for. He starts to read.

It all sounds fine, flags wavin' an' friends an' foes—just like a Fourth o' July or muster day speech. Puts me in mind of a Retreat an' Bugles blowin' his horn, an' Colonel Burgwyn with them snowy gloves on snappin' the guns back an' forth to the fellers in the line.

He reads on, tellin' about large numbers of so'jers absent, desirin' to see their friends an' homes, which is the God's truth I know. It even sounds like Vance. The Colonel had his own special way o' talkin'. I'd like to see him ag'in—show him Sam. I never know'd it when I was in camp but they say he had four sons. The fourth 'un died when it was jist a year old.

I lift a batch o' clo'es out on a stick an' drop 'em in the pan. I rec'lect the evenin' me an' Bugles walked to the Colonel's tent at headquarters together—how hot it was, an' I said I'd druther be in a burnin' hell than go to Virginny. Late last summer Pa Enoch brought me a letter that was left for me in the gourd at Chaney's house. I don't rec'lect just when it was—July, maybe— I know cabbages was headin' up. I ain't got many letters in my life an' I was impatient to find out what was in it. It was stamped Drewry's Bluff but inside it said Malvern Hill. It wasn't much of a letter. All it said was "Dear Sam—a burnin' hell is what it is. Bugles."

Reuben reads on an' has got to some bothersome words like coward, an' dangers. Then all at once there is the flat sayin' that all deserters who return to duty by the tenth of February their comp'nys will take 'em back, whereas all that *don't* come back by February tenth will be tried for desertion an' upon conviction will be made to suffer death!

Uncle Reuben peers at me over his spec's. "That's eight days from today, dar'ter. Seven you might say, leavin' out the Sabbath."

I shove the canteen down to the foot o' the crib. Sam's hot natured like Heese.

"Would you mind readin' that ag'in," I say, "about the childern's childern?"

He reads it over—about how they wouldn' do no good hidin'

out in the woods by day an' plunderin' neighbors by night, but would bring shame on the heads of childern's childern who will t'ant them as old men, sayin' your father skulked in the woods to keep from fightin' for his country.

"And there shall be no rest for the deserter in the borders of North Carolina." Reuben fetches up, folds the paper, takes off his spec's, sticks 'em away in his pocket. I go spit in the fire, lift the wash pot, open the trap door an' pour the water through.

"Uncle Reuben," I say, kickin' the trap shut, "I don't have as much time to talk as I us't to. My time is divided now by three."

"Is it just three, dar'ter? Or just how many *is* lyin' out there on the mountain?"

I'm boilin' mad. "How many *you* got out there?"

"Just me, dar'ter. Nobody but me. I come here because I'm anxious for your immortal soul. An' Heese's. An' this little lamb's."

It seems to me he's got things kind of confused, what's the Lord's or the church's, an' what's the army's. I rinse out the pot an' prop the door open. This room needs airin'. Reuben comes on past me then, pullin' on his cap.

I remember the oath we took. It was when we first got down to Kinston. The camp had been moved the day before from seven miles above Kinston to five miles below, but the mosquitoes was there ahead of us, an' officers worryin' about where the Unions was goin' to strike next, an' the surgeons busy with the wounded from New Bern, an' Captain Ballew had no paper blanks, so they give us the oath all together, standin' up. Heese an' me give 'em back somethin' between a salute an' a swat.

"Heese says 'it's he that writes an oath that makes it, not him that for convenience takes it.'"

"Fancy words," Reuben says, "for an uneddicated man—or woman." He steps off the door stone an' tromps away down the path. His shadder lies behind him like the ground hog's. Forty more days o' winter! Maybe him an' the groundhog is both wrong. Trees is shatterin' icicles down over the ground. The glass world is breakin' up.

At the house corner Reuben stops, raises his arm ag'in like he aims to bless us but says instead,

"Remember! The wrath of God is upon the childern of disobedience!"

I fetch a sigh, go back in the house an' look down at Sam. Then I pick him up, wrop him good in the shawl Chaney knit for him, carry him out the door in the sunshine. You can hear Reuben's crunchin' up the hill, fainter an' fainter. Seems like if a twelve year old young 'un would know enough to be took in the church, his daddy that's twenty seven orter know which side o' the war he chooses to fight on.

"I'll be glad, Sam, when you're five years old an' can carry a gun. Me an' you will sure have us a rabbit hunt!"

A drop o' water from one o' the icicles along the roof falls through the openin' in the blanket right onto Sam's nose.

"I reckin' that'll do you 'til you're twelve, son."

I jerk the kiver off the bush, give it a shake an' carry it an' Sam back in the house.

NEIL McCURRY

RIDIN' out on the mountain like we've been, you lose track of time, it's day, then night, an' nothin' to mark it when the talk gives out but how many times we've changed the sops on Heath Garvy's wound and none of it doin' any good. His arm's swole big as a ridge pole now, puffed plum to the shoulder an' beginnin' to streak red. It falls my lot to have to come down the mountain this mornin' to meet Heath's step-daddy, Enoch McKamie. He's bringin' us food.

Five days ago the militia come to Garvy's at night, thinkin' to find them home, and me too, maybe, but I'd already come off up here to the cave on the Grandfather.

Conscriptors didn't come in February when everybody expected them because Gov'nor Vance give everybody a extra month to think it over an' the law didn't take force until last Thursday. So that is when they come—the Browns from Forge Flats an' that school teacher son, Whang Brown, that's got a job now at Camp Vance, Camp of Instruction, they call it, below Morganton—and a Lewis and a Holloway from Globe. At least these was the ones Samantha reconnized. Heath very near got caught. He's so big he got stuck climbin' out the window of the loft to jump from it to the bank in rear of the house. The way Samantha told it she heard shots,

"They've shot Heath!" she hisses to the Buckhannon boy, Grantum, that come to stay with her in case Heath had to flee. He didn't want her an' Sam left by their selves. Buckhannons are rebels which Heese thought would throw the conscriptors off. Grantum's father, Laban, was home last week, first time in a long time, to get his roof mended, look after his family, then went back to the Army of Virginia.

When I tell old man Enoch that Heath's wound is festerin', he'll want to go right back up the mountain with me but I can't let him because he's often watched. Besides he's not been well, an' it's a hard climb from here even for a young man. The mother, Mary, can do Heath more good—he was out of his head last night, callin' her, cursin' his secessh uncles, cursin' conscriptors especially Browns, cursin' folks with food down in the Globe, and shoutin' for Samantha! I aim to send Mr. Enoch back for Mis' McKamie soon's I relieve him of the vittles.

It takes a lot of food for eight hungry men we got up there now. There's this red headed George Kirk that's raisin' a company for Dan Ellis to guide across the mountains, an' two men from Yadkinville that's just fit it out with conscriptors from a school house with twenty others, and had to flee because a secessh magistrate was shot. An' a scout. An' that peg-legged British sailor that got caught in Wilmington—he's a strange feller, that one, 'specially when he's mad. He gets mad when he tells how they tried to force him into the militia when his Queen already said her people don't have to take no part on either side this war unless they want to. He says "tyke" for "take," and "blockeyed" for "blockade," an' wants to get with Dan Ellis and on down to New Orleans an' join the outfit of some general name Farraguts.

And there's the foolish one, seventy if he's a day, woods are the only home he knows, the only South and North he knows is how moss grows on trees—don't know United from Confederate States but says he will support old North Car'lina, and any Gover'ment she belongs to. He's took the oath to all so many times they call him Swearin' Sam.

Wind is gettin' up now, scuddin' tags of rain clouds down the mountain, roarin' like a train through this big woods. Puts me in mind of the day I come home from Roanoke, March 10, a year ago.

My boots slide in the ravine where Haw branch has cut the rock twenty feet deep. We stay out of the old ox cart trail for fear of leavin' tracks. At each stride I sink up to my knees in mast that's wet a yard down from the rains. Hardest thing has been to get dry wood up there under the crag—we get more heat from hogs that's bedded up there in the cave than from any little embers we can blow.

My ankle turns, skids on a rock, it gives 'way under leaves and throws me flat on my hunkers in the mulch. Sittin' there crooked-up like a fool, I feel a beat in my behind like poundin' deer hoofs. I lift my gun but there's no sound. The wind lays, and fog comes driftin' in, closin' out everything but the nearest bush. I pull myself up to see if I have broke anything, an' stand listenin'. Fog drifts, then brightens, wind strikes from the west letting shafts of sunlight through the trees. I am close by the trail where old Man Enoch should come in. Framed before me in the V sides of the ravine lies Globe Valley, pretty as a picture, cursed last night by Heath Garvy, yet lying still, blue-green and peaceful, seeming to run out across the whole state plum to the ocean till you could almost think it is the ocean an' this wind slow breakers on Nags Head, leavin' water furrows in the sun.

I strain my eyes 'til I believe I see that hut on Shallowbag Bay, half toppled by some flowering vines that bloomed first yellow and then red, but always bloomed. Some called them chipperdales

—Patsy, Mollie and Miss Flo'—but they were good old gals. I feel blood prickle as I take the undrained path through liveoaks back of Supple's hill, the Hommock and the Marsh that no cart ever marked but only men who'd learned where they might risk their feet, an' many a man did wear the path, spendin' himself limber there to take an' give what they too took an' give, that no one else in all that lonesome barricaded bog of Roanoke would—a little joking with the hoe-down and the rum, the oysters and the she-crab soup, a little kindness too, till having left his ounce of scum behind, a man would feel his way by touch back through the quaking gromping stinging swamp and crawl into the fort again by day.

Miss Flo'—she was a refugee from Kinston, from one of General Branch's raids on Bright Street, Sugar Hill. She wanted peace, she said, as I guess other did. She'd never been further than Currituck Court House, having business there, but wished that she could see the mountings, as she called them. An' the snow, most of all she'd like to see the snow. So then the boys would tell of six foot drifts where men was lost an' not dug out till June, of bears and snakes and Indians, headless dogs that will not cross a branch, till half-believing they believed themselves, and were believed. But also learnt of phantom ships and Old Quawk Day when not a soul in Okracoke will venture on the Sound, and I tell you, old hill tales they are tame to them that has been brought in from the ocean!

In spite of war, the folks down in the lowlands have their fun, and that's the difference that I see between them and the folks up here—they'll have their fun even on a God-forsaken island waiting for a war. And that I miss! And that I tried to tell this flower from the McKamie Gap—this Margaret with the minimy mouth that I have tried to think but not to think about, and what it is her mouth is like and finally thought it's like the insides of a conch you'd pick up on Nags Head, half pale, half pink, an' smooth like that, and deep like that, but cold!! She is like all her folks up here —blood kin, that is, not Garvy an' Samantha—the Scotch that have prayed out the Irish in them 'til only church is left an' family, work and school and learnin' names of things that they will never see and afraid of names of things that they see every day, when all you need to know is touch, is deep, is holdin' nothin' back, is good!!

I jump the last eight feet from bank to trail—it stings my feet, but I am glad to have them sting! I wish 'twas summer now or even that I was back on Roanoke—I'd swim from Pork Point to Redstone, a good four miles with all the sunken vessels in between! It may be climbin' back this mountain with two sacks of food—I hope it's two—will take it out of me. I wish that old man Enoch would come now, his tall old carcass knotted in the joints swaying on the mule—how anyone so homely could have sired her! But he is good, I know. And she is good? or young, or both. A feller wants that? Even when he crawls through swamps to worsen them that lost it long ago if by chance they ever had it.

I strain my ears to catch a sound but all I hear is some dam' fool chickadee that's come back here too early, temptin' snow, an' Haw branch talkin' to itself the same it's done since me an' Joel McKamie used to fish here on the first bright warm-up day of spring. I spit an' wipe my gun an' settle my shoulders back against the bank feelin' the heat come through from rocks that's took the sun. I wish they'd come—old Thomas and his Indians! I just wish they would, or this yellow Pillow general that sneaked out on his troops at Donelson and maybe that is why he is so pressed for men he has to come now from Tennessee to hunt them out with guns without the law or right to do it, says Zeb' Vance, and then leaves his starving horses to eat up our grain. I'd like to see them come around this bend!

From down the trail I hear a sound that is not any bird though like a bird, a woman's voice a little daft singing a scrap of song flung out—I can't see her where the trail bends 'round the bluff but I know the song all right,

> "Send for the fiddle and send for the bow
> Send for the black-eyed Daisy—

>Don't reach here in the middle o' the week
>It's almost run me cra-zy!"

The tune's the same on mountain or on shore but there's some words I never learnt until I heard 'em sung on Shallowbag Bay but evermore will hear, and half hope this singer does not know them and will never sing, whoever she may be that's not afraid to sing in wilds where men are hid. And then I know! Before she comes in view of me, I know who 'twould be that thinks no more of caroling to birds and boomers than she would over washing suds at home.

She's there before me, her red cape with hood that frames her face, and my blood shames me striking like a breaker in my face then drawing back and spreading out 'til every part of me is faintified like some untried stallion.

She reins in the mule—both stop so still that I have time to wonder if my brain has played me false and I just conjured this up from little bits I stored inside me like some dam' squirrel, or like the spy glass I once saw in Globe had bits of colored glass, you turned it and made patterns, red and blue.

Her eyes look like molasses in the sun. She flashes one quick look that might say Go or Stay, but then takes on the stillness of her face. I'd like to wake that face—tear it, defeat it, win it or do anything but leave it as it is confounding me!

With one quick move she's on the ground. Sacks are roped to her side saddle on Shadrack's neck and rump. "Pa is not well, Ma let me bring the food." I have not moved, but now shove my shoulders off the rock and like a picket start towards her and the mule when she says sharp

"Turn your back!"

I'm not obliged to obey her and I don't know why I do, but next thing I know I'm facing the bank again, wondering if I'm to get shot in the back or play some dam' fool game like kids at school and her always the leader.

"Now you can turn back!"

I make a right face. There is not much changed except she has a package in her hand wrapped in white cloth the way I've seen her mother do when she goes visiting the sick. She brushes her long skirt down with the other hand, her skirt that is already smooth, and for a minute she is just the spit of any other girl blushing because she had the bundle hidden in her clo'es and made me turn for fear that I might glimpse her leg. For half a second it is like I see old Flo—I even blush and Margaret sees me and takes on her General Pillow air again,

"It's medicine. There's some money, too—a little," she holds it out to me.

Forward, left foot balance, shoulders still—the chickadee mocks from a hemlock—zirr-zirr-zee! Strange her folks would let her come bandadooing off up here by herself. For all I know there's nobody near for miles. The boys up yonder under the crag are a mile away. Thinking of Heath Garvy's arm steadies me.

"What kind of medicine?" It was Heath's day to come. She didn't know that I would be the one to come.

"Agrimony. For wounds," she says. "The money was brought for the pilot, Kirk."

She thought, I guess, that I would steal it? *Zirr-zirr-zee!*

"It's well your mother thought about the medicine. Your stepbrother has a very bad-festered arm."

Her dark molasses eyes grow darker and then cold. I tell her about Heath's arm, the shot is in it still. She steps over to the mule whose bridle hangs and starts to work the rope that holds the sacks. She works fast in the front. I go over and work slow at the back. Never in my life have I spent this much time deciding whether to grab a girl and kiss her, much less thinking about whether I'd do it atall. Why did you run away that Sunday at the spring? The words wont come. I'd make her like loving if she'd give me time. Miss Flo said she didn't always like it. "Women have to learn," she said, "Mister McCurry," she said. She was refined, Flo was, having waited tables at Nags Head Hotel before the war. Later she called me Mac.

I reach my right hand out and grab Margaret's fingers digging

« 126 »

at the knot. They flutter like a swallow I once caught in a barn, but they are strong and go free because the damned sack slips and I make a grab for it. After all, us men don't want to starve because I'm beyacking with an offish girl. She jerks away, the chickadee says "Zirr-zirr-zee" and flies off too.

"Tell me, girl, what are you made of? Ice? Old left over snow? I thought you were a little flirt when I worked at your house—and so you are! Why did you run off from me that Sunday at the spring? What makes you run from loving?"

It's as if her always-thinking face draws in all thought there is and holds it in the hood and it the only joke about her, and it not known to her—two little bits of hair that stick through holes on top like little devil's horns.

Then Shadrack lifts his head and brays one awful bray. The echo spreads and dies, and in the quiet that follows I hear the hollow clump, clump, that a horse's hoofs make on a forest trail. I let go the sack and reach for my gun.

"Get over to the side!" She does not move. "Get over there!"

And then around the bluff there plods the worst spavined horse that I have seen since I left Roanoke—a carcass that was took apart and never put back right—head low or withers high so that with sack on top, you barely see the rider, Tom or Thomas as they call him, Margaret's brother. The steed moves sideways as much as forward but comes plodding on and takes his place exactly by the side of Shadrack who gives out a joyful sound.

"Howdy, Tom! I'd not heard that you'd joined the caval-ree!"

"Don't tease him!" Margaret says behind me. Without glancing back I know that she is laughing at me—head tilted on one side and those two stick-up devil curls, she laughs at me, at Shadrack and his splay-foot friend. But not at Tom.

"The horse just came," she says, "left by some troops that crossed at Clark's Barn a month ago. It has made up to Thomas for the pistol Wash' is bringin' Thad. What we'll feed the horse—"

"Well, Tom—it does beat all the way he lined up then—right nose to nose. I bet he'll do things will surprise you. Close your legs in on the right. Now lift your reins!"

Old Sawbones, looking like an old swamp alligator half awake, brings up his head and steps out as quick as sev'ral months of untrimmed hoofs will let him.

"Thomas! Hurry!" It is Mistress General Pillow taking charge again.

"Halt, Tom. Now lift your wrists and rein him back. Say 'Halt' now!"

"Halt!" The boy's face shines. "What else can he do, Neil?"

"I don't know. I wasn't ever in the cavalry—just watched 'em drill an' heard 'em talk. If we had a bugle—"

"Thomas, hurry—get the bag down and give Neil the food. A bugle—that would be fine! Wake the whole mountain and militia clean down to the Globe. Heath is hurt, Tom. We have to hurry back and bring mother."

I put out my hand to stroke the creeter's face but he bares his teeth. The boy asks,

"What happened to Heese, Neil? Can I go with you? I could leave my horse here—"

"You'd haf' to, only oxes take that trail." I spit to rid myself of aggervated feelings, of wasted time—she knew we weren't alone. Why did I make a start—I'm so put out I don't even feel the three whole sacks I toss across my back.

"No, you'll have to go back with her, Tom—to pertect her!" I think I'll be leavin' soon, maybe go to sea with that one who is so stuck on Farraguts. "Someone will be here, General!" I salute her with my left hand. She's puzzled at the name I give her. "Someone will be around to meet your Ma. Thank her for the food, an' your Pa. I hope he's not very sick." She shakes her head. "We keep a picket out. Tell your Ma to sing the song you sung." I shrug the bags on to my back to start my climb. "Are those all the words you know?"

"The Gypsy Daisy? I know lots of words." She gives the cape a toss. "And lots of songs!"

"Give him a slap, Tom, see will he move!" The old nag stands there like a rock, just eyes us mean. I turn back to Rough Ridge. I'll bear the look of her longer than any sack before I lay it down.

« 128 »

HEATH GARVY

Fpt! A gun is shootin' far away. I count the beats in my ear—ear on my shoulder, shoulder on this rock—six beats, then comes the pain! So this is what it feels like to be shot! A thousand shots like this an' it's a war. A million pains like this an' somethin' might get settled—who's to be free or not be free!

Fpt! No voices with the shot. Nobody this time yells "Shoot him runnin'!" I jumped out of my loft, the ground was soft from all the rains, the muck weighed down my boots. I heard one say "It never failed to fire before—" What did they do after that, Samantha? Oh, Samantha! Did they steal? What about Sam? Oh, Samantha, give 'em hell! I know you did—the god-dam sons of bitchin' id'jits!

Fpt! There goes the gun ag'in! As far away as Globe, they're shootin', maybe to halt them that's seekin' food like the poor fools at Laurel. Battle of Globe. Battle to hold onto the hams an' bacon! That's funny! I would come, but it's me an' this arm now—a baby that wont rest no matter how you lay it—no place to lay the baby —this th'obbin' log that was a part of me is now against me. It's me an' it!

Somebody turns a stone warmed at the fire, tries to put it underneath my arm. "God dam' you, *stop*! I told you not to touch it!" Sparks burst out. "Warm wont do!"

Through the clickin' swirlin' sparks the pigs' eyes shine—the grompin' cave-held huddled mass of them, the front one seated on its filthy crup like a guard dog braced on six inch legs, eyes bloodshot from the smoke.

Turn east! Cold rock, cool my arm! Somebody went for somethin'—what? Maybe they're shootin' at *him*. What was it he went after? Food? Cold stone to my neck, stop-cock the bile—the noxious tell-tale weakness that the thought of eatin' brings!

Samantha! this is what it feels like to be shot. I've shot a thousand beasts, an' so have you—I never shot a man—not yet—but what has happened is not like to make me say I never will. It just goads me on to fight! to settle scores with them that's badgerin' me, like that measly rabbity scaly-varmint Brown!

If I could sleep! I have not slep' for two days. I'll think of all the words that say it—Sleep! Go to sleep. Rest, nod—the pain bears in ag'in, the burnin' pain an' far off gun! Him that was to be their leader is laid lower than swine under this crag!

I heer'd them talkin'—the one from Yadkin that's already killed a man, and the red-haired Kirk. "He might just lose that arm!" I think how it might be without it, my shoulder breakin' off to nowhur like the crag that roofs this cave. They thought I was asleep or fainted maybe.

If thy right hand offend thee, cut it off. I never understood the words. She'd read them at night before we'd go to bed, the grease lamp flared an' dimmed an' spluttered. Our three faces 'round the table—Enoch's an' hers an' mine. Hers I'd always know'd. It seemed I'd always know'd him, too. Whatever eased my oneasiness, that's what he tried to do, though he never said much. He was younger then, but never young. It was the happiest time, when I first came there. There were just the two of us—two men, that is—he said two men. "We are the men here, son." Evenin's we would play "Ant'ny Over," him on one side the house, me on the other, we'd heave the cloth ball she stuffed for us across the roof comb—"Ant'ny O-verr!" while she watched and laughed at us from the yard.

"The boy's left-handed, Mary!"

Is it good or bad? I look down at my hand. 'Twasn't long after that she read the verse. "If thy right hand offend thee, cut it off." For Enoch I would do it. I would do anything he said or wanted. I wanted to be like him. That's what I want today—the only man I ever know'd I could look up to, bein' as tall as me, an' taller every other way—the only man that I can look at in the eyes an' know I'm understood—an' more than that—such words don't come easy to a man—Yes! Loved!! Even when what he sees in me ain't just like he would have it, still him an' me are one. It was the happiest time—before the others came. Not that I minded

Thomas an' Jake. But *she* was differ'nt, Mar'git! He hadn't ever seen anything quite like her.

"Mary, it's like I see you growin' up, an' all those years I missed!"

From that time on, I led that girl a chase. The more he'd say "Not so rough, son, she is a leetle girl," the more I'd wear her down—corn rows, races, errands to the spring, till her face would get so he't up the wet hair drawed up like curly bramble shoots. The trouble was, I couldn' wear her down! She'd just come on like all the time she know'd just where she wants to go and aimed to get there, and to get there first. Then at the charity school she passed me. So I quit. Pa couldn' read. I wouldn' neither.

Fpt! One pulse, two pulses, three—four—count them. Let the damned pain th'ob to let me know my arm is still a part of me. Who went for somethin'? What did he go for? Haw thorns— that was it! Not one of the seven had guts to take his knife an' wash it clean an' lance the thing. The hatchet faced Kirk tried, an' Neil McCurry ducked away an' puked in the woods just from the sight. That's when I fainted.

Sleep. Sleep. It was a stone bruise an' I got dew poisonin' in it, my boy's foot swole to man's size. My mother hilt my heel in her left hand, took a long haw thorn in her right, an' told me it would hurt. I woulda blubbered hadna been for Margaret standin' there hopin' I would cry. Ma said, Never use a knife. No matter if it's b'iled there always is a trace of deadness about it. Take a thorn that has soaked up the rain an' sun an' bears its healin' to the very place. Scarlet Haw's the best, thorns stout, curved an' two inches long, tho' Dotted Haw will do—

"Go get some thorns! Yes, thorns is what I said!" They look at me like sheep, the outlandish sailor and all the rest. "Bring me some Scarlet Haw from down at the flat where the deer come to drink, there is a thicket—I'll sipher out the bloody pus myself."

Sleep. Sleep then. Fall back on the rock—doze, yawn—fire pops in the fireplace. Read. Read the healin' words. I set my bow in the clouds. Unto the hills. They are words I understand, not ones like death an' sin. *I can't sleep!* I have to get them where they want to go—help them get over on the other side. But war is everywh'ur. A man is safer in the Union Army than he is now at home. There is not time to sleep. Step in my steps now, down through the balsams, through the crevices—the rocks was rent long time ago, time of the crucifixion so they say. I never understood. A few stragglers drop out. Step where I step now—it's like a stairs, spread your arms out like wings and brace between the cliffs—flesh between two walls of rock, I've know'd that all my life. Fpt! Count—let the pain come to let me know I'm not turnin' into stone!

Linville Gap is next—the Old Bridge Place where William Mast an' his wife drunk poison, wild parsnip, a slave put in their coffee. Her name was Mill. She thought their death would free her to go with her lover to the Texies. It was a long time ago. She never got to go. They just whipped her an' sold her off to strangers. Sold her in Tennessee. Sleep, Mill—an' damn to them an' all that prosperin' kind.

The pain is less. The stragglers say "When do we eat? We're starved." "Only when we reach the Doe." They're always wantin' food, food for the peg-legged sailor, for the sandy Kirk. He has a baby at home less than one year old.

Next we reach Bull Scrape, crest of the ridge, where cattle come because there is a current of cool air. Stay left of Cranberry Forge an' watch out for rebels from Camp Mast at Sugar Grove, they're diggin' for salt petre under the Old Chimneys place, the smoke house site, the barn. Lewis an' Martin Banner are safe men but few knows it but Harrison Church and me. Learn to move fast—the Old Red Fox, that's what they call Dan Ellis. "Can't we just rest a minute?" "Not till daytime." Travel by night—no light, no fire, grope and crawl through miles of laurel no bird could fly through. I've never seen Dan Ellis but he's piloted enough men through to build a regiment.

The pain is less. Maybe I'm dead already an' don't know! Samantha! Maybe I'm dead already! I've heerd the dyin' takes a turn for the better just before they die. But I don't want to die! Samantha! I might not get to the same place as you an' Sam.

Or Enoch! Sam might not git to the same place as me—I know dam' well he wont! I ain't fit to die. Samantha—supposin' I was to, remember how I told you I'd druther lie between two rocks on the Grandfather mountain, up amongst the clouds—remember I told you, don't put me in no fenced in cemetery, heel to heel with them I wasn' clost to in my life, that's no blood kin to me! I won't have Reuben sing-songin' scriptur' over me, words I never understood. Church allers left me lonesomer than ever—'dead in yer sins' an' words like that. When I come outa quarterly meetin', all I say is, Thank God at least I never made no graven image.

Fpt! They're shootin' at us now. Walk in my tracks along Dark Ridge—watch out for Walters' long-haired greasy savages. Through the gloomy gorge past naked cliffs where the Doe tumbles, then we're into Tennessee! You can't sleep now, you'll freeze! Clothes hardenin' on you from the icy ford—the Doe is mushed with ice at Valley Forge. Keep to the right now. Longstreet's army has et up the food. But Aunt Sally Lacey will feed you near Siam. You'll see them crawlin' out from the dark hill above Dan Ellis's house—from brush piles under snow, from hollow logs—old man Tatem did, he that feigned death an' lived—they call him the Dead Yankee! Ely Mullican broke out of jail at Boon, walked twenty two miles. The jailer said, "It's cheaper to fight him than to keep him." You'll see them all—Dan Ellis, too. The Old Red Fox. Walk in my steps now—

Six steps an' then the pain Lord God! the worst it's been! Not even Samantha when her times was on her hurt like this! She could holler, and how she did! A man can't do that. Lord, I'm not always ding-dongin' at you like Reuben is. If you'll just save my arm, I'll not bother you rarely ag'in, if ever!

The ache strikes in, an' on the far-off gun, I jerk myself upright and seize the burnin' arm—

"Somebody went for somethin'! Who? Who did you send!"

The foolish one! He's there before me! Without a word, he holds out a bare branch of the Scarlet Haw. The grinnin' toothless one has brought the right splents back!

I take them. "You didn't need to go plumb to the Globe to get them."

The other six stare at me, an' the grompin' hogs. A drop of water from the cliff over our heads spits into the fire—Fpt! So that is it! that's what it was—no gun atall!

I take the strongest thorn, cut it the way she did—three inches of the twig with it, like a cross without its peak, straight handled like a gimlet.

"This will hurt—"

"I'm not afraid—"

See? The thorn between your pointin' finger and the third, knuckled like a gimlet. Steady now! All the way in—"It's the strong flesh holds it back," she says, "flesh that is healthy!" Not one of them would do it. All the way in until it meets—nothin'! Nothin'! God!! The point has pierced the bloody sack that holds the shot! Bring it out slow now—slow like she did—Hah!! It's free! It flows! I use my thumb to draw back the forearm flesh and gap the hole—the little gapin' mouth the thorn has made. See! It fills! It flows—it pours along my arm, the pulsin' purple yellow streaked stream and brings the shot. It drops in the dark puddle on the ground! My head goes light. I fall back on the rock.

Sleep! Doze while the veenom runs. Sleep! The fire is pleasant at our backs. A lazy spark or two snaps in the fireplace. To have her against me, smooth, all the way down against me, cradled and underset—milk soft, milk mild—Oh, Mary! Let me sleep! Keep me from hardening into stone before I'm whole again! Sleep pleasured, sleep breathless—downward, slide past the granite rock, warm, wanting, rejoicing, 'swaged! Sleep.

SOPHIA SMEAD to EMILY LEWIS

"Fair Forks"
Roane county, Tennessee
June 25, 1863

Dear Emily:

I have seen Yankees! From Illinois. We've been knowing since June 5th that something was going to happen because every horse and slave around here has been pressed to guard Loudon bridge. They even took Dolph to dig ditches, or maybe he just wanted to go, I blame Rosezetta with it all, she wont let him rest till he leaves us for good. Well Nat was driving me back from Loudon last Saturday where I'd been to try to get a box through lines to Abner. He is with Brown's brigade somewhere over near Tullahoma. We thought they were just more Florida or Georgia troops going to defend Knoxville. They came clattering past us, dressed in rough muddy clothing. I called out "Are you escaping from the Yankees?" "Madam, we are the Yankees." We were driving Old Yellow, only horse we have left, and with the patched harness I guess we looked harmless enough. Anyway they let us go.

Elder Kimbrough was at our house when we got home, had come to see Father and tell us what happened at Lenoir's June 19. Sanders burnt the depot that was full of guns and ammunition, precious leather. He captured part of McCant's battery, Florida men, and guns they had used to guard Bussell Ferry road and the great road in front of Lenoir's house. Henrietta Lenoir had just seen her father, Dr. Ramsey, off to Knoxville. As president of the Bank, he had to try to save it and the Confederate States depository there. Henrietta was walking through the passage to the back door after breakfast when she looked up and saw the blue coats coming. They rode forward opposite the house, got off their horses and went in the store and post office across the road. She knew the store safe had been unlocked that morning before Dr. Ramsey left. She said to the servant "Give me your bonnet, quick!" She put on the sunbonnet, walked deliberately across to the store, went to the safe, took out the big parcels of money, put them in the bend of her arm, covered them with yanks of yarn from an open bale and quietly passed out of the store, back through the house to a hedge near the beehives where she hid the treasure. The Yankees did not burn Lenoir's cotton factory and Mr. Kimbrough says 'twas because Ben Lenoir, who is a great Mason, walked around among the troops giving them the Masonic grip. Willie Lenoir never was a Mason but he says now he thinks he'll join the Masons to find out what 'twas Ben did. Well—I'm glad there is something to laugh about in the midst of all the trouble. We haven't heard the outcome from Knoxville except that every man left was turning out to defend the place.

I'm glad Abner is not here, though he will hear about this Sanders raid and worry more than ever. I think, though, he is where he wants to be, with the 26th defending Chattanooga. Since their flag was captured at Stone's River seems like they are more determined than ever to fight. Anyway our prayers are answered—he is not languishing in Camp Douglas. I don't remember if I wrote you—the mayor of Chicago feared he couldn't hold the Donelson prisoners in Camp Douglas and wrote General Halleck for help. Halleck replied "I took these rebels in arms behind their intrenchments. If Chicago can't guard them unarmed until they are paroled, it will be a pity indeed."

The Lincolnites are exultant here over what they call deliverance from oppression. They are coming out of their hiding places now that Federal forces are around. Elder K. says all is confusion at the railroad, refugees, some going north, some south. Old Mrs. Lyman has gone back to Massachusetts, the children took to fussing over the furniture so she just sold the whole lot of it to Klein's except the sofa that fell down when they were loading it.

We try to keep quiet and go about our business. Our garden looks well in spite of having no fences left. We will have peas next week. Have had lettuce mustard and onions. Father has been indulging too freely craves things he never would eat before, reminds me of the way Uncle Horace was before he died. Dr. Washburn was out to see Father before the raid, and Lizzie Fiske was right by his side. I believe he is getting in real good earnest. Mother has not had any return of the polypus on her face. So now you know how we are getting along in the way of health.

There have been several cases of small pox at Loudon, old Mr. Reid Lillard made light of it, caught it and died, leaving the sisters in a really desperate situation. Miss Maybell is almost inconsolable, Mr. Kimbrough says. She says if she was satisfied Reedie was prepared for the change, she could have given him up easier. Elder K. says the trouble is Sister Maybell was never satisfied on that subject herself, and after her brother was taken ill, there never was a time really when they could all sit down and talk about salvation. O what a solemn admonition this should be to us all to be always ready for we know not when we will be called hence.

I can take the big things better than the little ones, if you call drunken pickets and impressment agents little things.

We hear Lee is moving up North meaning to invade Pennsylvania. *Is this true?* Do write, because news you send us about Virginia is newer & truer than any we get around here. All we hear about is cave dwellers in the circle of fire at Vicksburg. I look for more bloody work this summer than has ever been.

Some soldiers (I don't know which side) are passing now along our one remaining fenced-in pasture, throwing sticks at our cows. One is starting to milk Katie! Now you see what I meant by the little things that are so big! I will run out and try to stop them. Write soon to your loving

S o p h

To THEOPHILUS LEWIS

Beyond Hagerstown, Md.
July 7, 1863

Col Theophilus Lewis
Globe P.O. Caldwell Co
North Carolina
Dear Sir

Your nephew Sgt. James Lewis asked me to write & tell you he was wounded in the first day Battle at Gettysburg A bullet past thrugh his thy. He is a doing all right is on the wagon train Going to Winchester by way of Williamsport but it is a raining & the wagons get boged down & he asked me to write you so you could tell his folks. Our 26th has suffered very much. It was a kind of accidental battle Our brigade was sent in to Gettysburg to look for shoes when we run into cavalry then infantry so Gen. Pettigrew turned us around and we reported back to our division on the Chambersburg turnpike. Gen. Lee was a way off. It was a nother Fredericksburg but the wrong way Before we knew it we were up against the whole Union Army. We had to fight a bunch called the Iron Brigade amongst the best the Yanks have We fought them in some woods and whiped them back thrugh the town but they fortyfied the hills east of town.

We fought them for two days in that place but failed to disloge them. Our loſs is very heavy but the Yanks is still heavier. Our Company F suffered very much. Your nephew was the 85 man wounded or killed of the 87 that went in that first day fight but I would ruther have been hit than Jim Lewis or many a nother specialy our Colonel H. K. Burgwyn killed. July 1 and 3 was worst day for our 26th. I did what I could July 3 to round up ambulance men & pioneers to fill our rankes till I got stund by a

« 138 »

shell at the stone wall & left for dead but by dark I got unstunded & crawled back over the battle field and Sir I can tell you a more sorrowfull sight I never saw poor fellows laying some in one position & some in a nother & little attention paid to them the Drs dont examin a wound unless amputation is necessary or it is very dangerous. But you can not blame the Drs the wounded come in so fast The next day July 4 I tryed to find all our Company. I found Jim in a field hospitle. He was some sunburnt from laying on the field all day July 1 & weak from thirst & loffs of blood. He is brave you & his family have cause to be proud of him. He was by the colors in the line during the fight and saw Col. Burgwyn sieze the colors when they went down the 10th time the bullet going thrugh his lungs & spining him a round so he fell in the folds He lived 2 hrs Jim heard him say Tell the General my men never failed me at a single point. I believe that is the truth.

Jim asked me to tell you evrything I could that you was a veteran and would know what to tell his folks. Well Sir all in all I beleive we have walked some uperds of 250 miles since we left Winchester that is, just forards not counting up & down & now we are traveling back. We stayed in a barn this side of Middleburg & rested well We are here in a Church I am writing this letter in a Church winder. Mr. Lewis Sir I think Jim is a going to be all right he is young not old like some such as Sgt Henry Coffey the 86 man wounded in Co. F Jim said you had been in a War & would know how to brake it to his folks. He is a going to be all right & said he will write you all just as soon as he gets to a hospitle Drs say it will just take time No doubt he will get a furlogh. He is in good heart says he wants to live to find out how come he was struck by a carbine 44 instead of a Enfield 66 when we was not fighting any cavalry We made out a list here of all our Co we could find out about from the Globe section of the county. I am writing on Yankee paper I found a whole portfolier & Envelopes when I was crawling back to our lines. Jim said to be sure to let Hickses know Sion is alive. Sion was detailed to stay behind with some worse wounded. The Yankees got him. So I will close.

>Yours resply
>ROBERT HUDSPETH, Sgt
>Co. F 26th N.C.
>Heths Div. Pettigrews Brigade
>c/o Col John R. Lane

MARY GARVY McKAMIE

It is a day of broken clouds. August sun has the look of fall. Up on the roof my apples dry—beans too, ready for stringin'.

Heath brought the child again for me to keep. He says,

"What are you goin' to do today?"

What are I goin' to do? If I had back all the days I've changed around for men an' young 'uns, I could start me a drug store like that Rousie feller told about in Lexin'ton.

"Well," I say, "I'd thought I might take some camomile an' ashes to Mis. McGillicuddy for her shingles."

Heath lifts his arm to swipe his face in the crook of his elbow. When Heath learns that Enoch's helpin' rebel families sometimes, it puts him in one of his dark moods. But he don't feel that way about McGillicuddys. Him an' McGillicuddy left here together to go to war over a year ago. They never found Mac after Gettersburg, not hide nor hair of him, folks that always had so much, and now all she's got left is land, no good without a man to work it.

Heath leans his gun ag'inst the bed and hands Sam to me. The baby waves his arms and kicks. He knows me better than his mother.

"Where's Pa an' the boys?"

"Gone to Foscoe. It is the salt agent's day to come."

"I'll get you salt."

I look at him, the odd look on his face, and go lay Sam on the other bed. They don't say where they go, him an' Samantha, nor who it is they meet, whether it's friend or stranger, black or white, though black are plenty since slaves were freed first of the year. It's like I lay my heart down with the child, heavy like him. It's common knowledge those who needed salt broke in a store to get it, in Madison on Shelton's Laurel. They were shot without a trial or hearin' of any kind, four women whipped, an' little Shelton boys thirteen and fourteen made to kneel and shot, and old Jim Shelton over fifty, Stobrod Shelton and six others.

Straightway the baby's arms fly faster, face gets red—at seven months Sam knows the up and down of it. It's like the woes of all this world meets in his squinched-up down-turned face.

"All right! All right!" I lift him back on my shoulder. Restless like his mother. Father, too. "Who takes him up so much he's got so sp'iled?"

"I do!"

The baby laughs through one tear, lifts his arm t'ords doorway and the sun. Along the fence my poppies blaze in the white light. The gum will bring fifty cents an ounce for opium.

Heath slips one finger in his baby's fist, raises it to test the pull. The little fingers reach but half-way 'round.

"I'll be back for Sam tomorrer. Or next day sure. I'll bring you salt—more'n you'll ever get from any agent."

I foller him out on the porch. They say folks in Globe is favored about salt, bein' for the Confederacy. "I want no stolen goods, son."

He turns on the lowest step, "They stole our men, foggin' their minds with lyin' talk!"

"It was the law. They had to go."

"The law's broke down. I tell you, Ma, in many a mountain cove now there are men who stroke their guns and say 'This is the law!'"

"There's some laws don't break down."

He turns and strides down the path past sunflowers and the barn, walks through sun and shadow as he has walked through my day. In the clear white light the poppies glow then darken as a cloud comes over. The mail man brought the seed and a paper

« 141 »

tellin' me how to drip the gum. I love to feel the watery seed pop between my nails, the greenish milk will ease the pain of some poor soul laid like those at Gettersburg on a barn door to lose an arm or leg.

Sam leaps in my arms. I pull up a chair, sit down and hold him out, head in my hand, elbow on my knee. Sudden a face looks out at me—I've put it by a hunderd times—the old half-promisin', half darin' blue gaze stabs me. Who shared his fury that could shake the earth! Did he have childern after Heath? If childern, then grandchildren too, maybe, and this is his! He'd be too old to go to war—not old as Enoch but too old to go—strange for I never think of him as old, nor think at all except when somethin' like this calls him up. Swifter than cloud chasin' sunshine the look is gone, the baby turns his head to stare at Queenie whose tail goes thump against the floor.

"Aunt Mary!" Sudden out of the woods a boy's call comes to startle me. "Aunt Mary!" Then the boy himself on a down path only the childern use, and pigs and dogs. It's Chaney's Thad, his jacket flyin' out behind his ganglin' legs. What now! Queenie pulls up, huffs and jogs out to meet him, her little stick-legged keg of body making but ten yards to the boy's forty from the woods. My mind starts sortin' all the kinds of trouble I've had to hear—deaths, snake-bite, shootings, kickin's by a mule—it's plain it's bad. I put Sam on my shoulder to brace us both.

Fast as he's been hurtlin', when Thad gets to Queenie the jean-cloth legs an' arms reel to a halt and he bends to stroke the old dog's stumpy ears. If only grown folks in this fam'ly know'd and understood each other plain as the childern do, an' dogs!

It can't be all bad, what he's got to tell, if he can take time out for this, but boys will do that—stop before the very gates of hell to pat a dog. The two of 'em walks on to the porch. Sam starts to jump as if he knows somethin' young has come to light his day.

"What is it, son? Sit down an' ketch your breath."

Thad drops down on the step, so hot he smells the way boys do—somewhere between a mushroom an' a pickle—and wipes his coat-sleeved arm across his face. His voice sounds hoarse,

"Aunt Mary, Princess is sick!"

I plump down in the chair with Sam. "Well!" I will not say, Is that all! I've had too many boys, and men that act like boys, for me to say it. I just give thanks it is not news from war, nobody's killed, scalded, p'izened, bit by a copperhead.

"How would you say she's tuk?"

"She jist lays there—"

"No acci*dent*?"

He shakes his head. "She ain't got a scratch. Her eyes are red—"

"Has she done anything out of ordinary?"

"Well—she went after a red fox over on Rocky Knob—"

"It's just a spree like that would set off nephritis in a old dog. A old dog has to drink about every half an hour."

"Oh, she drinks—"

"But not on Rocky Knob, there's not much water there, I've seen the day I'd like to find some."

"She drinks but she don't—"

"You mean the rest goes out the other way?" He nods. "And all the time."

"Princess is not so old."

"Older'n you. You know how dog age is reckoned, one year to a human's seven." If I recall, Princess was Queenie's second litter born the same year as Nannie's Mae, and same night old man Crump died. When I got home from helpin' lay him out, Queenie had it over with—six pups, each licked as clean and slick as any baby otter.

Thad sniffs the phleme back up his nose. I'd almost say tears mixes with the sweat but it takes a lot to make a mountain boy cry. By time they're twelve, fell out of bed, passed second summer, had ja'nders, stone bruises, cut feet an' broken legs, if they live atall, they leave tears to girls an' women. All they want's a gun—

That's it. Wash' said if Thad keeps Princess he will bring him back a gun.

"It wouldn't be surprisin', Thad, a female dog would be give out at seventy, if my figurin's right, 'specially if she's had a many pups as Princess, not countin' tangles with bob-cats, skunks an' other dogs—" and through it all, I think, havin' to fit her day to plans of boys an' men but that's one thing the blessed Lord seen to it comes nat'rul to dogs an' women.

"I promised Wash' I'd keep her—"

"Yes, I know—" I'd orter know, we've heerd it of'en enough from Jake an' Tom—some kinda Yankee pistol Washin'ton promised Thad you don't haf' to load but once for it to shoot five times.

Sam starts to buck, throws hisself back'erds, gittin' mad.

"If you'd come, Aunt Mary! I could carry Sam!"

The sweetish smell of apples dryin' in the sun comes down from the roof comb on the breeze.

"There ain't no doubt that Sam would like to go—" I set him on my hand, raise him up an' down. "I tell you what—you take this bucket, fill it at the spring, get you some water—" Thad's face starts to shine like spring sun after showers. "Douse your face good now while I tend to Sam."

What was I goin' to do today? To keep a old dog livin' so you can win a gun—well, not in all old folks is there that much profit, and Lord knows, there's little enough a boy can have up here now, even long life. Old man Trigger Crump had nephritis too. Maybe a little hydrangea extract or powdered corn-silk would help Princess. But it was age killed old man Trigger, not just gettin' drunk at the temperance meetin'.

« 144 »

JAMES LEWIS

My leg started swelling again after I tried to fish up Anthony's creek. Old Dr. Horace Rivers came, says there's still something in it from Gettysburg—some dirt, a bit of shell, a piece of bone. He put on a flax seed poultice and had them fix me a bed here by the parlor window.

The white curtain sucks in and out. I've climbed in and out this window many a time playing hide and seek. Without touching it, I can feel the gray sill under my fingers, ridged but smooth. The sand is fine and cool to your bare feet outside, below the window where rainfall from the eaves leaves a line of little holes.

Morning sun flashes on Johns River, but thunder is muttering back in the mountains. Uncle Theophilus says it is the equinox, September twenty second, but my father says there is nothing to that. I've heard them argue it a hundred times.

Uncle Theophilus comes at night, brings ice and the news. Home Guard has been organized under Colonel Walton at Morganton. Deserters and bushwhackers from the mountains swooped down two nights ago on Rader's farm, stole two mules and some salt. They go in companies of fifteen or twenty, are desperate for food, and one of the leaders is Heath Garvy, Margaret's step-brother. His wife goes with him, Sam, who was in our regiment at Kinston. When Heath's not whacking, Browns say, he's taking deserters and refugees across the Grandfather into Tennessee. Well—they know every trail and by-way.

Uncle Theophilus sits square in his chair like a bull frog, head shining like an egg between his side burns. When I first got home he wanted to know about Gettysburg, and I told him what I could, why everybody calls it Pickett's charge when Pettigrew was in it, and more especially Burgwyn and the 26th North Carolina—and most especially Company F with men from Globe and Watauga. He wishes he had been there. His black eyes snap. Well, we could have used Uncle Theophilus at Gettysburg.

He says Major McDowell with some of the 62nd just passed down the Globe from Tennessee, having refused the shameful surrender with Frazer at Cumberland Gap. They managed to push a Yankee cannon off a cliff as they came along.

Tom Norwood is back home in Yadkin Valley, was given up for lost at Gettysburg, laid on the field two days, was captured and put in a college but Tom said comforts there was divided by long division so he got out, stole some laborer's clothes, fell in with the whole Yankee army, learned a lot, walked forty miles, and ended having breakfast with General Lee and giving him a lot of information.

The curtain sucks and blows. Outside the window my little sister, Emeline Angel, and Kiz's grandaughter, Empie, make playhouses in the sand.

I wish I could get out of here! So much to do and fewer and fewer men and mules to do it with. I miss Pinckney—he is near Chattanooga with the 58th. Pendleton has gone with Wak to take a load of tax to Morganton—money has gone down until everything has to be paid in kind—beans, peas, corn, but no sacks to put it in. War was not here when I left. Now it is everywhere. Even old Dr. Rivers pays a tax.

"Boy, I pay fifty dollars for the privilege of curing you!" He looks smaller than when I left, grayer and more stooped. Everybody does, even my father and mother.

"Spell rabbit, Empie!" Emmy Angel is bossy.

This is the time we all used to start to school but there is no school now. The teacher, Mr. Charlie Dickson, has gone with my father to make up a warrant of distress for Mrs. Fleming. She hid her corn from the impressment officer. They have to prove she is not worth $1000. so she will be let alone—a queer thing to have to prove, looking at it one way. I saw her husband, Will, go down among the briars along Willoughby's Run.

"I'll spell it then! R-a-b-*rab*, b-i-t- *bit*, *rabbit*! You can do that, Empie!"

My mother, I believe, is a better teacher than Mr. Charlie Dickson. She tries to teach both black and white with all else she has to do. She wants to enter Pendleton in the Bingham School—he is fifteen now, but wants to join the cavalry. He sleeps in the barn with Taima, his mare, for fear she will be pressed, or stolen by bushwhackers.

I lift the poultice and take a look—there is no change, I sigh and settle back.

This room still smells the way it always did, like carpet and family prayers. I want someone my own age to talk to—maybe not a man. I will not say I went up Anthony's Creek expecting to find Margaret. But I went remembering how we walked there. In the Army it is so easy to run on kin or comrades, happens in the strangest ways, so wasn't there a hundredth chance—well, say a million, then—that Margaret might be there, gathering—what she said—ginseng, spignet—I did see her, or I thought I did—lighted like a red bird in the path. I have penned letters enough for men to girls to know how much has to wait till you are with the girl herself. There are some things you cannot tell a man that you could tell a girl, even about the war. I could tell *her*. Maybe she feels that way. How does she feel about her step-brother? Are they really scarce of food up in McKamie Gap?

Emmy Angel crows "That's two syllables! Now hear me spell in three!"

I can't see the little colored girl but I can guess what she is doing, her head to one side, sliding a little stick or pebble through the sand.

"P-o, *po*, t-a, *tay*, t-o, *toe*, potato!"

Empie starts humming a snatch of song I've heard since I came back, never before I went away,

> "Fol-*low* de drinkin' gourd!
> Fol-*low* de drinkin' gourd—"

The slaves stop singing it when they find you're listening.

Aunt Kiz comes in, flips a dust rag over the family Bible and the India shawl covering the round table. Her screwed-up little brown monkey face looks cross inside her turban. I've seen Kiz take a hickory branch and lash a daughter just to see her dance while other slaves looked on. To this day it makes me sick to think about. I ran and hid up in the graveyard. But she was kind to me always. She used to chant conjur rhymes for us while she stirred wash-pots down by the spring. I remember one—just the end of it,

>"Hailem, scalem
>Moojer, major
>*France*!"

She always bore down on that *France*—she'd picked it up somewhere, I guess it seemed an educated word.

"Sing the rest, Empie!" my sister begs.

The thunder rolls again behind Rough Ridge. Gettysburg! I wonder if it will always sound like that to me!

"I know the rest of the song!" Emmy Angel crows. "Mollie Dickson taught me! The drinkin' gourd is the Big Dipper! It's the stars! It's North where Dicksons' Sip has gone, and House Bob, and Doll—followin' the peg-leg man!" She sings in a high voice

>"Fol-*low* the drinkin' goad!
>Fol-*low* the drinkin' go'ad!
>For the old man is a-comin' for to carry you
>>to freedom
>If you fol-low—"

Aunt Kiz flies to the window. "Hesh dat!" She brings down the dust rag with a pop on the sill. "You Empie!"

Giggles and the sound of scampering feet in sand.

Kiz pulls back from the window, muttering.

"Tell me about that song, Kiz!"

"Hi!" she says. Kiz will say "Hi!" to anything—good news or bad, a broken dish, a gift—"Hi!"

"What is the drinkin' gourd?"

She moves about the room, a little mumbling witch, flipping her cloth.

"Make me a conjur rhyme, Kiz, the way you used to do for Pinckney and me on wash days at the spring!"

She laughs inside her turban, a wheeze turned outside in.

"Baid luck! I'll fix yo' haid." She plumps my pillow and I settle back. But when she leaves the room she turns at the door, sticklike arms and hands on hips, head thrown back and eyes half shut, she chants

> "One Zaw, two Zaw, zicka Zaw *Zan*!
> Bob-tail, bob-tail, tickle-'em-a-tan!
> Hailem, scailem,
> Moojer, major
> France! Hi!"

KIZ

Tramp de treadle, weave a spell—

Mis' Em sent me out heah git dis weavin' done. Took all cloths we had to sta'nch his woun'—Pen'elton! Shot down like a rabbit in de fodder! Pen'elton, de bes' lookin' one of 'em, shot in he own gyardin! Two of 'em layin' in de front room now, one shot in de wah, one r'at heah at home. Po' l'il rabbit!

Tramp de treadle, throw de shuttle th'oo—fo', *one*, fo' *one*! Mis' Em send evvybody out d'house dis mawnin' keep 'em f'um seein' her cry.

Tramp de treadle, weave a spell—

> Fish eye, hawk eye,
> Jerk 'er tight!

Midnight dey come! Storm clouds blowin' off de moon! Me gone to de back-house. Hear soun's in de big road—not movin' easy lak so'jers, not movin' wes' like niggers. Hi!

I squat behine boxwood. Niggers snorin' in de quahtahs. Moon on de big house roof, firs' white den dahk. Lil gals sleep upstairs on dey side de house. Jim layin' in de pahlor. Pen'elton gyuardin' he horse in de barn. Gyuardin' Taima.

Voices in de road! Voices mumblin', mumblin' lak de rivah. Soun' all mixed up wid de rivah—fo' *one*, *fo' one*! Slip, slop!

Moojer, major, *France*!

Den I see ole witch in shadder by de big privy! R'at wheah she standin' fust time I seen her, ovah yeah ago, hidin' her privates, pullin' up her clo'es—

Ole witch—
Shrinker an' shranker!
Jerk 'er tight!

Moon flyin' fas'—red aroun' de rim. Hit takes more'n white folkeses prayers to slay a witch. Hi! Mumblin' in de road gittin' loudah, Loudah by de gate. Den I see man climbin' on de roof—movin' strong lak paint'her, movin' heavy lak bear—Lord God, r'at to 'de l'il gals room! Whimb'ly, bimb'ly, str'rak him down!!

Crack! Gun in de road! Fire f'um shadders bunched at de gate. Man on roof jerk somep'n outer winder, runs back down roof lak cat. Runs back—goes in shadders on boys' side, comes out wid armful, runs back down roof. Jumps off! Whole lot yuther stuff piled on de groun', piled by de po'ch—Stealin' Mis' Em's stuff!

Crack!! Gun blaze f'um de pahlor! Jim shootin' f'um de pahlor—Lord God blessèd Jesus! Fo', *one*! Fo', *one*! Tramp—

Wak runs outa de quahtahs—ducks behime grapevines—Runs bent ovah—Runs to git to de house—Runs lak Chris'mus mawnin'! Ole witch crouchin' in shadders! Conjur dat ole witch!

Fish eye, hawk eye
An' jerk 'er tight!
Th'ow her tracks in runnin' watah!

Light flickers up in de house—Miss Em lightin' lamp—den Marse Andy's voice, sh'ap, tellin' her put it out. Fo', one! Fo', one!

Moon slides out bright, clouds sailin' fas'. Bear man on groun' now, lopes t'odes hill. Got whole pack o' stuff on he back—kiver outa Jim's room—Mis' Em's grammaw's kiver—whole pack o' stuff wropped up in ole kiver name Cat Tracks!

Stock gittin' stuh'd up—sheep bleats—all dem sheep an' humped up cows—fancy names f'um South Ca'lina.

Den I heah more mens—whole pack of 'em up on de hill—whole 'nother bunch of 'em up in de cem'teh! Robbahs in de grave-yahd tromplin' ovah Marse Jesse's grave.

Boom! Dat's Wak, got to de big house! Shootin' f'um de pantry—shootin' Marse Jesse's ole musky. Big hollow soun'. Ain' nevah shot 'cept on Ole New Yeah's. Wak in de back. Cain' git pas' him an' ole musky. Jim in front, cain' git pas' him. Marse Andy on de side—Hi!

Crack! Dat's Pen'elton shootin' f'um de bahn! Ole witch jumps —fust time she moves! Runs out in de moonlight—runs fo' de hill! Runs lak woman, holdin' huh ahm—Hit, by God! Runs r'at by me holdin' onto huh ahm!

Den Pen'elton stum'les outa de bahn—tries to git to de house— O blesséd Jesus! Robbahs comin' at him down de hill. Mules flyin' up an' down de pastuh—thunder-foot shadders wheel an' turn. Crack! f'um de hill—Crack! Crack! Pen'elton fall! He try to git up! Dahk head ben's down ag'in. Sinkin'. Boom! Dat's Wak— Marse Jesse's ole musky f'um ovah fiah-place! Mules feet thuddin' up an' down de fence!

Robbahs all 'round Pen'elton now—po' white trash f'um Mc-Cauthern's Gap—Home Yankees f'um up on de Gran'fathah! One say

"We didn' know dat was *you*!"

But dey leans ovah an' takes his gun! Pen'elton cain't git up! Po' l'il rabbit!! Lord God!

Grunts f'um de pastuh—"We got 'em now!" Dahk shadders po' th'oo de past'uh gate—all them fine-name stock f'um South Ca'lina—all Marse Andy's mules pressin' agents ain't already took! Boom! Ain' no use, Wak! Marse Jesse's ole musky won' reach dat fah. Robbahs runnin' fo' de hill!

Den I heah somep'n else—hosses' hoofs comin' up de Globe—clippity clap! Robbahs in de road flies aroun' t'odes de hill.

Clippity clap—clippity clap! Home Gah'd comin' up de valley, clippity clap! Whinny f'um de bahn—dat's Taima! Hi! boy! Robbahs ain' got Taima yet. Whinny ansuh f'um down de road—Gideon, Marse' Theoph' ole fat sor'l! Always whinny lak dat when he gits to de branch. Marse Theoph an' de Home Gah'd—can heah dey hoss guts now—Grump-gut! Grump gut! Come too late—

Mule bray up in grave-yahd. Somebody shouts gruff up in grave-yahd—"Come on, boys!" Gruff lak bear. Den he says "Sam's hu't!" Hi! De ole witch! Hit in de ahm! Blood on de trail!

Robbahs go skitterin' off—ain' no soun' now but Home Gah'ds—lights an' shoutin'. Robbahs done gone off in de mountains.

Took all cloths we had to sta'ch Pen'elton's hip. Brung all lamps in kitchen so Miss Em can see. See to bi'le things, wukin' lak doctah till doctah can git here—mebbe tomorrer, mebbe nex' week. Jim pretty good doctah—Marse Theoph, too—been in Revolution, Marse Theoph', seen lots men git hit. Hit! Cain' walk no mo'! Po' l'il rabbit! Fo', *one*! Fo' *one*!

Lights go out 'bout day. Moon goin' down. Moon winkin' on de rivah. Moon shakin' on de leaves. Ole witch hidin' off in de mountains. Witch blood on de trail—Nothin' won' grow dere no mo'—Hi!

>Fish eye, hawk eye,
>An' jerk 'er tight!
>Th'ow her tracks in runnin' watah!
>Slip, slop!
>Shrinker an' shranker!
>De ole hussy!
>Amen!
>Rapperhanner.

SAMANTHA

Heese holds another pumpkin slice over the hearth an' flicks the seed in the fire with his knife blade. Outside is fog—inside, too, it seems like. It settled in week after first frost.

I move my chair an' draw the churn clos'ter to the bed so I can rest my shot arm on it while I churn with my good arm. Butter is slow to come a day like this.

Sam has crawled over to Heese's leg an' is tryin' to raise hisself to the knee. If he makes it, it will be the first blessed thing anybody has got done in this house today. Ust to be, you done somep'n an' you had somep'n. You done somep'n an' it turned out right.

Heese lays the pumpkin slice in the skillet, hacks off another an' flips the seed in the fire. He's not us't to doin' no women's work no time an' it don't set well. Sometimes I think he'd do better if he'd go on *in* the Union army 'st'id o' tryin' to feed half of it an' nurse 'em on over into East Tennessee. When Grantum Buckhannon come to stay with me, he said his father said a *real* vet'ran don't feel right outa line, yet his place wasn' any bigger'n shoulder to shoulder. I guess Laban'd orter know—he's been in it since the first, soon be two years. He said it's just the green ones goes kyeyutin' off tryin' to fight the war all by theirselves.

Sam reaches up for the knife, holdin' on for dear life to his daddy's leg.

"Watch! He's after the knife!"

Heese jerks the blade back, then starts to move it ag'in, slow, t'ords Sam's fingers. He grins but the scowl stays. Sam frets an' reaches for it an' Heese draws it back ag'in out of reach. Sam don't know what to make of this, an' tunes up a sound between a laugh an' a cry. When Heese gets blocked some way, he gits mean, does things that hurt even hisself—like time he set our own woods on fire just 'to see the wild horses run!' That's what he called the fire. Well he seen it all right. It burnt plum on 'round the mountain, was about to take our house next mornin'—woulda hadna been for Haw branch an' a wet day like this with fog comin' in.

My arm pains an' I prop it with the kiver. It's the kiver we brought back from Lewis's in the Globe—gray an' white with ripples in it an' little reddish figures in between. Heese has been aimin' to give it to his mother but we've not been over there since the fracas down in the Globe, part owin' to us tryin' to harvest an' only three arms to do it with, an' Sam determined to walk, an' the conscriptors all about.

The kiver looks old, but strong, too—had to be to hold all the peach brandy we brought back from Globe. That was a month ago an' all we got to show for it now is this kiver an' my sore arm. An' Heese's bad temper. We've not seen all them fine cows an' sheep since we lef' 'em at McCauthern's. Kirk took the mules right on to Shell Creek where he's makin' up a regiment. God knows we couldn' feed stock. Meal an' meat was et up by outlyers. I reckon I'd a-died sure hadna been for the brandy. I used it outside an' inside.

Sam is howlin' now so Heese pries him off his leg, sets the skillet holdin' the pumpkin an' knife on the table, an' throws Sam his little bloodstone on its thong that Sam dearly loves to play with. He beats it on the floor, so we don't notice the knocks at first.

"Mister Garvy!" It's a man's voice.

Heese quick grabs his gun, raises it an' backs up to the fireplace. I shove the churn in the corner, grab Sam with my good arm, plop him 'way back on the big bed an' pile the kiver around him to hold him in.

"Mister William Angel Garvy!" It's a commandin' voice.

"Who'd know your whole name for-God's-sake?" I hiss at Heese.

"Open the trap door, Samantha!" he says. We feed the hogs down under the floor sometimes, an' after Heese got sqez' in the loft window an' shot, we planned he'd go out under the house next time rather than get shot ag'in. He motions with his gun bar'l for me to peek through the side o' the shutter.

"There's five of 'em!"

"Rebels?"

"I don't know—they're bearded. Old worn out store clothes—boots cut up—"

"Guns?"

"Nothin' but staves—less'n they've got arms—they got satchels, an' the youngest one, Yes, sir, he's carryin' what looks like a cam'ra over his shoulder!"

Heese looks at me kinda pityin', then tips over an' peeps out. It's the truth! A big black box he's holdin' by the legs. The tallest one is leanin' over, got his black-brim hat pushed back an' long nose jutted 'most into our latch hole.

"Mister Garvy, we're friends! Your father says tell you the sorghum is ready!" Whoever he is, he talks different from folks around here.

Heese waits a bit, then keepin' his gun raised, walks over, unbars the door an' steps back to the fireplace. Long Nose nearly falls through the door an' straight on through the trap door as others push in behind him. One of 'em has on some kinda old dark blue army cap but the band is still shiny an' got some kinda little crossed hooks on it.

"These are gloomy times," says Long Nose who seems to be the leader.

"Yes," Heese scowls, "but we look for a better."

It's the richwal—the one Heese ain't got much use for any more. First time I heard it, I asked him how come so many stragglers to say the same thing.

" 'Lie lows to catch meddlers,' " he says.

That makes me mad, him puttin' me off that way. "I thought me an' you was ust to sharin' everything, or is that gone up, too, 'long with all in this war?" It was soon after he come back from a Peace meetin' in Wilkes. I couldn' go on account o' carryin' Sam.

"It's a richwal, Samantha. Women folks ain't supposed to know about it."

This kind of married talk he knows I don't pay any mind to. "What's a richwal?"

"I dunno—that's the name was give to me, same as your name's Samantha."

Now I've learnt it all by heart. They say

> These are gloomy times.
> Yes, they are gloomy.
> Yes, but we are lookin' for better.
> What are we lookin' for?
> A red an' white cord.
> Why a cord?
> Because it's safe for us an' our fam'lies.

Then one of 'em may bring out a little piece o' red twine or a rag but Heese never had much patience with this kinda play-actin' even at the first.

One day the richwal changed. Heese would just say "Three—" an' the other feller would say "days," an' they would shake hands with two fingers across each other's knuckles for the grip, an' that would be it.

Heese was feelin' meller that day because we still had some o' the brandy, also some Union feller had left him a little terbaccer.

"A richwal," he says, "is somethin' you change when too many gets to mouthin' it."

After a while I noticed him an' Enoch had made up one o' their own. When strangers pass an' say "The buckwheat is ready—" (or the sorghum or the peas—ever what crop is in season) we say

"Good, an' I'd like to have some too for Uncle Jake," though God knows we ain't got no Uncle Jake no more'n Enoch has maybe got molasses.

Long Nose peers down through the trap door. "Many rebels 'round here?"

"Home Guard," says Heese. "Old men an' boys tryin' to guard bridges an' passes. Most of the fightin's over in Tennessee now—

there's four armies drawed up over there." Heese walks over an' kicks the trap door shut. "We feed pigs down there sometimes."

"Ah? Well!" He holds out his hand an' gives the grip. "We're cor'spondents, Mr. Garvy—" I can tell this don't make sense to Heese any more'n it does to me. The rest start tryin' to give the grip but Heese just brushes 'em aside.

The youngest one has let his cam'ra legs rest on the floor, an' is holdin' the box over his shoulder easy like holdin' a baby. "War cor'spondents," he says. "Most newspapers have 'em." I can't tell whether he's makin' fun of us or not. Long Nose is not. He pulls his hat off an' speaks polite,

"I'm Junius Henry Brown of the New York Tribune. This—" he says pointin' to the wide-awake lookin' black-eyed feller with the flat hat an' fringes o' hair over his ears that's carryin' one o' the valises, "is Mr. Richardson, my—" colic? or somep'n, I couldn't make it out. "This is Captain Thomas E. Wolfe—" he motions to the one with the gold hooks on his cap, "late of the U. S. merchant ship Honduras, taken by rebels off Belize. Behind him there is Private Charles Thurston, 6th New Hampshire, and late of the Salisbury prison bakery. The gentleman with the camera is Mr. William Davis of the Cincinnati Gazette, our rescuer."

Each of them bows real polite when innerduced. Later I got 'em to write down their names. Whatever they been through, you can tell they still got a lot o' spunk and are real educated gen'lemen —the most of anybody we ever had here. The colic, Mr. Richardson, tests the trap door with his foot before he sets down the valise.

"We are escaping from Salisbury," says Junius Henry Brown, "slep' last night in your father's stable. He gave us the passwords an' told us you might be so kind as to guide us over this mountain."

"Or *around* the mountain," says Richardson, "or *through* it." He is settin' straddle of the valise like ridin' a horse—a lively horse, too, an' he's lively with snappin' black eyes that take in everything. "We been *over* enough mountains."

"What was you doin' to git put in prison?" Heese asks.

They all chuckle like this was a big joke. Sam, 'way over in the back of the bed, catches on to their laughin' an' starts bouncin' up an' down in his nest o' kiver.

"We were consigned to Salisbury as general hostages for the good conduct of the government," says Brown.

Richardson has been lookin' curious at my arm in the sling, at my Confedrit coat hangin' on the wall an' my hair switch over it. Mary McKamie found my hair on the woodpile day after we chopped it off when we went away to the war. She kep' it an' Enoch sewed up the ends neat with fine black shoe twine.

Heese lets his gun fall loose through his crooked elbow, leans down an' picks up his bloodstone Sam has left on the floor an' stands by the fire twirlin' it the way he does when he's makin' up his mind about somep'n. If they're tellin' the truth, they must be pretty important fellers, but truth or lie, they're friendly and seems like they brought a breath o' fresh air in with 'em, 'specially Richardson, sittin' there with that flat hat perked up at the edges an' those sassy tags o' hair.

The New Hampshire feller sniffs the air, "Pumpkin!" he says, "Pumpkin pie. I've not had any o' that in over a year."

The Navy Captain, Wolfe, has gone to the water bucket and is drinkin' a gourd full. Ones comes from Salisbury never can get enough mountain water.

"Well, it ain't to say *pie*," says Heese lookin' in the skillet, "I been heatin' some raw in the pan. My old woman ain't much to cook. Help yourself."

My face turns red—him runnin' me down like that to strangers and I snap "Maybe you'd bring home somep'n to make a crust out of, I'd make as good pumpkin pie as anybody!"

Long Nose—or Brown—makes a bow, sweepin' his soft black felt hat down. "I'm sure you would, Mrs. Garvy! Thurston's not hungry, really. Your father and mother fed us well. Very well. Remarkable folks. Your mother showed me her herbarium and told me she'd once known the botanist, Asa Gray."

Thurston pokes at the raw pumpkin in the skillet, "Asa Gray was from Massachusetts."

"She's my mother-in-law." I says. "That's right. She's not ever forgot the meetin'. Nor has any of the rest of us."

"He was not so from Massachusetts," says Richardson, "he was from the Mohawk Valley!"

"His folks were from Massachusetts. And Vermont. How do you cook this pumpkin?" Thurston goes over to the fire stool an' Heese shows him how to hold it over the coals.

Sam has started to play peeky boo with the cam'ra feller, Davis.

"What is it—boy or girl?"

"Boy!" You'd think he could tell.

"How old is he?"

"Eight months."

"How'd you git outa prison—tunnel?" Heese asks. We had some stragglers done that.

"Tunnel!" They chuckle same as the other time. The Navy Captain lifts the gourd t'ords the roof like it was a mug of good liquor. "Tunnels!" he says, "the noblest work of man! We've seen tunnels from Vicksburg to Richmond to Salisbury. We've seen 'em dug with case knives, old rusty hinges an' bare hands. There was at least four finished at Salisbury when we left, three unfinished. But we did not come out of a tunnel. I wish we had—we might have brought more gear with us."

Thurston with his mouth full holds up a piece o' hot pumpkin an' waves it on the tip of the knife. Seems like they all understand each other real well, an' kinda keep aigin' each other on.

"That's right, Mr. Garvy," says Brown. "Far from wishing to harm a hair of your head, your safety has become our safety. These valises contain Mr. Davis's photo-chemicals, our apparel and a few pens and paper. Search if you like."

"How *did* you git out of prison, then?"

"Well, we owe our escape to Mr. Davis here who owes his to a Herald correspondent who left him enough good U. S. dollars at Libby to buy his way out. He came on and aided us. Richardson, Wolfe and I were for eight months volunteer hospital orderlies in Salisbury prison. The only difference in prison and hospital is that the hospital has straw on the floor. We were detailed to go for straw. Private Thurston came out by way of the bakery."

Richardson keeps lookin' at my arm. "What happened to you, ma'am?"

I look at Heese. "A bullet boomeranged off a spy," Heese says short. "Where was you wantin' to go to in Tennessee?"

"To the East Tennessee an' Virginia Railroad. If it's still runnin'. From there we can get down to Greenville and the Union lines."

"What's the baby's name?" the cam'ra man asks.

"Sam."

"I got a boy six months old I've never seen."

"Ain't that too bad! Ain't you even got a pitchur of him—an' you a photog'apher?" He shakes his head. "I been wantin' a pitchur o' Sam but—"

"The railroad was runnin' last week" Heese says, "least I guess it's the one. Two rebel deserters come through here, they'd been in a big battle somewheres over about Chattanooga, some Injun name I can't call—"

"Chickamauga?"

"That mighta been it. They was mad at some rebel gen'rul name Brag for not follerin' up a Yankee they called Old Rosy. These fellers was bein' took to Virginny to keep 'em away from gittin' to their homes aroun' Greenville an' Rheatown, but they point black didn' aim to go, an' escaped from the cars at Jonesburr."

"If you'll just start us off in the direction of Dan Ellis's—you know him?"

"I know *uv* him. I know them that knows him."

"Tell me—is it true he's piloted hundreds of men into Kentucky?"

"That's what they say. There's loyal people all along the way that's helped him though. Some from right around here. I can't take you to Valley Forge, or Siam, that's where he lives. But I can start you off."

Thurston, chewin', raises another piece of pumpkin an' waves it like a flag while Brown bows his head an' lays his hat over his heart. "Through the dark clouds of war, Justice an' Mercy shine!" he says like a prayer.

"Wh-ups!!" Sam lunges t'ords the edge o' the bed. Davis lifts him back on.

"How come you to name him Sam?" he asks.

"That was my name when I was in the Army." Heese looks at me warnin' but I don't keer—I'm still mad at him about my cookin'.

Richardson clears his throat. "Which Army was that, ma'am?"

"The Confedrit Army. 26th North Car'lina Regiment! *Volunteer* Regiment!"

Richardson gets up an' bows an' starts fiddlin' with the straps on the valise.

"Samantha an' me are loyal, all right!" says Heese. "We was tryin' to git over on the Union side. I'd a-thought Pa woulda told you."

Richardson gets the satchel open but its full o' bottles, tin and glass. A kinda sweetish spoilt smell comes outa it. "Swap me that other valise, Junius!"

"What's the last pitchur you took with that cam'ra?" Heese asks.

"Libby prison."

"I'd like to see that."

"It's not finished yet. I'm hoping to do the final washing in Knoxville—or Greenville—if I can find some studio. I hope it will be good, I took it in rather a hurry."

"What's the next pitchur you're gonna take?" Heese asks.

"My first glimpse of the Stars and Stripes!"

"Whyn't you take a pitchur of Sam, you're so interested in him," asks Thurston.

Richardson finely gets his pen an' paper out from under some clo'es in the other valise. "I'd rather have a picture of Mrs. **Garvy!**"

"Never move out of range 'till you've completed your notes, eh, Albert?"

"Let's get the whole story. Why not make it a family group?"

"Are you foolin'?" Davis asks.

The captain says "You can't argue with Albert, Bill—he was a prominent member of the Libby Prison Debating Society."

"You fellows think snappin' a picture is all there is to it. There's the little matter of light, and preparin' the plates, to say nothin' of holdin' the subject still." He looks at Sam. "You couldn't put head clamps on *him*, even if I had 'em."

"I will entertain Sam," says Thurston. He sets the skillet down, picks up the deerskin rug. "Looky here, Sam! Gr-rr-rr!"

Sam don't know whether to laugh or cry.

"I couldn' have no pitchur took with this arm in a sling—"

"You want more light or less light?" Heese asks.

"More light."

"We can light the grease lamps then."

"Well reely, I—" I b'lieve Heese has been holdin' out on me. I b'lieve he wants a pitchur o' Sam as much as I do.

"I believe 'twould be better just to open the door and windows," Davis says. "But we'd have to have a dark room—"

"How 'bout down there?" Richardson waves at the trap door.

"An' a sink—"

"That's somethin' we ain't got," Heese says. "We just use the woods."

"I mean—where do you wash the dishes?"

"Why here, of course," says the Captain, lookin' to see has he drunk up all the water.

Brown opens the door and peers out. "Well whatever it is, boys, we better get on with it. This fog is not liftin' any."

"We've worked under pressure before—"

"An' been bribed before."

"An' done some bribin' ourselves," says the Captain.

"Well reely—" I rub my hands down my pants.

"Now Samantha," says Heese, "There's never been a cam'ra in

this house an' it's unlikely there ever will be again. You been sayin' for years—well, one year, anyway—you wanted a pitchur o' Sam an' now's your chance to git it."

"Well, I just never figured it'd haf' to be done in such a hurry!"

"Oh, it can't be done in a *hurry*," says Davis. "The subject—Sam or whoever it is—will have to sit perfectly still for *at least* ten minutes!"

I turn to Heese. "I don't think we oughta be *separated*!"

"How much you figure it will cost to take the three of us?"

"Never mind about that," says Brown, "I'm sure the Cincinnati Gazette will be glad to pay for it. If not, the Tribune will."

"Is that so!" says Davis.

"*And if not*," Brown says "I have a book of my own in mind."

"But we ain't *dressed* to have our pitchur made!"

"What finer record of your service," Richardson says, layin' down his writin' an' goin' to the wall, "than—" he brings my uniform coat an' throws it around my shoulders,

"Take that off!" Heese bellers.

"Oh for God's sake, don't get him stirred up!" I say. I'm close to cryin'. *Me!*

Heese growls "She can just have it took in her reg'lar waist."

Richardson still has my switch in his hand, drawin' it from one hand to another. He raises it to his face an' looks at me, pullin' it across his mouth, and that flat hat o' his perkin' up at the edges. "It's been a long time since I felt a woman's hair."

"Samantha!" Heese says sharp, "Go get Sam!"

Davis has got his cam'ra stood up, a black cloth throwed over it an' he gets under it an' then out ag'in about five times.

"Now I got to prepare the plate," he says, an' swings the valise up on the wash shelf, takes out little brushes an' panes o' glass an' bottles, an' makes more to-do over it than I would washin' Sam, or Reuben would over communion. "It is a delicate operation," he says, "Poison—the slightest breath of it—would produce a blank spot." The stink gets worse.

Richardson has rolled my switch an' made it in a soft knot.

He holds it up, turns his head on one side an' looks at it an' me. Thurston is sittin' on the floor with the deer hide over his shoulders. "Let's try the shig-non on," he says.

I ain't ever worn it though I think Mary an' Enoch wisht I would. Richardson sets it on the crown of my head.

"Hm-mm-mm," Thurston says, "I believe it becomes you more, Mrs. Garvy, to leave it off." I let it slide off on the floor.

"Let's quit foolin' around," says Heese. "If we're gonna get to Linville. Samantha! did you hear me tell you to go git Sam?"

I go over an' pick him up. "We'll have to kinda let him set in front of my sling. Where'd you want us to sit?"

David holds the wet plate between the insides of his pa'ms. "Let's see—I've focussed on that wall. Right over there. Do you think you can brace your heads ag'inst it?"

Thurston gets down on all fours again, pulls the deer skin over him.

"Better not do that," I says, "Sam's scared enough to keep still."

"He's *not* scared," Heese says, "he's just sleepy!" I wonder how come him all at once to know so much. I feel to see if Sam's dry. For once he is.

"Wouldn't Heese have time to put on his plaid shirt his Ma made him?"

"No—we're ready."

"I don't like the pose," says Thurston.

"What's the matter?"

"It's customary to have the lady standing with her hand resting gracefully on her husband's shoulder."

"You heard the lady say she wants the injury concealed."

"Go on an' take the pitchur!" Heese is breathin' as if he'd climed Grandfather. "We got a two hour walk ahead o' us. Four for me."

"If there's goin' to be any pi'zen blank spots, let 'em come out where my hair is, or ain't." I say.

"Not quite so tense! Smile now! Keep your heads firm against the wall—Ho-o-old till I count—Ready? One— two— three—"

At ten Sam starts to wet, slow, warm, hot—it gives us both somethin' to fix our minds on anyway.

"Ho-o-old!" Davis is rattlin' his little plates. "Now! Fine!" He comes out. I don't know who's sweatin' the most, me or him or Heese.

Richardson lifts the trap door, Davis climbs down, Richardson looks after him, salutes, an' lets it bang shut.

Heese gets up an' starts collectin' his gun an' things. Sam is startin' to fret. Thurston lays the deer skin back in place on the floor, goes to the door an' looks out.

"Must be a pretty view from here judgin' from the mountains we climbed to get here. How does it look—I mean when you can see?"

"I wisht I could say." I put Sam down on the floor, he runs across my switch an' sits there feelin' it. "When the fog closes in, there's nothin' but it. When it lifts, there's no words can tell it."

"What's gonna be the name of your book, Junius?" asks Richardson.

" 'Four years in Secessia.' "

David knocks to get out. Richardson lets him up, helpin' him keep the plate safe. "I'm afraid there will be a lot of spots," he says. "Ain't it kind of unsanitary, feedin' hogs under the floor like that?"

Heese is countin' out his bullets, placin' 'em in his cartridge case. "We never lost a hog."

"Can we see the pitchur?" I ask.

"Oh—I'll have to do the final finishing in Knoxville," he sees how disappointed I am. "*But you'll have it—I promise!* You'll have it, and all fixed up in a pretty case, if we have to pawn the Tribune to get it for you."

He packs the pitchur plate in a tin real careful, gathers up his little bottles an' stuff. Richardson puts the papers he's scribblin' back in the valise an' hands me the names he wrote down for me.

"Goodbye, Private Garvy," he says. "I hate unfinished stories."

"So do I!" I'd like to see Bugles an' Company F right now.

Sam has not made up his mind whether he likes the feel o'

my hair or not. He sits there gittin' it off one hand an' onto the other.

The men gather up their staves. "I'll see you before night," Heese says to me.

Time I finish churnin' the fire's burnt low an' no dry wood—I haf' to put Sam in his box an' go out to the woodpile. Whole blessèd world still buried in fog, only now an' then the air gets kind of pink-like, like it's tuk on the color of leaves we've not seen all week, then dims dark as November. I hi'st two wet sticks up under my good arm. I'll be glad when Sam gets big enough to do chores. I need me a boy like Grantum Buckhannon, the one come to stay with me when Heese was the one got shot an' hid out on Grandfather. Serena needs Grantum, though. An' Heese wouldn' have no rebel around now anyway.

I stop at the door, lissen for a sound—hick'ry nuts fallin', a squirrel chompin', anything to break the quiet but there's just the drip, from trees you can't see. Except for meetin' some interestin' people, this day's not brought me a thing. Ust to be you done somep'n an' you had somep'n. You done somep'n an' it turned out right.

The sweetish smell is still in the house. I stop at the table an' read their names Richardson wrote down. I never was so drawed to anybody on such short acquaintance as him—seem like he's the kind o' feller you'd like to go right on to a hoe-down with. I wonder if he's got a wife an' childern—why didn' I think to ask him! I pick up my hair switch off the floor an' hold it up to my nose. *Ker-choo!!* I guess it's dusty. I give it a shake an' hang it back on the nail.

Heese gets back before dark like he said, an' I've worked up a bad case o' cabin fever, 'specially when he th'ows down two squirrels. Time was, we'd a-been out shootin' together.

"How could you see to hunt in fog?"

"Fog run out at Linville Gap." He gets a knife an' starts cleanin' the game.

"Do you b'lieve those men was what they said they was?"

"Well, what did they say they was?"
"*New*spaper cor'spondents is what they said!"
"A-ah, law! You better ask will they git to Greenville. Or Knoxville—just ask that to start with."
"Do you b'lieve we'll get the pitchur?"
"If we don't, it ain't my fault. Linville River was up. I had to tote Davis across on my back an' the cam'ra, too."

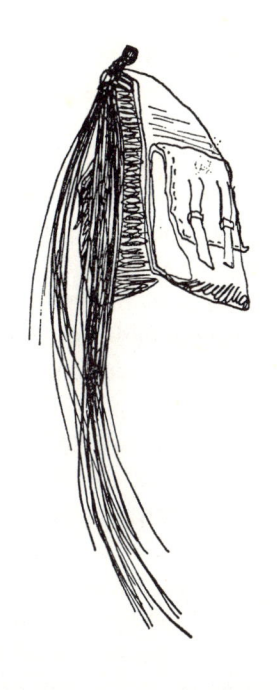

Sam is slurpin' mush on the kiver. "Scrape that off. I aim to give that kiver to Ma."
"Heese," I say, "if you was in the real Army, you wouldn' be the only man feedin' an' guidin' the whole dam' Union side. I'd hate to see you go, God knows I would, an' me an' Sam prob'ly couldn' go with you this time. But there's worse ways than miles to git divided. You wouldn' haf' to think no more. You'd even

get paid for not thinkin'. Your duty wouldn' be no wider'n the space between you an' the next man's shoulder 'stead o' the whole dam' mountains an' on over into East Tennessee."

He opens the trap door an' throws the entra'ls down. Some o' that sweet spoilt smell comes up.

"Grantum Buckhannon said—"

He fills the pan from the water bar'l, sets it on the wall shelf an' washes his hands. Behind him I can see the trunks o' trees now, the fog is beginnin' to lift in long trailin' curtains.

"Grantum Buckhannon says what?"

Sam sees the door open, starts wrigglin' off the bed an' I haf' to catch him. "Ne'm mind."

Heese drops one o' the squirrels in his jacket, gets his gun an' starts out again but stops by the bed to free the kiver from Sam, the one we brought from Globe an' tosses it over his arm. "I'm goin' to see Pa an' Ma a little while."

It's exasperatin' he can't stay home for one hour! We been needin' a good scrap. Maybe tonight is the night we get it. "Mayhap you'll be back to eat this other squirrel? An' feed the cow? An' get in some wood?"

He sets the gun down a minute an' rubs his face on mine, rough an' not been shaved for two days, an' his big ole hands all over me an' Sam too. Sam yips like a happy pup on the aidge o' fear! The sun's come through on a yeller hick'ry tree. I fix my mind on that to keep down the old lickerish tickerish feelin's Heese knows he can raise in me at will, but then I can raise some too.

"Hadn' you better bring us back a new richwal?"

"Don't no richwal work lessen it means the same thing to both sides."

JAMES LEWIS

NATH' Gibbs hadn't been gone an hour 'til I wish I had the note back. And I knew that before I gave it to him, saying to myself out loud so I'd hear it like somebody was warnin' me,

"If you send that note to Margaret McKamie, you'll be sorry. She is your enemy—hear? Her step-brother and his gang lamed your brother Pendleton. Remember that? That he's not dead today is no credit of theirs. And now you're asking to borrow his horse, Taima, that means almost more to him than his power to walk, and ask this girl you have not seen for two years and a half—no, two years, 6 months and 8 days—to meet you on Beacon Heights!" I try to see her then, a whole company of Margarets, all my enemies, coming at me through the mist at Sharpsburg, or in McPhareson's woods at Gettysburg but I can't because that is not where you would want any woman to be even in your imagination and besides, there is only one of her in the world or I would have run across another in Virginia or even Pennsylvania instead of always seeing that one face against tent walls, barns, cornfields or whatever godforsaken place I've slept—and all I notice is how straight she walks and that she is not an enemy that I would care to meet, so what am I doing trying?

MARGARET McKAMIE

MA READS from the Bible. " 'And he came down with them and stood in the plain, and a great multitude of people came to hear him—' "

The corner of his letter sticks into my breast when I breathe in, so I keep breathing—*in*, out! just to feel it. Jake looks at me funny.

I know the letter by heart,

Dear Margaret—

I have spent many thoughtful hours before I've written this note. In a week or so I will be going back to join my Regt in Virginia. It would afford me great pleasure to be in your company for a few hours before I go. If tomorrow Thursday is a pretty day will you meet me on Beacon Heights? I will be waiting there at noon. I know how much has happened to divide us but I believe that I would understand it better if I could talk with you for as times are now I don't expect we will have the opportunity of seeing one another for quite a long time. I know I am asking you to come thrugh danger on acct of all the prowlers in the woods but I know you are brave and smart and I am sure you will know a safe way to get there and I will be waiting and praying for your safety and for you to come, so I will see you like a red bird on the cliff. I have a heap to tell you more than pen and ink can describe it. Nath Gibbs says he will give this right to your hand. So do not tell anybody else but please come Margaret.

Your friend
Jim Lewis.

What will they say if I change my clo'es and it not the end of the week? How will I get away!

The sun set clear. It will be pretty weather, all right. Today when I would look up through the smoke of boilin' molasses, the maples were red like blood spilled in the gold, and the sky so blue—! We finished the sorghum, there is no more cane. Now Ma and Pa will give it all away.

" 'If thine enemy hunger feed him—' "

If that's true, why do they keep readin' it all the time?

Is Jim my enemy? He says "how much divides us." I guess he means Heese raided their place. Samantha was in it too. James's younger brother got shot. So did Samantha. Our fam'ly started it. His never would—if I haf' to call Heese an' Samantha fam'ly, an' I guess I do.

Well, I want what the valley people have. But not anything

you'd steal if you was the stealin' kind, more how to talk, and learnin', and to be yourself without havin' to prove it, unless in a war.

I need to get off an' think, up in the loft an' think. Maybe in houses like they live in down in Globe everybody don't know what everybody else is doin' the way they do here, everybody doin' the same thing at the same time or else somebody's head pokin' up in the loft, Jake or Thomas or Bennie, to see why I don't come on down an' do it.

I breathe hard to make the letter prick my breasts again.

Nath' Gibbs called me out today, making excuse to get me down to the gate, away from the rest, away from my brothers. We used to watch for Nath' there, swinging and singing my songs. He would stand me against the gate post, measure how much I'd grown before he'd give me the candy or whatever else he'd bring, some nuts or a paper doll, till no more post was left above my head to measure when I lifted my chest and chin, and one day Heese saw Nath' staring at me so I never did it again.

Ma will have a fit when she finds I'm gone. She will send the boys after me, hollerin' theirselves hoarse—like as not they'll find us—but two sides can play that hide-an'-go-seek.

What is it James can't tell me that pen and ink can't describe? He's remembered a long time. Well, so have I!

I sashay my toes on the floor, my foot strikes Jake's bare toes under the table. "Wow!" he hollers just to raise a disturbance. Ma peers past the grease lamp, then reads on,

" 'Give, and it shall be given unto you; good measure, pressed down and shaken together, and running over, shall men give into your bosom . . . ' "

The hair on Jake's face is pale in the lamp like fuzz on a mullein leaf. He's growing into a man and pesters me nearly as much as Heese.

I draw my hair over my nose—it smells like molasses and wood smoke. How will I get it clean and be at the cliffs by noon!

What does he look like now? He was just a boy when we

walked from the Globe to the Bluffs, first of the war. Nath' said Jim was shot in the battle of Gettysburg and lay on the field all day. I remember him low and fair—not swarthy like Neil McCurry. At thought of Neil I wipe the hair from my lips as I'd wipe Neil off my lips and out of my mind and— an' unwanted man pressing into me against my will!

Bennie is almost asleep. Pa sits with his shoulders in—he is tired. Ma is always preachin' "Ask yourself how it is goin' to seem afterwards—maybe long afterwards—whatever it is you're going to do and are not sure about." But what has she ever give me a *chance* to do that I could see beforehand how I was goin' to feel about it later! Nothin' worse than fightin' my brothers or sassin' kin or holdin' back pennies at church. I want to learn for myself! Everything!

" 'For he is kind to the unthankful, and to the evil,' " Ma closes the Book.

Which am I? Unthankful? Evil? I need to get to bed, draw the covers over my head, lay on his letter, think! plan out my day!

What will he say? What is the very first thing he will say?

JAMES LEWIS

I AM standing with my back to the gorge and Margaret's glance keeps kind of sliding off my uniform—the new one my mother made for me to go away.

One thing I'm sure of right off—she is no enemy of mine. I'm not sure what else she is, only she is not my enemy and she is here. There's only one thing I'm disappointed in,

"You didn't wear your red cape."

"It was long ago knit up into socks."

She is pretty in the black one, though—brownish black, the color of her eyes. Now we're together I have to brace myself like a fool to keep from trembling. Maybe it's the height or maybe I'm not as strong as I thought which is what I told Pendleton I wanted to try when I borrowed Taima to come up here today so at least there is that much truth in it!

Things I saved up to tell her have gone like the mist went in such a hurry this morning—we're just standing here under the openest noontime sky you ever saw and all I can think of is something like "I see Nath' gave you the letter—" when how would she be here if he hadn't.

"It sure is a beautiful day," she says on a kind of sigh.

I step over beside her and we stand together looking out over the gorge. "We couldna had a better!" The fall color is so bright—reds an' purples an' golds—seems like it's got loose from its roots and is floating right up to us. I rest my gun stock on the cliff to steady me. She's no higher than my shoulder.

"You've growed," she glances up sideways. I can look down on her the least bit and what I see is good. Everything about her is the right size—little bitty nose, little bitty chin. She looks down at my leg as if she expects to find it wood or something.

"I'm sorry you got hurt."

"I'm all right now." If I'd known—but then, how could she have known—not while I was lying on the field, anyway. "How did you know?"

"Nath' Gibbs told me. Besides—" she kind of shrugs her shoulders, "up here everybody knows everybody else's business, sooner or later."

"That's not just up here."

She glances down at the rock then, left and right, and sits down spreading her skirts, causing the cliff that is shut in with huckleberry bushes and laurel to become like a playhouse and I haven't asked her in it.

"I'm sorry! I reckon you're tired!"

She shakes her head, the dark hood falls back, curls roll out on her shoulders.

"I don't much get tired."

Well I don't either usually but sitting down by her is sure easier than standing up. It's all come about so much easier than I expected, in a way it makes me feel guiltier than ever t'ords my folks. On the other hand, it does seem as if the Lord was actually approvin' of it.

"I thank you for comin'. I'm glad you came safe."

It is one of those days of cloud shadows dipping up and down over the Globe. On the southeast horizon lies a faint cloud bank. Taima grazes among the red galax, splutters her nose in dry fern. Margaret turns to look and one curl rolls down across her cape. The black hair has rainbows in it.

"That's a pretty horse."

"She's my brother's—Pendleton's."

She looks me straight in the eyes. "I'm sorry about that."

"He's doing all right. I guess."

"Pa tried to stop 'em." Her chin sets in a way I remember. "I'll have you know my folks want no part of raiding."

"I know it. If I'd thought different, I wouldn't of asked you to come."

"Was he bad hurt?"

"Pendleton? Yes." There don't seem to be any call for us to be saying anything but the truth to each other. "At best, he will always walk sidling."

She faces back to the valley. "All for some mules an' sides o' bacon, an'—" she stops short.

"Is food scarce up here?" It is anywhere, though.

"It's never been much—only what we could make. Pa feeds as many widows' fam'lies now as Yankees and outlyers." She unfastens a button at her throat and lets the cape slide back on the rock. She is wearing a white waist made of some kind of thin stuff with big sleeves that leave off at the elbows. "To Pa, hunger don't wear no special clo'es."

"Heath an' Samantha just naturally likes a fracas," she goes on. "They'd both be better off if they was about twelve inches shorter!" I look at her, all five feet of her and all vexed. "Just his bigness makes men foller him—and Samantha backs him right up."

For a minute it's like I'm back at Kinston, it's reveille and Mason is holding off from blowing his horn until Sam can get over the sand hill swinging her bucket that is her excuse to get to the sink only she knows where it is.

"I got to know Sam—Mrs. Garvy—right well when we were at Camp Ransom. How is she?"

"She's not been over. She got shot too. In the arm. She don't come around us much when she's been up to somep'n she knows Ma wont approve of. I guess we'll see her, though, now Heese has left."

"Where has he gone?"

"To Tennessee. Walked. To join the 13th Tennessee Volunteer Cavalry. A whole company for it was made up in Mitchell, now the Unions have come back into East Tennessee."

"Well, that's what they always wanted . . ." I can see them, creeping along in the night, staying away from Thomas's men.

"Is Samantha going to join too this time?"

"Right now she's hilt back on account of her arm. No doubt she will, though—they've got one sayin' between 'em, him and her—'*Always together!*' Where one goes the other goes!"

"Isn't that the way it should be—man an' wife?"

The side of her face next to me flushes pink. She hugs her knees, the thin sleeves fall back from her elbows, and she rocks a little looking out over the gorge. An orange butterfly is hopping up and down over some purple thistle blooms that stick up above the edge of the cliff.

"They'll prob'ly leave Sam with us—that's the baby. He's a fine one, Sam is—fair like Heese an' smart like Samantha."

"I've been pretty sure what your step-brother's been doing doesn't make you like him any more—"

She shakes her head. "We've never got along. Oh, I guess *I* could—but Heath—I don't know what's the matter with him. I think for one thing he'll never get over it I'm more kin to Pa than he is. He *wor*ships Pa!"

Sun beating down overhead and heat coming up from the rock make me feel as if I'm going to melt like a candle in this uniform and run right on off the rock. It is easier to stretch out on my left side, prop my head from my elbow, and look at her. If it wasn't you'd not want to compare a girl to a horse, I'd say you get the same pleasure out of looking at Margaret you do from looking at Taima. I mean for one time the Lord Almighty didn't go wrong a quarter inch—though I guess He didn't in other things like a trout or deer, or even that fool butterfly hopping about those thistles as if there is not a thing under him but five hundred feet of air.

"Why do your folks stay so strong for the Union?"

"Not because it's easy, sure. Pa's brothers are for the Confederacy—two of my cousins—one, Wash, is fighting in Virginia. Joel got killed at Fredericksburg. Most folks up here don't own slaves—Pa's never believed in anybody bein' one, or dependent any way. I guess it goes back to the Revolution. Pa's grandfather fought in it—"

"So did mine."

"I don't know—" she waves her hands. "I just want it all to get over with an' people stop fightin' each other!"

"I do, too. I think, though, after a while something like war itself takes over and we all get caught up in it."

"Why do you go back, then?"

"Just me stayin' away wouldn't end it. Besides, you get the feeling you owe it to those that's died. Like Burgwyn. Or those three sets of twin brothers from our Company killed at Gettysburg—"

"I knew the Woodall twins—"

"Or old McGillicuddy—"

"Mrs. McGillicuddy is one Pa helps—"

But over and under whatever we're saying is knowing this is real, not mixed up with any march, just a face between you and a muster roll. "Fix it in your mind," something says deep down in me, "you're going to have to remember this a long time."

"Margaret, what do you want after the war?"

A sweat bee is pestering us and she slaps at it. "I want to go to school. I'd like to know how music's wrote, and played. I don't want to be like Ma, lookin' back some day, wishin' I'd had more schoolin', or waited to—to get married."

"I guess I'd know your mother if I saw her. It's been more than two years—"

"She's dark—'bout medium height—looks taller though because she walks so straight. Dark hair down in kind of wings over her ears. But she can look a hole through you."

"So can mine!"

"You said you look like *her*."

"When?"

"That Easter day we walked up the mountain. You said she was short and fair, and dumpy. But you are not so dumpy any more!" The sweat bee is back. "I reckon there is a time for everybody when your learnin' starts. For Ma it was the day that Mr. Gray come through the mountains lookin' for plants and stayed at our house. I was just a little girl then but I remember them as furriners. You know—a woman in the mountains don't get much chance to know whether she has much sense or not. It's all you can do just to keep up with men an' dogs. Unless you happen to be somebody like Samantha that just joins 'em. I guess there has to be somethin' in you, though, for the learnin' to take hold of. Ma already knew where plants growed, kinds he asked about, so she took him, and showed him others. He taught her names. She's got it all written down in a book."

She lifts her hands, pops the sweat bee. It falls on the rock. An old hemlock tree in back of us makes wig-wag shadows on the rock. She fishes in her skirt for a handkerchief, rubs her palms with it and little clear beads of sweat from under her nose.

"Want to move further back in the shade?"

We scramble up—me kind of shaky-like. I reach for her hand—it feels the way I remember. She don't draw it away. We stand letting the waves of color roll over us, and dark blue cloud shadows drifting toward the cloud bank in the east.

"Margaret, you would never guess how many weary miles there is between us and that bank of clouds." She squints her eyes. "It's prob'ly risin' over the ocean—right about Fort Macon."

"I know about Fort Macon."

Already I've forgot what I told myself to remember—that a

girl as nice and pretty as Margaret would have lots of fellows coming to court her.

"How?"

"Somebody who was there told me—"

"Best quarters we ever had, that old Fort. Nighttimes we'd build fires in the casemates, sit around spinning yarns—Well, I guess the Yankees have it now."

Taima walks up behind us, snuffs at the tail of my jacket. We turn, her soft nose moves up our arms.

"I b'lieve she's thirsty."

"A long cool drink of water is the best thing I can think of. Is there a spring around here? My mouth is as dry as this rock."

"There's Nameless," she nods her head to the left. "Just a little old branch."

"Let's go find it."

I draw my gun out from between Taima's hoofs. Stepping into those woods is like going into a church—quiet, the sky shut out and a pale yellow light over everything.

She tells me about her family—about Bennie, the little one she's same as raised. About the 'strangement between her father and his brothers. About her Aunt Harriett, not mean exactly but loving land and goods almost more than her own children yet lonesome too. About how hard it is for families to be divided, the days going on under each roof same as before but now not shared when there's so little to share up here at best. It's as if she's tellin' it all to herself at the same time.

She's a good listener, too, even when I tell about fellows I've known, like Wesley Cannon's white mule Simon that never got tired, could live on nothing and had more sense than a General—then, mule-like took a stubborn spell right when surrounded an' Wesley throwin' his arms around his neck to yell "Simon, for God's sake go *some*where!" Only I don't say 'God sake' to her. About Sion Hicks seeing the blue line rise before him at Gettysburg and flee, dropping his gun butt to the ground and leaning on it with his long neck stuck out, *"To-look-at-'em!"* But they took Sion at the stone wall.

About how pretty Pennsylvania was when we went in—such plenty, and the good Dutch bread and the people very kind, but more from fear. They never knew anything about war till we invaded them.

About battery drills, "A full six gun battery going across a plain at a trot is something to see, Margaret—seventy two horses suddenly halt at the bugle—then limbered up, horses and men seem to fly in all directions. The horses get so they know the calls and can carry them out almost without drivers."

"We had an old cavalry horse was left up near White Springs. He wandered off, though, lookin' for his kind—or stole by those that's makin' up to go to Tennessee. Big as Thomas is, he cried!"

At a sudden sound in the woods we both stop short—I slip her the bridle and raise my gun. But all is quiet again.

"A deer maybe, or a wild hog—" I lower the gun between us and she runs her fingers along the barrel. Her fingers are strong and square at the ends. "Tom would like that gun."

"You know what the barrel is made of?"

"What?"

"Church bells. From Savannah. My cousin in Georgia sent it to me. I lost mine at Gettysburg."

"Better they'd stayed so—the bells."

"An' me go to Virginia without a gun?"

We are standing under a giant beech tree—the prettiest tree of any I think—can't make up its mind whether to be gold, green or brown so holds to what it can 'til spring. I pat the smooth trunk. "We'd ought to carve our names."

She glances up through the leaves, into the sky, "*What time is it?*"

I haven't even thought about time. "*How long can you stay?*" Even to ask it makes the end seem closer.

"Not much longer. Ma will have a fit. She'll be sending Tom and Jake to hunt me—"

"Oh, Margaret—*if time would only stop!*"

She turns, a smile on her pink smooth lips, "Do like Uncle Reuben does! There's a rock east of his place—a big rock like a pulpit—where he practices his sermons and says mornin' prayers. He yells at the sun "Stop! *Stop!!*" It keeps comin' right on up. He says he does it to feel the power o' God!"

Well, I don't much feel the power of anything now but her. One thing strikes me about her, she is serious yet gay, sees the funny side of things without your having to spell it out for her the way I would Pinckney or my sisters.

We have been going down among the rhododendrons, dog hobble and cliffs to the branch where there is a good sized pool held back by two big moss covered stones before it riffles away down the mountain. Taima drinks long and sweet, one hoof raised dainty the way she does because her neck is short. We wait for her to finish, then I throw the bridle over a stob.

"Come on—let's drink!"

We lie full length on two touching rocks—our faces rise to meet us in the pool, then break up when my stone teeters. We suck, turn to each other laughing as water runs down our noses and chins. Her wet lips are close.

"Margaret! Margaret!"

Then soft on soft—cool, new but known a long time, I kiss her. It's as if my muscles melt and run on with the stream. Then the moss gives away under my hand and down goes my arm into the pool, ripping my flesh on the rocks. A fine rope of blood swirls away into the riffle.

She opens her eyes—"*Oh—!*"

She pushes herself up, braces her boot in the rocks, fishes for a handkerchief, finds it and knots it 'round my arm.

"It's nothing—" The stream sucks in the hem of her skirt. With a broken stick she twists the handkerchief in a little cloth rope.

Then with her broad-tipped forefinger and thumb she draws back the cut. "It's not deep."

"Here—let me—"

"Are you bad to bleed?"

« 180 »

"No—look! Your skirt is getting soused!"

I take the tourniquet from her.

"Best not to touch the cut—leave it open to the air."

She hauls her heavy skirt hem out of the branch, it's soppy as a sponge, and tries to squeeze it dry.

"Margaret—" I reach my free hand out and take hers, "Tell me—have you been kissed before?"

She raises the back of her wrist to her mouth as if she might ward off another kiss—

"Yes? Or No?" She just keeps her wrist there.

"Yes—and No."

"What does that mean?"

"You mean kiss back?"

I stop to think. "I'd kill the fellow got it just one way. Or two ways, come to think of that."

"James—" she starts like she would get up.

The dad-blamed arm! I push the stick down in the circle of cloth to hold it and we both scramble up but I don't let go her hand.

"Margaret! Is there another fellow?"

She lowers her wrist from in front of her mouth. "How about *you*?"

"*No*. Nobody!"

We have both stepped away from Nameless, back on solid ground.

"I'm not talking about any gram'paw's kiss," I say.

"I have not kissed anybody back." Way down in those dark-molasses eyes is a glint the way a grain of mica in a stream will catch the sun. "I have not kissed anybody back a not-gram'paw's kiss!"

"Are you teasing me or telling me the truth?"

"I am not teasing. I am telling you the truth."

I reach out for her hand and draw her to me. She is light and slim, part of my very self I've always known, always been coming back to, know now I will have to start from wherever I go but always to come back. I groan and hear the blood churn in my ear against her hair—and hair soft against my cut arm on her back.

"I've seen your face against a hundred barn doors, tent flaps, ledger sheets—"

"I know—"

"You know? Me!" Me always shortest in the line, moon faced, always taken for younger than I am!

She puts up her hand. "I like your face. I've seen it in lots of odd places, too."

We're both close to crying. I draw her in and kiss her—the earth goes turning around but I just let it go on any way it wants to go. Finally she pushes away breathless "Jim! I must go! For one thing, I don't want them askin' me about it. Or worse still, comin' on us. I don't even want any more to remember right now—"

"You're easier satisfied than I am," but I let her go, and then I groan for across the back of her shirtwaist is a line of red blood broken where her hair kept it off!

"Margaret! I've bled all over the back of your shirtwaist!"

She skews her chin around and tries to see.

"Margaret—you're goin' to have a time explaining *that*!"

"Oh it's all right—" she says, "my cape will cover it—let's see your arm—"

Then like some duet we say "*Where is the cape?*"

"Back at the cliff!"

"Gee! I'd thought I could go home from *here*!"

"We'll have to go back now. Good!"

I pick up my gun, un-sling Taima's bridle. "Did you ever know one little branch to do so much devilment in two minutes?"

"We ought to find it another name."

"Bloody Breathless!"

We don't talk much on the way back but it doesn't seem to matter. We're walking in a new world. When we do talk, it's more to plan how she will answer when I write. I tell her how a regiment moves and gets its mail.

"What will I think about you doing while I'm gone?"

"Oh—the same old things, what any woman does, I guess up here. What do your sisters do?"

"Work. Now. We all do." Her face is raised, framed against the trees. I kiss her then the way I'd kiss one of my sisters.

"I love you, Margaret."

"I love you."

"You said there is a time everybody's learning starts from. I'm older than when I came up here today. Are you?"

"Yes—"

"For one thing I didn't know there were so many ways you could kiss a girl and all of 'em different yet all meaning the same thing."

The air is deepening and I feel her shiver in the thin waist. But when we come out on the Heights warm air meets us, dry and smoky as some old sun-warmed chimney.

"Well there it is. Nobody stole your cape!"

I put it around her and we stand looking out over folds and folds of rich colored foothills mottled purple. My arm's still around her.

"Margaret, there is one nice time in the Army. It is when we're going to bivouac at night. Word goes down the line, every man grabs a rail from the nearest fence, throws it over his shoulder and steps into the camping ground. In no time at all little camp fires shoot up in the meadows and on the hills, acres and acres shining with them."

"Things you tell me about the war don't make me any satisfieder with the McKamie Gap."

I draw her to me, fold her into the brown cape like a creature wrapped for winter.

She speaks muffled. "I don't blame Samantha for goin'. It's like Jackaroe—she's a girl in a song."

I look down in her eyes where there is no glint now. The thought of that camping Army's next day business comes over me like a cloud. "No." I say, "No."

She swings out at my side "Whichaway will you be goin' when you go?"

Mountain speech suits her the way green spines suit a chestnut or bitter crust on walnuts in the fall.

I face her to the northeast. "Thataway! Over there's the Yadkin, then the Dan, the Staunton and the James. Finally the Rapidan. And a hundred bogs and branches in between."

"Like Nameless?"

"Worse than Nameless!"

Her arm is about my waist, "You might get shot!"

"Maybe the bullet is being molded that will hit me but I think if it had been it would of before this time and one more thing is this war is not going to last forever—"

SAMANTHA

Hog-killin' weather set in ten days after Heese started walkin' to Tennessee to join the Army. Me an' Sam and the wildcats that try to push their noses under the eaves at night is each lonesome in his own way, but nairy one of us has enough in common to do the other much good. Finely I says to myself, If you got empty days to fill up, get somep'n big to fill 'em up with. So I hitch the ox to the sledge, set Sam on it an' him an' me take to the woods and hunt down one of our old wild sows, shoot her, haul her home an' slaughter her.

If you want your man to come home, just start doin' somethin' it ain't convenient to have him come into and he'll show up inside a hour. That hog was spread all over the place when Heese come in. I seen right off his trip hadn' done him no good—he don't so much as say Howdy, just moves the crocks off the bed onto the floor, pulls off his shoes, crawls in bed an' sleeps till this evenin'.

While I'm puttin' some o' the meat away in the spring house, I make a little discovery. There's half a demi-john of good whiskey settin' on the shelf, the likes of which we have not seen since Vance decided everybody needs bread worse than liquor and wont let whiskey be made even out of sweet potatoes, not even for the Confedrit gover'ment. After I try a little in a gourd with some spring water, I decide I'll bring the jug on in the house and from there on out my work goes a lot smoother. By the time of evenin' Heese stumbles barefoot out of bed, I got the whole place cleaned up, Sam washed an' chewin' a rib while I'm ready to set down an' listen to Heese tell about his trip just any way he wants to tell it.

He takes one look at me, limps over to the water bucket, walkin' on the outsides of his feet like he da'ssent put any weight on the soles. He holds up the jug, lets late evenin' sun slant through the west shutter on the liquor that's clear as new cider.

"Samantha, you been drinkin'."

"I figured you'd not want a good glass jug like that left on the spring house shelf where a boomer might come along an' knock it over. Or was you savin' it for a little surprise?"

He sets the demi-john down, swallows a coupla gourds of water and starts outdoors, remembers his shoes, sets back down on the bed stiff, looks down at them wore off-sides, picks one up, peers at me through the hole in the bottom, then the other—same way.

"Samantha, I been all over this world."

I hold out some dry socks. "Here—I darned these while you was gone—they'll hold you to go outside while I dish up your supper."

He comes back with a armload of wood, dumps it in a corner, punches up the fire, goes to the shelf and takes a nip.

"Can he walk yet?" He points to Sam.

"Mighty near."

"I'd hate him ever to haf' to walk where I been." He seats hisself down and makes a big burp. "I'll tell you how it goes. First there's the Doe an' the Watauga. A Humphrey boy keeps a boat there to take Union men across. An' if the Holston ain't too swollen, you can ferry across it at Old Pactolus—Elihu Embree's boarding house. That's the last you'll see of any boats. But not the last of mountains. It's just the start of mountains. First there's the Bays and Clinch, with Clinch River besides. Copper's Ridge and Copper's Creek ain't so bad, they just limber you up for Powell's Mountain. Then there's Wallen's Ridge, Wildcat Mountain and Powell's river before you get to Cumberland Gap."

The room is warm, the fire is bright, we got meat to eat, whiskey to drink, somep'n to talk about an' Sam beatin' his bone on the floor. We're all back together ag'in. "Come on, Sam—patty cake for Daddy!"

While I'm clearin', Heese rassles some with Sam. "Seems like he'd ought to be walkin'."

"He does when ain't nobody lookin' at him." After a while Heese sets Sam down, throws his little bloodstone for him to play with, an' we both set down by the fire with mugs.

"Samantha, I ain't a-goin' in the Army after all."

I sip an' look at the fire. I didn' know how much I been countin' on us gettin' outa here where there's more goin' on. All time he's been gone I been same as packin' up the stuff in my mind.

"You wouldn' like it either," he says, readin' my mind like usual. "All hell's broke loose in East Tennessee. Burnside an' Longstreet together has stripped the country—there ain't a thing in three miles of any road but dead mules. Farm's neglected, horses stole, it don't make no difference how this war comes out—in East Tennessee *every*body's lost."

Sam tries to climb up Heese's leg. He lifts him up on his lap. They are two of a kind if I ever saw 'em.

"Samantha—I seen somethin' else."

"Do tell."

"I seen Dan Ellis. He come in at Camp Nelson with a bunch of recruits while I was there. They say he's piloted two thousand men through the mountains in the year he's been a guide, not to mention all the mail an' messages he's carried. When I laid eyes on him I said to myself 'There's a man I can foller.' And that's what I aim to do, Samantha. You know I never did like sol'jerin'. An' the camp officers said I could do 'em more good bringin' in fellers to fill up this new 13th Tennessee Volunteer Cavalry than I can do standin' guard duty an' drillin' an' all such piddlin' stuff as that. Some o' the Aldridges an' Testers that went from Watauga with the 13th had done told 'em about me a-guidin' men across the Grandfather. So when Ellis was ready to come back, he asked me to come along with him so I come."

"What kinda feller is Dan Ellis?"

"He's 'bout thirty five—older'n us, anyway—six feet, dark, keen eyes, wears a huntin' shirt loose so he can get to his two pistols fast. Every man, woman an' child of every loyal family in East Tennessee knows him. They'll hide him, feed him, work for him, fight for him—an' when you know him, you don't wonder. The words 'Dan Ellis says so' is good as gold from here to Kentucky. There's just one thing he's got no use for an' that's a rebel. He don't see they've got no right to live atall. Of course they've got a price on his head too. Some of Dan's friends have tried to get him to move to a safer place but he wont budge. 'I worked and paid for this patch in Carter County Tennessee,' he told me, 'an' I aim to stay here 'til the Confederacy is moved down an' toted out to sea an' sunk where there ain't no bottom. What's the use o' me movin'?' he said. 'I've only got to stay here a little while longer and there wont be any Confedricy to move out of.' An' that's so, Samantha. A lot of rebels are goin' over to the other side now the Union men they run off last year are comin' back home.

"I'd git paid somethin', you understand. Ellis is makin' a right good thing of it—people always wantin' to pay him for carryin' stuff for 'em, letters, boxes, an' the Union Army pays him some, otherwise he'd *haf* to go in the Army. He's got a bunch o' childern."

"I reckon you didn' get no pay for this trip?"

"No—but just gittin' to know Dan Ellis was pay enough for me. I learnt a lot. Why?" he says innocent, "Was you needin' somethin'?"

"Oh, *no*!" I says. "Only salt. Dressin' this sow has took nearly all we had. Clo'es for Sam. New pants for you an' me. Looks like you might be needin' some leather, too."

"We'll get those things if I hafta make another trip down in Globe."

"Not me." I rub my arm. He can tell I ain't overjoyed at the thought o' bein' left up here while he goes gallivantin' off all across Tennessee an' Kentucky. He dribbles some more whiskey in our mugs. Sam has fell back asleep.

"You reckon you better save a little o' that likker ag'in I might get lonesome up here with just Sam an' the wildcats?"

"I can get you more. It come from Howards' on Little Doe River. I stayed with them last night—or whenever it was. You remember Tallison Howard? The feller come through here about a year ago, same day Uncle Reuben was here pesterin' us?"

"Yes."

"Well—rebels murdered Howard's brother David last winter. David an' Tallison run in opposite directions. David got shot, but Tallison sunk hisself in the creek, he stayed under a hour, just come up now an' then for air. He didn' even feel the cold, he said."

Heese keeps talkin' the way he does when he knows I ain't believin' half of it nor agreein' with any of it.

"Samantha, you know who's over in East Tennessee now? Them same dam' two old Generals was fightin' each other when we was at Kinston. Ransom and Foster."

"You mean our old Comp'ny is over there? Bugles an' the rest of 'em?"

"I don't know about them, but it's the same Foster was pushin' us in the sand hills. Now he's fightin' in cornfields around Jonesboro."

"What do you mean, pushin' *us*?"

"I give it to you as it was give to me. Dan said a General Ransom is guardin' the Salt Works an' Foster is after him. Them two old bastards had done fit plum around the world an' got back to East Tennessee."

EMILY LEWIS

AT NOON these brief December days there is a pause in all the work and I can bring my darning and sit with Pendleton at the front window. I draw up a rocker, sit and search my bulging mending basket for the precious needles.

"Has there been any passing?"

Pendleton is sucking a persimmon from the pile the children brought. The seed will be used for buttons or if any left over, for chess or checker men. He spits out a clean seed, lays it with the others on the stool. Of all things now, we ask "Shall we eat it, wear it, convert it, or hoard it against an even leaner day?" We may be eating persimmons green to shrink our stomachs. Flesh of these is orange, lavender misted, brown rosettes on the book Pendleton has been reading, "Great Expectations."

He holds a bent nail against the iron shoe-last between his good leg and his cast, raps it with the hammer and drops the straightened nail in a little egg basket on the stool. Our home is a factory now, every hand needed for four jobs at once, even I will not say it—the hands of a cripple.

He goes on crutches now, yesterday all the way to the gate to see James ride away on Taima. Theophilus came to go with him as far as Happy Valley. There were a dozen of us, all that are left now except field hands that come only when they feel like it. None of us shed a tear but Kiz, throwing her apron over her head, chanting and lamenting as usual.

I stood where I could see Pendleton's face to try to read what we will have to cope with now all he could make motion with is gone—his limb, his horse. But he told James to take the horse. And

I saw only his pride in Taima's slender legs that hardly touched the road, so delicate and light beside old Gideon bearing Theophilus in his Mexican war uniform.

I pull out a skein of yarn now—it catches my fingers, they are rough to soreness. We shun self-pity like the plague, the subterranean trickle that undermines even bravery, saying how hard it is, how lonely and how—useless? But our private griefs are in some measure merged into the public calamity so some of the keenness is taken off.

There is no motion anywhere outdoors, the ground iron-frozen, only softness the hoary old heads of clematis along the wall and near the gate a single patch of hardy dark red late chrysanthemums.

Pendleton takes another nail, wipes the rust off it with his tallow rag and like an old blacksmith lifts the hammer. Suddenly there is a man's shout from the gate and I catch his arm,

"Look! Isn't that the iron wagon from Forge Flats?" Something ponderous long and heaving is moving behind the fence. There is the clank of iron, cracks of whip, an ox's head tosses above the palings, then another until the team of six comes in view guarded by conscripts from the Camp at Morganton.

PENDLETON LEWIS

The front door slams as my mother goes out. I see her trot down the front walk, drawing her cloak around her.

A man comes through the gate, he is short and stocky, dressed in Confederate uniform—Whang Brown from up at Forge Flats. He and my mother meet halfway on the path, he sweeps off his cap, showing his slick black wavy hair plastered down. I bet there's many an officer in Marse Robert's Army not dressed as well as what Uncle Theophilus calls this bumpkin from the conscript camp—gambler and horse-trader, horse thief, maybe. He once tried to buy Taima from me. 'Twas after he came back from the war at Kinston. I wouldn't sell so he threatened Taima would be pressed. But Uncle Theophilus saw to it Colonel Avery pressed Whang instead into the Camp at Morganton.

While he talks with mother, a woman appears at the gate. She wears a dark cape and has a package in her arms. Brown seems to be telling my mother something about her as she comes on up the path. She is tall, her cape and skirt swing slow. Whang Brown steps aside, the woman stops, faces my mother, says a few words and lays the bundle in mother's arms. I know her. She is Mrs. Mary McKamie from McKamie Gap. I've seen her at camp meetings, a sort of doctor woman and mother of the Margaret that James is sweet on and can't forget and I believe he went to see her the week before he left. He claimed he wanted to try out his hip and give Taima some exercise. But he was gone all day and came back looking like the cat that has swallowed a bird.

Men are gathering at the gate. They wear dingy butternut uniforms. They are conscripts that guard the iron.

Mrs. McKamie stands tallest of the three, dark like her daughter, and her eyes seem to bore into my mother whose back is to me. But my mother's back can say a lot, too. Mrs. McKamie turns, then—starts back down the path. My mother must call to her then for she stops, turns as mother holds out a hand to her. For a minute the whole thing is a picture frozen in the window— two women, the stocky Whang and the soldiers at the gate. Then they break up. Mrs. McKamie stalks down the walk and out the gate, Whang Brown joins my mother holding the package. She asks him to come in I know, but he shakes his head, smoothing his hair with a stumpy hand before he pulls on his cap.

My mother turns and with the bundle in her arms walks slowly back to the house. A whip cracks at the road, men shout, the heavy loads of iron move along the fence again. Mrs. McKamie sits atop the first pile, jolting, but her back as straight as an arrow. She seems to ride along on top of the boxwood hedge.

The front door slams, again, my mother comes back in the room, pokes at the fire, takes her chair, sits down, the package in her lap.

I pop another persimmon in my mouth and wipe off another nail.

She folds the papers back—old copies of the Raleigh Standard, the Holden newspaper that is causing so much trouble now with peace talk. Wrapped in it is that old quilt that always stayed on our beds upstairs—gray and black and red—the one the 'whackers took eight weeks ago the night—

This nail is bent so bad no hammering will straighten it. I lay the sucked seed on the stool and find another nail.

"Where was Mrs. McKamie going, perched on Confederate iron?"

"To Lenoir with herbs, she said—alder for maggots in wounds. They have to let her ride, purveying drugs. She brought back your great grandmother's coverlid—"

Women set great store by things like that. I wish it had been my gun.

1864

SOPHIA SMEAD to EMILY LEWIS

"Fair Forks"
Roane county, Tennessee
March 10, 1864

O my dear Emily,

Surely you guessed your November letter telling of the disgraceful raid on Globe and Pendleton's injuries did not reach me! Our Provo Marshal took to drinking about Christmastime and much went astray including precious packages intended for our men at Dalton. Of *course* you would have heard from me—you and your dear ones are in my thoughts many times each week. In a way I'm glad I *didn't* hear, though, since I'm now reassured Pendleton is better and James able to return to the Army of Virginia. Thank God and General Lee that all seems quiet there for the time being.

I just finished baking and sat down to write Abner when Mother called to tell me there was a letter from you and I tell you I did not sit long there. Now my thoughts and prayers fly across the mountains where I still try to see the eternal in the hills despite the feet of strangers and vermin that infest them. What can I say that our Holy Scriptures have not already said! "These are they that came out of great tribulation!" At least, Emily, your boys are alive—not strewn along Chickamauga creek and Missionary Ridge, or by our Tennessee creeks like those of so many of our neighbors.

'Whackers have been around on their circuit here too, went out to old Mr. Pat Dismukes' a few weeks since and took him out and hung him three times to make him tell where his gold and silver were but he said he had none & they made him give them several thousand $$ in paper money. Even if they catch bushwackers now they turn them aloose again, will not let a rebel swear against them. I declare I don't know what it's all coming to. We hear there is a regular underground railroad through the mountains, Dan Ellis from Carter county is the head of it. Do you know of him?

We worry about Nat, 16 now and going to school at Luttrell's in Sweetwater, staying at Pattons, though I must say he is more interested in the wooden machines Wm. Patton makes then he is in Latin.

My dear Abner has been near Dalton since Chickamauga, they are building fortifications, are on half rations but Abner writes he does not mind that as much as the itch. As the train came up this past Thursday it was said cannons were heard firing at Dalton, but lines have been pushed back to Cleveland and everybody thinks there will be desperate fighting for the railroad junction there soon. I know you pray for the safety of our loved ones as we do for yours and for a return to peace, but I fear it will have to be on *their terms*—the Yankee military seem confident of holding Tennessee now—nobody knows where Longstreet is, certainly he is not helping Joe Johnston that we know of. Our lower meadow is literally covered with tents, Union troops that have been brought across the river to be ready to go to the junction at Cleveland. Soldiers say that is what they are here for, to open up the Chattanooga branch and guard it. They *can't* be here long— I can't see where they forage now. Tennessee is simply *eaten out*! We succeeded in geting 50 bu. corn last month from Lenoirs for $1.50 per bu. and made breads and rice pies and sold them to the pickets and got green back enough to pay for the grain and have a few $$ left. It would be right amusing to you to see Mother trading with them, they all have a little something they don't want to take with them, tea, a little sugar, coffee—they get plenty of rations now and have a much greater variety than the citizens do.

We hear a negro regiment is coming on the other side of the

river. They have issued an order to take all the negroes that belong to rebels & put them in regiments. There was a negro recruiting officer here the other day and later a white one stayed all night, he did not tell his business till morning, that he tried to get Dolph and Joshua to enlist. Dolph came and had a long talk with Father about his affairs. I wrote you his wife Rosezetta was among the first to go off but Dolph promised Abner he would stay, but Rosezetta keeps writing him she can get him a job cooking for some men in the telegraph office. She writes kindly to Mother but says some of the most impudent things you ever heard to the rest of us, says they are living a mile from Knoxville in the house of white rebels that refugeed to Atlanta rather than take the oath. All are going to school (it was Mother taught Rosezetta to read and write in the first place) has everything her heart could wish and doing much better than when she was here "waiting on rebs." She says she has only one mistress and that is herself and a great many other such things. Father talked to Dolph like he was one of his children and Dolph cried and I was sorry for him—the others going would not affect us like he would. For one thing, he knows everything we have and think and say and he could repeat it.

I think by warm weather all the negroes in the country will have left. I heard the other day that Esqr. Heiskell's had left. I think all Mr. Owens' are gone too—their Rilla died in the negro house in the hotel yard at Loudon, she was living with some of the men that stayed at the General's headquarters, now the rest want to come back but Mr. Owen is not going to let them. Klein's settled it in typical fashion—turned them over to the government and got three hundred dollars apiece for them.

Loudon is just crowded with trash, especially Saturdays, but I expect some of them are really suffering and I pity them from the bottom of my heart, but some are so trifling I can have but little sympth for them. They Camp on our land and out in the edge of the woods are full of them too. There are women in Town that are known not to have done a days work in four months. I had no idea there were half as many such people in the world. I know some of them are really objects of Charity but I do think instead of taking from honest citizens and giving to some of them where the men are able to work they had better give employment and insist that they work. There is poor encouragement for the farms to raise provisions for such people and cannot get them to do a day's work.

Well, you remember I told you about Lizzie Fiske setting her cap for Dr. Washburn—or *his* cap for he has been literally keeping her in hats and clothes. He can buy without taking the oath but everybody else in town has to take it, even ladies. Well in February Lizzie got word from the Relief in Kankakee that her husband missing almost 3 yrs is finally given up for dead. Just as she takes a long breath and gets ready to marry the Dr. he ups and marries his housekeeper, Lena Potter, a nice girl though rather pale and spinsterish. Jule Lenoir says Lizzie was *flabbergasted*! Some Yankee cousins of hers are here, a Major and Lieut. and the talk is they introduced Lizzie around—anyway the Upshot is that Lizzie, not to be outdone, marries a Yankee officer she'd known just two weeks! Well—I say Potters are nice people but plain and it does seem a fine man well-educated like Hugh Washburn might have picked one of his own station like dear Miss Maybell or Miss Constance Lillard who are in desperate straits since Reedie died. Last time I heard from Maybell their negroes had left and she was out sewing oats and about to work and fret herself to death. Well, there's no accounting for tastes!

As for me, I try to keep myself in obscurity and make my old duds do a while longer and not be known anywhere any more than possible. I get frightened when I hear of them talking of arresting ladies. All the Wilkerson women came near getting arrested. A funeral procession passed their house, a federal captain's but they did not know that, and Eva said to Blandina, suppose it was one of our brothers and Blandie commenced to cry and someone in the funeral procession, they do not know who, saw them and reported they were making sport of Yankees and there was an Investigation and they were warned they could be arrested without any ceremony and their home would be burned down. Eva and Blandie were frightened nearly to death!

Sally Vaughn Etheridge heard about this. She is a red hot rampant rebel as you know, and last Sunday at Service when Mr. Thornehill prayed for the President of the United States, Sal said clear & loud "the President of the Confederate States" and some Illinois troops heard her and one of them was going to report her but one of the others knew her and said they could not please her better than that.

Well, Emily, I have used up nearly half the portfolier of paper one of the soldiers gave little Laura and I will have to make it up to her maybe let her go with Mother to visit the Camp again. I declare it does beat all how little girls will be little girls and flirt and love a uniform even at the age of six! I hear that Beaver Reagan is to be our new postmaster so I will be almost afraid to send this on, and heaven alone knows when you will get it but long before it finishes its journey up through Georgia and South Carolina my love will have found a way across these mountains to each of you in the dear old Globe. Tell Theophilus I wish I could find some means to send him some Madiera a Union officer pressed on Mother for darning his uniform. She refused, being a teetoler, but Father accepted it for communion wine which Mother thought blasphemous. But I bet the presiding elder will get some of it on his next circuit around.

As ever your
Sophie

JAMES LEWIS

Co. F 26th NCV
Orange Court House Va.
2 April 1864

Dear Margaret, The last letter I receved from you is dated Feb 15 and I answered it the day I receved it and have been looking for an answer from you to it in deep suspence for I did not know if what I said was exceptable to you or not. But it does not really matter now since I can't come home after all. There was a while any man could put in for a furlow that would bring back an ablebodied recruit that is not a deserter but then came that forray to Madison Court House and I had my furlow and was feeling good for soldiers do feel good sometimes and I asked Captain Tuttle should I go on and take my furlow but he left it up to me so I thought it all over and I felt I could not go and leave the rest to march some of them barefoot and wind cold enough to shave a man so I sent Taima on home by Sion Hicks. Horses are scarcer than men here now and little to feed them on, there is not a tree among the camps has bark below where a horse can raise his mouth. I had hoped to come home and see you but now that Grant has been put over all the Union Armys and the streams are going down I think we will get a big fight soon and not just another snowball fight eather. We cannot give details in a letter but it looks like this part of our Army has the longest rest we will ever have & I do not think we can be quite much longer. The Co. are all in good health though a good many are barefoot and likely to remane so as a shipment of shoes just came in with leather turned faceside in and had to be sent back by order of General Lee who said that was contrary to nature. Sometimes I think all the mistakes in this Army pile up here in this QM tent but then I get to thinking about him having to fool with things like that to say nothing of meat stolen off trains and speculators and farmers wont plant because they know it will be pressed and then I start willing to do my part & more.

    Well Margaret it is 10 pm and I am coming to the end of this sheet It has been a pretty day here the Trees are beginning to leaf out and everything goes to show that spring with its beauties has come at last. Two things ther is plenty of in this Regt since we have had time to sit down and think, One is Marrying and the other is geting religion. But I will not write about eather of them now but I have been doing lots of thinking. The asurence of a sweetheart's confidence and affection have a great effect on a soldier's spirit an give him something to look forward to.

I would like to do what you say and make up a song to ease my disapointment about not getting to come home but in the first place I never could even spell much less write and second I don't know any song any body could write after packing 59 pr of wrong built shoes. So I think I will go to bed and hope to dream I am back with you on Graggs Bluff with the leaves coming out there below us in the gorge and you in your red cape but I like the dark one too. There is a better day coming when we will not have to write letters but can see each other maybe every day. Untill then I am always the same.

J i m

P.S. I will have to write this crossways. I noticed what you said about discontent at home and Peace meetings and am sorry to hear some of the Home Guard got there eyes blacked out but Margaret there is one thing I am inhopes of and that is you will not let your step brother and his gang go back down in Globe for they will kill him sure and I dont know what that would do between our familys which is in doubt now but one more time is something nobody could forgive. Anyway that is the *wish* of your true friend Jim and I know there is nothing you can do to stop them but anyway try.

WASHINGTON McKAMIE

In Line of battel   Wilderness Va.
May 7 1864

Mr and Mrs Martin McKamie
McKamie Gap   Caldwell Co N C

Dear friends

I seat myself to in form you of the death of your son Washington McKamie he was wouned on May 5 a bout five oclok in this place called Wilderness and died in a bout an hour after he

was wouned. I carid him out of the woods it is painfull in dead for me to state to you the misfortune. He died on the way before I cud get him to the field horpitle he told me he had to die and to tell his Mother he had been a faithful soldier and always dun his duty. He give me a duble barl Yankee pistol and said it is for his cusin Thad McKamie that kep his dog for him while he was gone. I beried him you can not get any plank in such times to make a box. This Wilderness was one of the awfules places I ever saw and the woods and thickets was on fire and cracklin like a furnis. I beried him as good as I could I ropt him up in a blanket and beried him in a elbo of a little branch where no fire couldn get to him. It was as much as I could do to get his body out of the woods. Our Co sufered severly we had 3 kiled that I know of for sertin our Maj John T. Jones and J.A. Coleman and J.A. Sheril is the wonns that was kiled Larkin Coffey W.H.Fowler H.C.Keller was wouned and captured and the Frazer boys is missing no others close aroun Globe & Wataga that I know of Mr. and Mrs McKamie what Wash says is the truth He was quiet and a hard worker and always dun his duty. The 22nd bore its part well You can also tell my folks I am safe yet and wod write home if I had a chance but there is right smart skirmishan on the line this morning I will keep the pistol safe as I can and send it by the first man passin to go home. I must clos you have the sinceer simpathy of your true friend   A.C.McRea
　　　　　　　　　　Wilcox Divn
　　　　　　　　　　Scales Bgd
　　　　　　　　　　22 Reg NC

PENDLETON LEWIS to PINCKNEY LEWIS

Riverside
Globe N C
July 6, 1864

Pvt. Pinckney Lewis
58th N C Rgt
Stevensons Div Hoods Corps
Army of Tennessee
Ga.

Dear Pinckney, We have had a battel here at Morganton Camp Vance Tuesday a week ago. Kirk (capt) yankee with band of Indians torys & deserters swooped down on Camp Vance captured the Junior Reserves (250) burnt a engine and cars everything in the place all but the hospitle, stole grain stock wagons & guns which they gave to prisners freed and negros along the way back to Cool Spring. Home Guard under Col Walton chased them to Brown Mt up Starcase Mt. Uncle Theo. joined band of militia from Caldwell & overtook their rear guard Said Kirk put our boys behind to cusshon the fire Tommy Haliburton wounded also Finch Beach and B.A. Bowles, drummer, killed. Main battel fought out on Rip Shin Mt Col Avery badly wounded also Calvin Houk and Philip Chandler crawled of & died they found his body near a stream. Uncle Theoph's old horse Gideon shot under him he borrowed mule from Perkins to get home. He talks fit to turn bark on trees. Mother had to take the girls out of the room. He says Kirk is a renigade trator scowndril vaggabond says all had finest guns Spencer repeating rifles. Heath Garvy was in it also David Ellis brother of Dan Ellis the Yankee pilot. All got away into Tenn. burnt Col Palmers house on the way because Palmer had burnt Kirks mothers house in Tenn. James asked me to write and tell you all this he was home 2 days to get recruits he said tell you he will answer your letter soon. He said looks like

« 203 »

you are doing the same thing in Georgia he is in Va fighting & falling back, fighting & falling back but wait till Gen. Lee and Joe Johnston get together it will be a different story. Pa is begining to wonder is the cotton safe in SC. I am in the Home Guard now Capt Lindsey is our Capt but he can not be here much Most of the time me & Jade & Billy lay out in the woods and meet Pa and Uncle Theoph at night we go where needed. I can walk pretty good but James leg is bothering him some he cannot march the way they move in Va now so he is going in the 1st N C cavalry I let him take Taima because theres a chance he may get on Hampton's Legion. Im pretty sure James is sweet on Margaret McKamie up in the Gap but he did not go up there that any body knows of When those folks are mentiond specialy the Garvys my folks faces just go blank you know how they are yours too. [Go back to page 1.] Zeb Vance made a powerful speech at Wilkesboro on loyalty and habus corpus. Well if you want me to give any messages to Isabel Hicks just tell me & I will. Jasper has got over his Chickamauga sclap wound and is charming them all at Camp Douglas with his fife playing. Well I will keep you informed about any more battels around hear and I know it is bad to say but it is also more interresting with some thing going on and I hope you will do the same is the wish of your cousin
                 Pendleton Lewis

PS Col Avery died Sunday—3 days ago.

1865

BENNIE McKAMIE

QUEENIE scratches at the door and I run open it. She trots in with a field mouse in her mouth, drops it on the hearth, sits back pantin' an' grinnin'. Margaret is ironin'. She goes over to the fireplace, sets her cooled iron at the coals and takes another one. Passin' back she flicks the mouse off the hearth with the toe of her boot.

"Dead," she says, "first livin' thing she's brought in in a long time. Winter must be breakin' up." She taps the hot iron with her wet finger and it spits.

As soon as Margaret finishes ironin' we're goin' to turn the spiles back up on the sap buckets. We had to turn 'em down durin' the freshet. You can tell how far along Margaret is by how loud she sings. She pitches in with Awake You Drowsy Sleepers. Now she's singin' One Morning in May—just a old love song. There's still a pile of clo'es because of no washin' during the freshet.

I heave a long breath and go over and lie on the floor by Queenie and the mouse. Ma and Pa and my brothers have gone over to Aunt Harriett's. I didn' want to go. Since Wash got shot everybody is sad and Uncle Martin is sick. There's one good thing, though, Aunt Harriett and Uncle Martin are not mad at us any more.

I poke the mouse with my finger and it moves all one piece of soft gray fur. Queenie pricks up her ears. "Dead," Margaret said, "the first livin' thing she's brought in in a long time." How can a thing be livin' and dead too? Queenie stretches out her throat on her paws and falls asleep. She is ninety one. She does not hunt alive things much any more. Thirteen dog years times seven people-years is ninety one. Margaret teaches me numbers on days like this when we're by ourselves. Pa is fifty, Ma is forty, Margaret is eighteen. Heese is in between there somewhere but he does not live with us. Baby Sam is three. I don't know about Samantha. Jake is 15½, Tom is 13½. I am seven people years. Next October I will be eight.

"What month is this, Margaret?"

"January."

I count up. Thirty days hath September, April June—no, that is something else.

"Is it 1864?"

"1865!"

"What day?"

I have to think. The freshet started on the 10th. It makes me ashamed when I can't answer right up. The bridge washed out a week ago. This is—the twenty third of January? There are four kinds of feelin's—shamed, glad, mad and sad. Sad feelings I can push under, like about Wash' bein' shot. Everybody cried. It was bad. I think it would be better if Pa and Ma just let Aunt Harriett and Uncle Martin push it away down for theirselves an' not go over there. Besides, Wash is not really dead. He'll be back in the spring, maybe when they have the funerals. Joel, too. They will walk around with the rest amongst the graves decorated with flowers for all that died this year—really died like old man Eagles. Thad went in the back room where old man Eagles was and touched him. Thad said he was as cold as a rock. It was scarey. Scarey I love but sad I hate. Wash will stand off with the men at the edge of the woods and talk while the women fix dinner. Wash sent Thad a Yankee pistol.

Margaret sings,

"They took hand in hand and went on together
But where they did go, that I do not know where.
Then said the lady, Let's go to the spring

> Where the waters are sliding and nightingales
> sing."

"Aw, Margaret, sing John Hardy." I lift the mouse's hind leg, but the legs don't part, they just come up together, stiff. I think it's a boy, though. I think I will have a funeral for it out by my rabbit trap. I'll put red galax on it.

Margaret leans across me to change the irons. Her breasts fill up the open neck of her dress. I look away at the wall. Margaret is very much of a girl. Then she almost trips as Queenie gets up under her and huffs. Huffs again, trots to the door and barks. I un-sling the gun from the wall, Margaret sets the iron on the table and runs to crack the front shutter.

"It's Nath'!" She grabs her jacket. I lay the gun on the stool and the two of us and Queenie race out to the gate to meet the mail man. Nath' is one of the glad things that happens. I don't know how often he comes—days and weeks he is not there, then he is just there again like chestnuts or blackberries or snow, but oftener than those. Usually he brings us somethin' besides the mail.

Margaret throws open the gate but Nath' is already shakin' his head to let us know there is not any mail so we wont be lookin' for any. He gets off stiff and draws Jarvis's bridle forward. I do not know how old Nath' is. He has a little pointed chin and fine-wrinkle face more like a woman's without any hair. When he talks to Ma he's her age but when he's with Margaret he brightens up.

"Good mornin'! Howdy Benjamin!" He sees me eyein' the pouch slung over his shoulder so I look away. "How many rabbit skins you got now?"

Margaret is disappointed about the mail. Whenever Nath' brings her the letters she sings. Now she has to make the most of it.

"You've got a new coat!" she says. Usually Nath' and Jarvis are all one color of brown, but today his coat is Confederate gray.

"We're in the Home Guard now, mail carriers—sworn in and everything. This is Zeb' Vance cloth." He looks down pleased she noticed. "There wont be any more, though. A fort has fell that guards the coast, Fort Fisher, below Wilmin'ton. Blowed plum up!"

"Come in, wont you, Nath'? Ma and Pa are not here, they've gone over to Aunt Harriett's."

"I'll come in an' warm a little. Benjamin, you wouldn't have any fodder, would you?"

"We got some oats." I take his old bent-up bucket and run for the crib. I don't mind missin' the sad things he has to tell—somebody's baby's sick or died, or cow—but mixed up with that is a lot of other things that are interestin', like that Fort.

When I get back I see it's all gonna be sad! He and Margaret are sittin' at the table straight and still the way grown folks look when they have bad news and haf' to find some way to meet it. Margaret holds her knittin', she and Ma never sit down without that, but she's not knittin'. They don't even notice me comin' in. I lift the gun from the stool where I left it and hang it on the wall.

"You'd might as well figure on your step-brother losin' his eye," Nath' is sayin'. "Andrew Lewis is a example of what a mild mannered man will do when he really gets mad. It was powder, ball *and* buckshot this time, enough shot to throw Heese's aim off so only one bead struck Jim Lewis's shoulder. Heese was shootin' from behind the big pine up in the graveyard. Lewis's buckshot caught him right in the eye."

Margaret's eyes are storm dark. She knits harder. "This will kill Pa an' Ma." Kind of under her breath she adds "Why, oh, why!"

"Two things. They meant to capture whatever kind of Home Guard is down there, in*clud*in' Jim Lewis. And they needed bacon."

"I told Heese. But you can't tell him anything!"

"Foragin' is as old as war, girl, an' hate makes hunger bitterer."

"That's not all! It's just *him*! Why can't he stick to pilotin'—!"

"He wont be doin' that for a while. Besides, things is pretty well et up along the Elk and the Watauga—Bingham's men and

Thomas's Indians both over there. Not to mention the Yankees."

"Was Samantha in it?"

"Not that anybody seen. And they would of. It was broad daylight this time. Breakfast time they come. They're gettin' bolder. The Home Guard boys had just come in from the woods—the crippled one, Pendleton Lewis, and two of his cousins. They wanted to see Jim Lewis once more before he went back to Petersburg. No doubt the whackers had been spyin' on 'em."

Nath' sits and looks at Margaret. You can tell when somebody likes somebody. Even a old man like Nath'. Ma likes Pa, Pa loves Ma, and Margaret. Jake and Tom like each other. Everybody likes me, I am the youngest. And Nath' likes Margaret. He is old but you can tell. He is sorry for her. I am sorry for her, too. I'm sorry for us all if Heese has lost his eye.

It's as if Nath' has told his story but if she needs to hear more he will try to add something to it.

"The shot struck Jim Lewis in the soft part of his shoulder. Jim was due back at Petersburg Tuesday with conscripts and Doc Rivers thought he wouldn't probe for it, it would just stir things up worse. Same with Heese's eye, McCautherns tell me. They was in it, too!"

"All of us are in it." Margaret stands up sudden.

"Yes, girl, the tides of war is tollin' in upon us. Up to now we just had the trickle. Some Mitchell boys in Kirk's command told me all Stoneman said when he reached Knoxville was 'I have come here. I have a score to settle.' "

"Bennie, run down to the spring house and bring some milk. You'll stay and have a bite to eat, wont you Nathan?"

"I thank you, but the freshet's put me behind. North C'lina just about washed away. As if the war warn't enough. I promised Mis' Harriett an' Martin I'd stop with them. Is she doin' pretty well since Wash's death?"

"Aunt Harriett? She didn't take it in at first. You know Aunt Harriett's mind is always on *things*, land, stock, that land she thinks is still unclaimed. Aunt Chaney's stayin' with them helped. *He* is the one I feel sorry for. Uncle Martin."

Nathan pulls the pouch around. "Oh, Benjamin, I brought you somethin'—" He draws out a littel calico bag and fishes up two pieces of candy wrapped in brown paper. "Mis' Harper at the store sent it. She makes it for young 'uns along the way."

I peel back one end. Molasses taffy. There are only two pieces. Would there be any use to save only one for Jake and Tom?

"If you don't have any mail to go, I guess I'd best be movin' along. If Stoneman's not cut the railroad above Abingdon, I'll see you before too long—"

We walk with him to the gate and wave him off. "Nath'—don't tell Ma and Pa about Heese, if you see 'em. I'll tell 'em. Or wait 'til they find it out soon enough—"

"They'll not hear it from me. But you children keep your door locked. And barred. Don't go runnin' out just because the dog barks. Home Guards may be old men an' boys, but they got help. I got a letter here Major A.C. Avery has wrote to Major Bingham sayin' how things are—"

We walk back to the house. I wonder how Heese can see with just one eye. I shut one of mine to see.

"Margaret, can Heese see with just one eye?"

"Maybe he'll see to do less devilment," she snaps.

The candy is sticky. "Would you like a piece, Margaret?"

"No." She is not thinkin' about me. "Thank you." She kind of turns her head away. I run ahead with Queenie to the house. At the fireplace Queenie sniffs the mouse like she never seen it before. Margaret comes in, hangs up her jacket, goes to the fireplace, takes up an iron. She don't wet her finger but I hear it spit. I look to see if she is cryin'.

She flicks the mouse with her boot. "*Move him!*"

I pick him up by the tail, carry him outdoors and fling him as far as I can send him. God can bury him, I guess, same as He did Wash. I tear off the rest of the brown paper and pop the last piece of taffy in my mouth. It tastes salty at first then sweet.

THOMAS McKAMIE

I keep it all straight because Uncle Martin says we may have to tell it in court.

It was about dusk the Home Guard come. It was a Sunday, Sunday February 26, 1865. Ma wrote it down in the Bible. They musta come up from Anthony's Creek because they'd already took Ed McCauthern. But Uncle Martin says in court you tell only what you seen, not what you think. It was gittin' on to dusk. Pa, Ma an' Margaret was in the house with Samps' Calloway that had come over to get some medicine for his wife's flux. I was playin' Ant'ny Over on one side o' the house against Jake an' Bennie on the other. It was a pretty day but muddy like spring, so we was slidin' about an' hollerin'. I never noticed till the ball quit comin' over. I heard men's voices but I thought it was just Pa an' Samps' Calloway. But when I peered around the house I seen 'em—ten men on mules. They was Whang Brown with one o' those Creek Indians from Forge Flats, Abram Lewis who is a officer at Camp Mast, an' Franz an' Wilts Beech an' Pat Mast from down in Globe that a slave poisoned his father and mother, an' I can't say the names of the rest because I didn't know them, except they was from the Home Guard camp at Morganton, Major Avery's battalion they call it.

My brothers was just standin' there with their mouths dropped open, holdin' the ball, while the ones I named, includin' the Indian, got off their mules an' went inside the house an' the rest stayed outside to guard Ed McCauthern.

I quick slipped around an' whispered to Jake an' Bennie to get Beulah, our cow, an' lead her off in the woods the way we'd always planned if rebels or 'whackers should raid us. McCauthern looked over at me an' winked—Ed is noted for havin' the keenest hearin' of any man in these parts. They ust to try him out on Muster Days or camp meetin's.

I slipped in the house. Whang Brown was standin' in the middle o' the room, a little stocky feller, real self-important, with slicked-down black hair an' a good uniform on, and I remember lookin' at the back o' his trousers because I've heard Pa say the Browns has set on their forges between the two armies the whole war an' never even got their pants split.

Pa was standin' by the fireplace, quiet an' strong the way he always is. Craziest thing, though, was Samps' Calloway. He was in the bed! Ma was settin' by it feedin' him medicine with a spoon. Every once in a while Samps' would let out a groan like he really had took sick except Ma was doctoring him outa the flux bottle, an' I never know'd no man to have nothin' like that.

Whang was askin' Pa a lot o' questions about Heese, an' about Brooks an' Smoot, two preacher-men who pilot by way of Elk's Cross Roads and Cut Laurel Gap. Pa wouldn' answer any of it. Then they turned to Samps', askin' him about Kirk's 3rd North Carolina Cavalry, an' while Wilts Beech tried to jerk the cover off Samps', Ma hilt on to it an' said for shame, a man took too sick to even lift his head! And besides, she snapped, Kirk's men was nothin' to Vaughn's rebel cavalry—pretendin' they had to get to Newton for horses an' all the time they just wanted to stay outa danger in East Tennessee an' plunder all the way to Newton an' back.

Whang has been lookin' at Pa an' all at once he kinda wheezes "Why don't we take this old Enoch McKamie? He's fed more deserters an' run more men through to the Union lines than anybody 'round here."

Captain Lewis said "We don't want him, he's too old."

"He could carry water," Wilts says.

At that, Ma dropped the bottle an' run to Pa, an' started tellin' 'em how many *Confedrit* Volunteers' widows he had fed—an' Pa not sayin' a word, just standin' there tall an' quiet like always. But they tied his hands behind his back, an' he bent down an' kissed Ma an' Margaret, an' told me to take care of Ma, that he would be back an' he wouldn' mind carryin' water or anything else if it would end war and hate. With that, they took Pa out an' put him with Ed McCauthern between the guards an' marched 'em off in the direction of Clark's Barn, toward Shulls Mills.

An' that's the last we ever saw of him. When they got over about Clark's Barn Ed McCauthern escaped. With those sharp ears o' his'n, he heard the captain say to the Guards "We're gonna fall out," an' soon as they did, he dived into some l'arls. They shot at him once an' one bullet grazed his hip—then they shot ag'in but there wasn't no more chance o' stoppin' Ed than a fox when once he got in some woods.

Ma set down in a chair an' throwed her apern over her head an' cried, an' said maybe if she'd only helt her tongue an' not said that about Vaughn's cavalry they'd not a-took him, an' Margaret tryin' to comfort her, an' fleem comin' up in my throat an' me shakin' all over, but Samps' Calloway hopped outa bed an' followed 'em an' they went on over past Clark's Barn to the Tom Henley place an' camped, an' they tied Pa to a tree, but it was awful cold an' nothin' Samps' could do ag'inst two armed guards, an' he got to thinkin' about his wife, or maybe all that medicine got to workin' on him. Anyway he decided to go on to Foscoe an' warn an' maybe head 'em off in the mornin'. Next day, though, there was a fight over at Foscoe between the first o' Stoneman's Yankees and those that escaped from Camp Mast when it surrendered on the 5th of February. Some was killed on both sides, an' Pa' wasn' forgotten exactly but they just didn' have time to hunt him up.

Ma dried her eyes after a while an' sent me to find Jake an' Bennie an' Beulah an' milk her an' put the fence back where it was trompled down an' the yard all mucked up by mules' feet, an' Margaret cooked supper but nobody could eat but Bennie, an' after supper Ma had prayers same as always an' read outa the Bible the 23rd Psa'm, "Thou preparest me a table in the presence of mine enemies, thou anointest my head with oil, my cup runneth over . . ."

Early next mornin' she got on Shadrack an' rode first to Heese's house but he had gone to Strawberry Plains to join up to the

Union Army shore 'nuf, said Samantha, because with the Yankees as close now as Banner Elk there wasn' no need for pilotin' any more an' Heese thought he deserved a pension after losin' his eye, an' all the rest of the hell he'd been through, an' Samantha said she thought she did too.

So Ma went on an' rode five more days huntin' Pa—all 'round Shulls Mills an' Foscoe an' even as far away as Boone an' Blowin' Rock, but wasn't no trace of him. So the seventh day was Sunday, an' that's when it happened.

We slept late, Ma bein' so tired from searchin' an' us from waitin' for her to come home, so it was past daylight when we heard Queenie scratchin' an' whimperin' at the door. Tom let her in an' she trotted over to the hearth an' I heard her drop somethin'. With that Jake let out the awfules' yell an' dived back up in the bed between me an' Bennie, jerked the kivers over his head an' laid stiff. I raised up, rubbed my eyes, looked over on the floor. Queenie was lickin' herself. She was all scratched up. Then she went to whimperin' an' waggin' her stump of tail. The fire was banked so I couldn' see good. I rubbed my eyes ag'in.

It was a hand! A human hand chawed off at the wrist with dried blood!

"Ma!!" I yelled.

Then everything got all mixed up. We was all outa bed, shakin', freezin', starin' at that hand stretched out t'ords us with the p'am up like it was pleadin'.

Margaret grabbed a long splinter, stuck it in the ashes till it flared, lit the grease lamp, then helt the rest of the splinter above the hand.

Ma leaned down and turned it over. It was all black with a faint white scar across the back. Ma give one awful cry, grabbed the hand up ag'inst her breast an' set down in the chair rockin' it back an' forth an' sobbin'. We was all 'round her—Jake an' Bennie had jumped outa bed. Each of us in his own way put together that it was Pa's hand an' the rest of him was not likely to be alive. I was cryin' like a baby but still an' all I remembered what Pa said about takin' care of the rest so, shakin' like palsy, I un-banked the fire an' got it built an' burnin'. Margaret was kneelin' with her head on Ma's shoulder, the two of 'em just rockin' back an' forth same as if they was hushin' a child, an' Bennie stood like a knee baby in front of 'em, not takin' it all in but knowin' he was part of it too. Queenie flattened out on the floor an' went to sleep, dog tired.

"Leave her be," says Ma after a long time. "She's got to take us back to find the rest."

MARGARET McKAMIE

What was left me an' Ma brought home in our aperns, the head with the bullet holes in back, an' the good arm that the dogs an' buzzards hadn' et because it was stretched out from the cliff over the Globe—the cliff me an' Jim sat on that day before he went away. We don't know how Pa come there, we guessed at the day, an' Aunt Chaney carved it on a head-board,

>
> Enoch McKamie
> b. Burke co. March 28, 1815
> d. Watauga co. Feb. 27, 1865

March wind was gustin' down from the Grandfather. For once Uncle Reuben didn't have much to say. I remember just one thing,
> "Mark the perfect man and behold the upright,
> for the end of that man is peace."

Heese come over when he got back from enlistin'. Little use as I got for Heese, he put me in mind of a big chestnut tree that trembles then falls. It sh'uk us all.

After two days he rose, burnin' like flame, or ice. He never cussed even once. He just said he aimed to find the one done it if it took forty years, and he would kill him.

> "Down in yonder green field
> There lies a knight slain under his shield.

>His hounds lie down at his feet,
>So well they can their master keep,
>
>His hawks they fly so eager-ly
>There's no fowl dare come him nie—"

But there is no song in me. There is no song.

MAIL MAN

ED MCCAUTHERN says a clearer case of self defense he never seen. It was about close of day, a pretty May day, and Whang Brown had been to take some plow points to Andrew Lewis's down in Globe. Seems like the country is in a stooper since the war ended but people have to raise food.

Whang had that Creek Indian with him, his body guard, folks say, because Browns know Heath Garvy's been closin' in on Whang ever since he decided Whang was the one who murdered Enoch McKamie or anyway know'd who did it. The Indian didn't help Whang much this time though. He just disappeared in the woods an' has not been heard of since, a fact most folks think is suspicious in itself.

Margaret tells me Heath come to their house that mornin' an' told his mother somethin'. From the way she walked the floor afterwards, he must have told her he was goin' to get Brown. When Heath come outa the house, he says to Jake, his half-brother, "Come on an' go with me an' Ed down in Globe—my dog's got a deer at bay."

"Heath, you haven't got a dog!" Bennie, the little 'un, piped up.

Heath give Bennie a look then Margaret says nobody will soon forget.

Andrew Lewis had told Whang he thought it would be safer for him to go home by Hatley's an' Harmons, not knowin' Garvy would be comin' down that way. So it took place just beyond the foot log in a little flat near a big rock.

Garvy shouted "Is that you, Whang?"

Whang answered "Yes!" at the same time strikin' out with a stout hickory stick he was carryin' with a clout on one end that even a little runt like Whang could have killed an ox with. The blow was aimed at Garvy's head, Garvy shielded his head with his arm and caught the blow on his left wrist, then fell back about fourteen paces with Brown followin', strikin' at Heese with the club ever' step. Finally Heese got room enough to level his seven-shootin' Sharp's rifle at Brown and shot him.

Heese told Ed McCauthern to roll Brown's body over. There was no life in it. Then Heese turned and went back up the creek by Hatleys an' Harmons an' told 'em what he'd done.

There is no law or justice in this country now. The courthouse at Boone is closed, its windows broke out by Stoneman's men.

Garvy will be examined by Major Walcott, one o' the new Yankee military commissioners sent out to investigate persecutions of Union men in Watauga. But with times like they are now, there's about as much likelihood of Garvy ever bein' brought to trial as there is of me bein' Postmaster General.

MARGARET McKAMIE

Tom and I have picked down from White Springs to the Old House Gap leavin' four baskets back on the trail to take home by sledge if the bees don't eat 'em first. They will bring ten cents a gallon at Lenoir. With what Jake an' Bennie pick at home, we'd ought to have $1.50 for Ma to spend when she goes for Heese's hearin' before the military commissioner tomorrow.

It's the thirty first of July, a real scorcher—no breeze, no sound but now and then a jar-fly—six weeks 'til frost, they say, when you hear that sound. We could get more for the berries by dryin' 'em an' waitin' till fall but there are too many things we need now. There's hardly anything we don't need.

Blackberries are bigger down here the way they are around old barns an' gardens. This is the old Crump place. It has a beautiful view of the Grandfather that makes you wish you'd been here in old Revolution times when the log barn an' outhouses was new, the ox cart comin' in at dusk, an' children jumpin' about over the big rocks in the ferny pasture.

We've not stopped but one time an' that was when we heard a chirrin' sound. I looked at Tom to see if he noticed—too high off the ground for a rattler but not lazy like a jar fly either—a sizzlin' sort of sound. Tom listens—then his hands go back to pickin' above a tumbled dry wall where phlox flowers planted by some old Crump years ago still try to bloom through the weeds and blackberry briars.

'Twas then we see the people come outa the woods—a young man, a girl about sixteen, a old colored woman wearin' a big white turbin, and a horse—I know that horse! It is Taima! A girl about nine, plump and tow-haired, is ridin' her, and as they all come on up to the patch she is like James ridin' t'ords me above the pink flowers!

"Hi!" the old woman cries startled. The sound dies with the jar-fly. They all have pails, and a gun and lunch basket are strapped to the horse. The older girl is dark and pretty.

The old woman says somethin' else more like she's frightened than speakin' to us. Ends of her kerchief stick up above the bushes like rabbit ears.

The young girl rides right on up to the wall like she mighta been one o' the owners of the place, and sits starin' down at me. She's bound to be James's sister, even to the light freckles. Taima looks older, heavier, a little gray in her mane. She stretches out her neck, then draws back like she's scared and splutters her velvet nose. I want to reach out and touch it, stroke her, love her, speak to her—but she backs away. My fingers start to tremble an' I drop a handful of berries, stoop down to pick 'em up, put my foot through the rent in my skirt and tear it some more.

The young man asks "Mind if we pick here?" He talks nice and common.

Tom kind of shrugs as if to say it's as much your'n as our'n. The last Crump heir died about two years ago in a place called Bristoe Station.

"You have many snakes up here?" the boy asks. There's somethin' familiar about him.

"They're on the move this time of year. And dry weather's brought 'em out."

At that, the old woman jerks her knotty hands back from the briars and peeks through at us. She has a little monkey face below the rabbit ears.

"I'm Pinckney Lewis." Another wave of heat goes over me. That's what it was—the family look between him and James! Then an ache comes—that I can't tell him James talked of him— why, I've even read some of his letters 'til I feel as if I'd walked all that long way from Tennessee to Georgia and back up to Nashville again! True, part of what James said about him you wouldn't want to tell, like he was kind of simple-minded an' suspectless, but there was no doubt Jim thought a lot of this cousin of his.

"This is Miss Christy Hoke," he says. "She's from the rebel state of Rowan." He grins like it's a joke between 'em. "That is Kiz over there, an' the one on the horse is Emeline Angel Lewis. She's my cousin."

And she is James's sister! I nod, still red in the face, and go on pickin'. My brother Tom mumbles something. It's unmannerly of him not to tell our names, but maybe better to spare 'em knowin' who we are to them—Who are we? What! To them?

"They were bound to come blackberrying so I had to come along to protect 'em." He grins at Miss Christy Hoke. Her lips are stained the purplish color of her dress that is some thin stuff with thick braid in curlicues down the bosom—not the kind of dress to come blackberryin' in, an' what with eatin' and pullin' herself loose from briars, she's not gettin' much fruit but I guess that don't matter to her the way as it does to us.

Emeline Angel Lewis just keeps sittin' on Taima and starin' at me. Settin' on a horse always puts a body to advantage, 'specially a horse as pretty as Taima, an' Emeline is no different. Though I couldn't be damper, I sweat some more. I know I look awful but Ma says apologies are only if you've hurt somebody. I've sure never harmed Emeline Lewis or anybody else that I know of. I decide I'll just do a good job of ugly. I pull a curl under my nose for a muss-tache an' make a face at her the way I do at Bennie. She says slow

"I know who you are. You're Margaret McKamie. You're the girl James liked."

They stare, all but Tom—his back says plenty but he goes right on pickin'. The old woman lets go of a branch with a "Hi!" that sounds more like a hic-cup.

"Your brother shot our brothers," says Emeline Angel, not mean but dreamy-like the way Bennie would tell me a hawk caught a chip-monk.

"Emmy Angel!" Pinckney Lewis frowns. Miss Christy Hoke stops with a berry half-way to her mouth.

"Your brother's bullet is in James's shoulder an' our father's bullet is in your brother's head!"

"Emmy Angel! Did you come up here to pick berries or a quar'l?" Pinckney Lewis speaks sharp. "How 'bout gettin' down from there an' givin' Taima's back a rest?"

Emeline plucks a wisp of damp hair off her hot cheek. "James wont be seeing you any more," she goes on in the same dreamy sing-song. "He's goin' away. To Kansas. He's goin' away and stay for a long long time."

The old woman breaks out in some kinda gibberish. Taima is splutterin' her nose at the flowers, ears pointed like she's fixin' to shy. Emmy Angel jerks the reins.

"Your brother is a bushwhacker. That's what he is."

My brother turns away. As he does, the sizzling breaks out on the wall right under the little girl's leg. This time there's no mistakin' what it is. Tom whirls back, takes one look an' reaches down for a stone. A timber rattler is coiled big as a hen's nest on the wall among the pink flowers not three feet from Emeline Angel's fat leg!

"*Look out!*" Tom yells, "Get *back!*"

Taima rears and whinnies! There is a sharp gritty strike! Pinckney Lewis lunges for the bridle, half mounts and clings to Emmy Angel and the saddle as the horse wheels and lopes away down the hill. Miss Christy Hoke screams, throws her pail away and takes out after them, the thin purple dress spreadin' behind her like butterflies' wings.

Pinckney Lewis stops Taima at the woods, jumps off and runs with his gun back up the hill to us. But the rock was sharp and already the snake's pink entra'ls are spreadin' out amongst the flowers.

I'm spell-binded—sick an' faint! Yet you can't help feelin' sorry! Sorry that such a strange powerful creature—its body beginnin' to loosen on the wall—what came between us? Fear! We done what we had to do. There's no way to explain.

Lewis pants and stares. "*Jimm-i-nee!*"

Tom drops his second stone, picks up his basket an' moves away up the hill t'ords another blackberry patch.

Lewis tips up to the wall like he's not sure the snake wont still bite. He looks around for a stick, draws out a pocket knife, chops off a staff of locust an' trims it. "No matter how often I see one, I'm always scared stiff!" he says like he'd ought to explain it. The snake's tail twitches. Pinckney Lewis runs the stick under the heavy body an' lifts it. The shale split the back neat.

"Four feet long. Twelve rattles." The rattles shake feeble. "You don't mind if I have them, do you?"

I shug my shoulders, go on pickin'. "It sure don't belong to us." He pushes the flowers away an' slides the body back on the wall, straightens it to look as if it's alive an' crawlin'. His knife is gold-decorated with letters "U.S." on it, an' a number. He cuts the rattles off neat below the flesh, leaves the glassy stump. It fills with blood, glows like a ruby on the wall. He holds the rattles up and shakes them—they don't sizzle now—then drops them in his pocket an' looks at me as if really seein' me for the first time.

"You *are* Margaret McKamie, aren't you?"

I jerk my sunbonnet forward. "Yes."

"Is that your brother?" he nods t'ords Tom's back—blue jeans ag'inst blue Grandfather. "I'd like to thank him. The snake might have bitten Emmy Angel!"

"I wonder it didn't!" He don't take it like I mean it.

"Because he *killed* it," he answers innocent which is what James meant about Pinckney's bein' simple. "You mustn't mind Emmy Angel. She didn't mean all that the way it sounded."

"I guess most of what she said was the truth."

"Such as James likin' you?"

I'm so aggervated I could fly apart. All I want is to get on with our berryin', finish so Ma can take 'em tomorrow when she goes to the hearin'. But I hold in. They wont stay much longer. Or we wont.

Down the hill the women are comfortin' Emmy Angel who has got off Taima and is on the ground boo-hooin'. The old woman never lost a berry when she took off at a limpin' trot down the hill. They call up to Pinckney Lewis—he waves his arm an' shouts he's comin'.

"What other part was the truth?" He cleans blood off the knife by scrapin' it on the wall.

"*What?*"

"What other part of what she said was not the truth?"

"Bushwhacker!" One corner of my mind thinks, Strange for me to be takin' up for Heese.

Pinckney Lewis snaps the knife-blade shut, drops it in his pocket with the rattles.

"It's just a word. The war's over, anyhow." I think to myself I'm glad Heese wasn' here to hear that word! Flies are already comin' to the snake—bees too. He strokes the stick along its back. "James ust to talk about you." I start pickin' clusters then, stems and all—I'm so mad!

"But he don't any more. You know why I think he don't?"

"I'll not lose sleep over it."

"Because it goes deep." The women are shoutin' at him. Vine

shadows move across the snake. They make him look like he's crawlin', or swimmin' in deep water. "Should I bury him?"

"Buzzards will take care of that."

"I'll tell Jim I saw you."

"Please don't."

I shake my basket down. Even without the stems, it's full. I call Tom. If we hurry we can go back by Thunder Hole an' wash ourselves.

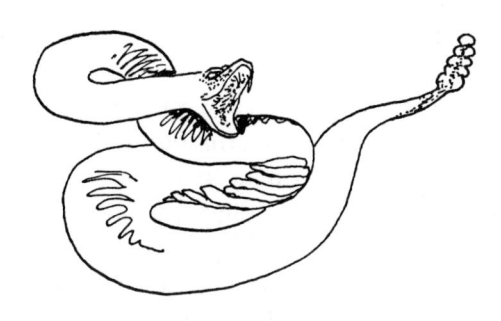

JAMES LEWIS

PINCKNEY sends me word he needs to see me, but when I go over to his house, he has gone to Piedmont Springs Hotel to take Miss Christy Hoke back to her folks.

Uncle Theophilus receives me in the back room. He has one foot propped in a high chair because his gout has come back on him due to him having to decide whether or not to take the oath.

"To be a good citizen and continue as Justice of the Peace, Jim, it is necessary to begin with perjury." He squinches up his face as Aunt Saphronia pours hot salt water over the swelling. "When do you leave, son?"

"Next Monday, August 7th, sir."

"I've got a load of corn I want taken up on the mountain to some Volunteers' families. It wont go far but it will help some.

They are pitiful. Pitiful! Where's the list, 'Phronie?"

"At your elbow under the medicine glass."

Uncle Theophilus starts pawing around among the brandy and medicine bottles hunting for something else. "Pinckney has become unaccountable lately for some reason. He's gone now to take Bob Hoke's daughter back to Piedmont Springs." Uncle Theophilus knows exactly why Pinckney has become unaccountable lately and he is not displeased. When he says 'Bob Hoke's daughter,' I know what he means. He means what any of our family mean when they have weighed any visitor's character, worldly goods, religion, politics, military record, crazy ancestors and number of generations you've known 'em, and come up with a *Yes* or a *No*. From what I have learned about Miss Hoke, I'm sure it is going to be a *Yes*, but all this before Pinckney has maybe ever kissed the girl. It's the kind of managing I want to get away from. I don't mind taking one more trip up the mountain. The nearer time comes for me to go West, the restlesser I get.

"I'll haul the corn for you, Uncle Theophilus."

"I'd appreciate it, Jim! I guess those Newton cavalry mules will pull."

Aunt Saphronia purses her smile, casts her eyes at the ceiling, "He named the mules 'Pomp' and 'Circumstance!'"

Uncle Theoph gives up pawing around. "Phronie where are my glasses?"

Aunt Saphronia steps behind him, slides the steel spec's off his head and down on his nose.

"Read this." He gives me the list. "Terrible, terrible."

There are fifty names, mostly women. The margins say "Destitute." "No means." "Husband (Vol.) died in the Army." "Able to pay." "Some bacon." "Able to work." "Husband in prison, reported dead." "Destitute. Son large enough to work." Size of families varies from three to twelve.

"Start at Younce's, then make it stretch as far as it will. I hope those layed-off mules will pull."

So that is how I happen to be in this two-mule wagon hauling corn up the East Prong of Johns River on this Thursday morning,

August 3rd. I came early while everything is fresh, and so I could have the day to myself by the woods and streams. Maybe it's because I'm leaving that everything looks so good, sourwoods and black gums begining to redden. Dust is like velvet from last night's heavy dew. It's rained all around us this week but not a drop in Globe. A garter snake crawls across the road and leaves a wavy trail—Pomp and Circumstance prick up their ears but I speak to them—old cavalry mules are as sensitive to tones as any mule can be.

Here is where Pendleton, Jade, Billy and Pat Mast hid out when they were in the Home Guard. Here is the big poplar cornering the tract my father has willed to me, along with slaves Bob and Doll, but Bob and Doll have gone to Ohio. Only the land is here, including my great grandfather's peach orchard—the one he made pay twice for his Globe land. The orchard needs pruning and cleaning up.

Over there is the foot-log in the little flat near the big rock where Heath Garvy shot Whang Brown. It is sad. For one thing, nobody knows Whang was the one that actually carried off and killed Enoch McKamie. Most think while he might have had the will to do it, he put the job off on the Indian and the Indian's disappeared. Whang used to strut like a little martinet, yet he'd barely started to live! Never married—

Well—how about you? Be honest now. Well—maybe there's some big-footed home-steadin' Kansas gal . . . For a minute I picture myself gettin' in bed with a big-footed home-steadin' Kansas gal, an' my first thought is to get right back out again. Each day I'm unsurer why I want to go 'way out there by myself, atall.

We're startin' to climb. It's slow work, and since I forgot to bring anything to read, I take out the list Uncle Theophilus gave me. Down the right hand side of the page is listed what the families have—a little more wheat than corn. Less flour, but those who have flour have a good deal. Enoch McKamie's family's name is not on the list—or maybe Reuben McKamie just left them off a-purpose. The church drew up the list.

"Enoch McKamie's daughter." I say it out loud just to hear it.

The mules prick up their ears. "Enoch McKamie's daughter—Margaret McKamie. Religion, Baptist. Character, good. Worldly goods, little. Politics, Republican. Crazy ancestors—" well, Heath Garvy's not an ancestor but he'll fill the bill.

A man's shout! The mule's start. As if I've called him up, Heath Garvy is there, swaggerin' down the road like some giant out of a fairy tale, but he's real. Real for two reasons. He's got on his blue Federal uniform and his eye—well, it's one thing to hear a man has had his eye shot out and another to see it.

But the eye he *has* sees me, and he shouts again, calls my name friendly and strides on down to where I've stopped the wagon. He is armed and I dangle my hand down in the wagon bed above my own gun, just in case.

I've not been close to Heath Garvy in several years. He's aged some, same as everybody has in war-time—is about thirty years old to my nineteen, two hundred pounds and more to my hundred and fifty. The blue uniform becomes him. What shreds of gray I had after Spotsylvania are on Wak.

He grips the side of the wagon bed with one of his big hands. I look at it, rub my chin and wonder if it comes to a pull which will move off with the wagon—him, or me and Pomp and Circumstance.

He fixes me with his single light blue eye and grins. "Now you don't hafta be afraid o' me. The war's over! I don't intend no harm to *no*body—never did."

I would feel easier about this if I didn't smell whiskey. The war was over, too, when Major Bingham's men charged the Hamby house and General Clark's son from Lenoir and Henry Henley from Watauga got shot by bushwhackers and strumpets from the inside. You never know for sure how much you want to live 'til you come smack up ag'inst a good chance o' dyin', and that's somethin' I had to learn over every battle.

He pounds his big fist on the edge of the wagon bed. "You an' me both fought for what we believed in. We got a right to walk now as free men. If you'd a-been some old bushwhacker layin' out in the woods, I'd a killed you!"

So. I think how my mother quotes to us " 'Consistency, thou art a jewel.' " But I let that pass. Instead I say,

"Well, I'm free all right. How did your hearin' come out at Morganton?"

"Aw—they've sent the papers to Statesville." He moves his shoulders, grins like an embarrassed kid. "Why, they ain't gonna try *me*! Red Kirk ain't goin' to let 'em try *me*! Me an' Red Kirk piloted together too long for that. That's *Colonel* Kirk, you know —3rd North C'lina Mounted Infantry. That's how him an' me got started. Did you know that? By pilotin'. Red's close to Governor Holden, too."

He peers in the wagon, sees the gun, tries to appear he didn't, sees me eyeing his. "I'm goin' down in Globe to get me somemore char*ack*ter witnesses. On a paper. Thought I might kill me some game along the way." I wonder what kind of character witnesses he's goin' to get in Globe and him in Federal uniform too. 'Course there are the McCautherns—some of 'em married an' livin' in Globe. The girls are all pretty. He carries his rifle loosely through his right arm.

" 'Course I *know*," he says, serious as politics, "it takes a war a while to die down. I tell Samantha, 'It'll be a while before Garvys an' Lewises is visitin' back an' forth.' I tell people that." For a minute he shows grimness or resentment, then he brightens, " 'Course Samantha ain't much for visitin' anyway, less'n it'd be a hoe-down or somep'n. Just visitin' by itself she ain't got much time for. She'd druther be out a-doin' somethin'!" He looks at me, his one eye red and earnest. "No sir! You needn' be afraid o' ole Heese any more! Looky here—" He snaps the lever on the bottom of his rifle, a beautiful gun, lets the bullets fall in his hand, thrusts them in mine. One drops in the seat bed. I don't stop to go after it. "See? I don't mean no harm. Never did. *I ain't no murderer neither!* You an' me both just done what we had to do, the way we seen it, *at* the time!"

It is hard not to be disarmed by him. I try to fix my mind on Pendleton's hip. But this man has lost an eye. He must have been some man to survive it, or else Samantha was a better nurse than

I'd think she'd be. The little pellet I feel when I soap my shoulder is nothing.

This is Margaret's brother, too—her half brother. He may have been with her late as today. Coming down this way he prob'ly would. Can bein' near somebody rub off on a person? Did you ever look at him and wish it could so you could see her? If you could do that without her seein' you, that is.

"Here, take your bullets." He fingers them down neat into his cartridge case without ever glancing down, draws out some kind of little watch fob and whirls it around his finger on a thong. There is a low rumble from the West, and we both look up. "I believe we'll get some rain." A big thunderhead looms white as cream above the trees, slatey blue in the folds.

"Haven't I seen that somewhere before?" He drops his talisman in my hand, a half ounce bloodstone worn beautifully smooth. "I've heard you wet one of those and the red comes out brighter."

"That's right."

"Throw it in the fire an' it will turn gray."

He takes it back. "Ain't nobody gonna put *this* in the fire. A old man gimme that when I was four years old. I've carried it ever since. Where you goin' with all that fresh corn? Not distillin' I know." He chortles, slaps his big thigh with a pop that echoes in the rocks. The mules jerk up their heads. "If you *are*, I got somep'n ready made to he'p you 'til you get there." He swings a big shoulder canteen forward, a canteen brand new like all the rest of his gear, unscrews the cap, waves it under my nose and waits, serious, for my verdict. "Best that's made on Shell Creek."

I push it aside. To soften this I ask "You haf' to go all the way to East Tennessee to get good liquor?" The way things are now, you pretty nearly would.

This tickles him. He slaps his hip harder than before. "Me walkin' to Tennessee ain't no more for me than you walkin' to your barn. Well—excuse me." He tilts the can, drinks, gasps and rasps. "I forgot you was a teetotaler."

I glance at the strong columns of his legs ending in boots so big even the U. S. Army must have had them made special. I've always been interested in pilotin'. So much of it went on here near the woods and streams I love. I've seen the mountain gorges between here and Tennessee when we would go to visit Smeads. Sometime I mean to hear Heath tell all about it. Right now, though, the cloud column bumps and rolls again.

I say "I guess I better be movin' on."

"Aw, you don' haf' to go. Remember all that hell at Kinston? Dogged if I don't believe that was the easiest part of the war I was ever into."

I nod. "But it didn't stay like that."

"No. That's what I tell Samantha—Sam—you remember her? Whenever she gets restless or me pilotin' an' gone so much an' starts wishin' she was back at Kinston or anywheres except Haw Branch, I say 'Samantha, it didn' stay that way.' No sir-ree! 'Course she has Sam now. That's my boy!"

"I bet he's some boy." Bachelors do have the advantage of married men some ways. Sometimes but not all the time.

Heath Garvy's one eye beams. "He'll be three come next January. He can do mightn' near anything we can. An' some we can't." He props his gun against the back wagon wheel. "We got a pitchur of him."

"*No!*" I wonder where anybody around here these past three years could have a picture taken. I wish they might. I know one I'd like to have. Without thinking, I say "Was that in Kinston?"

His one eye looks at me pityin' or reproachful, "You know we didn' have no boy at Kinston! Least—not so's anybody could *see!*" This tickles him more than anything yet. He stamps around, shuffles a dance step or two, goes into a fit of laughing—he's light for such a giant. He slaps his thigh, the mules start to pull.

"Whoa, boys! Whoah!"

He calms down, wipes his eyes. "Yes, *sir*. It would take some cam'ra to show *that!*" Even the slit has cried a little. "Naw. Some reporters took the pitchur."

"*Where?*"

"At our home! Where'd you think? Samantha woulda perferred one like she seen at Kinston—stretched out, you know, the

« 231 »

baby—on a sheep skin? All we had, though, was a old deer hide. They thought we'd all three ought to be in the pitchur, an' since they was in a considerable hurry escapin' from Salisbury, they put all three of us in for the price o' one. We've not got it yet, but we better git it. I toted that smallest feller, David was his name, across the Linville river on my back, him *an'* his cam'ra. They was from some New York newspaper an' one in Ohio."

I let out a long breath. "I hope some day I see that picture."

"Oh, you will. We aim to have a hoe-down before long. Maybe it'll come by then. We'd be pleased to have you come—any of you'ns feel like comin'. You was good not to tell on us at Kinston. 'Bout Sam's bein' a woman."

He digs the canteen out of the corn, raises it to me in a sort of toast.

I don't know anything about acting except shows the boys put on first of the war. My folks think the stage is sinful. But this fellow is an actor. I don't mean Heath Garvy *puts on*, or moves himself all over or anything like that, though his whole body says whatever he's got to say so you can read it like a picture book. It don't come from drinking either. Drunks never have appealed to me, and besides, some preachers have it. I just mean when a person has this power, he can make you give attention, and I don't blame Heath Garvy's wife for follerin' him to the war, or men across gorges, though I'd never say that to my folks. And I wouldn't be surprised if folks don't remember him long after some Watauga Colonels and Majors are forgotten.

It seems a good time to get one thing off my mind. "I did tell one person—about Sam's bein' a woman."

He sobers. "Who was that?"

"The bugler—Mason Byrd."

"Oh, *him!* he laughs. "Old Bugles! Say, did he finely git in the Band?"

"Yes. Second cornet."

"I'll tell Samantha." He nods his head. "Where's Bugles at?"

"He's tryin' to start a store in Globe. And he says someday he's goin' to start a hotel at Blowing Rock."

He nods again. "Me an' Samantha been thinkin' 'bout startin' a store. Takes a lot o' money to do that though. I hope she don't hear 'bout no *ho*-tel. There's nothin' Samantha would love more'n a *ho*-tel less'n it'd be two *ho*-tels. 'Course we'd have to git somebody to cook." He shakes his head.

Maybe the liquor fumes are workin' on *me*, makin' me expand an' get confidential or maybe it's just this man. "Mason—or Bugles—will be all right. Some of his folks hid cotton down in South Carolina that Sherman never found. It'll bring a lot of money soon."

The words are hardly out of my mouth until I wish I hadn't said 'em. The effect on him is startling. He flushes red, then blotches purple and he lets out a string of words that cause Circumstance to lay his ears back flat.

"Now don't you go down there tryin' to find it!" I beg, " 'cause the money's hid good as the cotton was. You'd just get me in trouble an' I'd like us to stay friends." I would indeed. But I wonder if I have not hit on something sensitive in Heath Garvy's character for he brightens like a new cleaned lamp. His moods are as unpredictable as March. I never saw a fellow can change so fast. To get his mind off the cotton, I ask

"What outfit did you join, finally?"

"Tenth Michigan Volunteer Cavalry. B Company. Captain James Minihan's." He comes as near attention as his muscles will allow but his foot slips down the bank and he has to pull himself straight with the help of the wagon bed.

"I guess they were a pretty good outfit?" I know damn well they were. He's started me cussin' too, though not out loud.

"Lord God!" He spins out some more of it and Pomp and Circumstance both lay back their ears. "Best in the world. Wherever was a job, the Tenth Michigan was there. Bridges! Railroads! Salt works—or just scoutin' or skirmishin' in some la'rls, you jest give 'em the job an' they'd finish it."

He turns his attention back to the load of corn, picks up an ear. Now he is a farmer, judging crops. "I've hauled corn for General Lenoir down in Happy Valley. An' for Norwoods, on over in Tennessee. There's nothin' goes down as fast as a load o' fresh corn. You take cabbage, now—or apples—they'll hold up pretty good. But corn—!" He chooses an ear, pulls back the tender husk and silk, examines it, takes a bite and chews thoughtful. "We ust to live on this stuff when I was pilotin'. Worst corn's around ole rocky Bay's mountain. Best's hid below Powell's mountain—that's Wise county, Virginny. Did you grow this?"

"No, we—" then I think, I wont tell him any more. How do I know he wont raid us the third time? "My Uncle Theophilus grew it. On down the valley quite a ways."

"Mr. Theophilus Lewis? Shu-rr-e! I know nim!" He spits out hulls like a snow flurry. "He comes around to see us reg'lar 'bout election time, him and Mr. Mason Byrd. That's Mr. Mason Byrd, *Senior*—Bugles's daddy. Say tell me, do you think it was politics got Bugles in that Quaker Band?"

"It was a Moravian band, don't you remember? Captain Mickey's Band. Quakers don't allow musical instruments even in their churches."

"Do say? Well I never did think Bugles could play too good, only the Calls. Where did you say you was takin' this corn?"

"I never said. But it's goin' to Volunteers' families up this way."

"You just *givin'* it to 'em?"

"Yes."

"Well—that ain't bad politics."

"Politics has nothin' to do with it. Who around here has any chance in politics now! These are church people. Hungry!"

He chews, one way or another showin' most of his teeth.

He says "I bet you've never know'd what 'tis to be hungry. Even in the Army."

"As a matter of fact, I haven't."

"That's what I thought." He points the cob like a teacher's ruler. "I ain't talkin' about coves an' hollers up here in the mountains where there ain't a man left between fourteen an' sixty. Dead an' gone! *All* of 'em! Bulls Run, Seven Pines, Fredericksburg, Stone's River, Gettersburg—"

"*How do you know 'em so good?*" He ignores this.

"Only money crop mountain folks got now, after blackberries, is 'sang. Maybe a few apples. An' I ain't talkin' either about them that went to war late and is just as dead or worked just as hard to make the country more endurin'er than what South C'lina had in mind for it." He is swelling up like a toad. "All I'm sayin' is, there's some folks never worked, don't know how to work, an' wont work. And I tell you another thing!" He shakes the cob under my nose, "Our fam'ly's name ain't never goin' to be on no pauper list. Which is not to say there ain't plenty of things we need an' would like to have. But as long as this one eye can see an' my limbs work, an' see that *theirs* works, we don't aim to get on no such list—the church's nor nobody else's! Pa taught me that much."

Breathing hard, he walks around to the front of the wagon. He sticks the cob in Pomp's mouth and comes back. "We don't waste things, neither." His voice has dropped lower with a break, nearly like he's goin' to cry. He lifts the canteen out of the corn.

"If you're goin' to Globe for character witnesses, hadn' you better lay off that stuff? What's left of it?"

He turns up the canteen, swallows, smacks his lips, goes into a deep study, then speaks matter-of-fact. "What do you aim to be doin', Jim, now the war is over?"

'I've been plannin' to go out West. To Kansas."

"Me an' Samantha been thinkin' the same thing—that is, if we don't decide for me to run for the legislatur'. Or start a store, or she don't get wind of any *ho*-tels. How long you figure you'll stay out there?"

"I don't know. I've never been further West than Tennessee."

"Goin' to find you a womern?"

That big Kansas gal is still right there in bed. By herself. "Maybe." He prob'ly likes big women.

"I told Margaret that's what you'd do," he scowls.

It's like he's brought her name right down out of the air where I left it.

"*Told who?*"

"Marg'ret." He drops it in a pool between us. "Margaret! My

step-sister! Miss Pepper Pot! *You* know. I told her she'd just as well stop settin' her sights on Globe Valley people that don't mean ever to have more'n passin' acquaintance with us, however much marryin' may have gone on for generations, churched or unchurched!"

"You *did?*"

I stand up in the wagon bed. The mules lurch forward and I topple right back down in the seat. I have to pull and shout to hold 'em. Garvy's gun drops under the back wheel. He stoops for it, and I give the reins an extra twist under my arm and reach down for mine.

"You've not done much to help friendly relations along," I say.

He blows dirt off his rifle, takes two unsteady steps backwards to be even again with me and the wagon seat. His good eye has narrowed until it and the slit are the same except for a glint of blue.

"But *you* have!—writin' her all the time. Oh, I know when it started! It started when you was kids, four years ago. You an' her walked home from church where me an' Samantha an' some others was havin' a little disturbance out in the grove, an' we couldn' find Marg'ret but I learnt later how it was because one o' the McCautherns was servin' out likker down at his still in the gorge an' seen you both holdin' hands out on Gragg Bluff. And she ain't never forgot. It's just made her more hoity-toity then ever. Well. Now Pa's gone, *I'm* the head o' the fam'ly an' I'll be the one to say who's in it. I aim to turn her around an' set her straight an' turn her hopes in the direction of somebody more her kind. *A sight better lookin', too,* whether he's eddicated or not, or got bottom land, or cotton hid away so good not even Tecumseh Sherman could find it!"

His face is livid. With a jerk, he thumbs the canteen strap back around his shoulder. Thunder rumbles. The big cloud has shut out the sun. He tosses his gun over his shoulder, stalks off down the road. There's no way I can warn them in the Globe who is comin'. I groan, let the brake rod fall back, and cluck to Pomp and Circumstance. But when I look back at the turn, I see him plunge down a path west, right of the road, one I had not even seen.

MARGARET McKAMIE

THE first thunderstorm goes around. The second hits, an' him right in the middle of it. As he bursts in the door it splatters, and it settles to a roar when he slams it behind him. Drenched, he knocks the water out of his little blue so'jer cap, tosses it on the table. I move my muslin aside. I don't want it dripped on. Ma brought it from Lenoir to make me a new waist.

"Good evenin', Heese." If he can't speak civil I can.

"Where's Ma an' the boys?"

"Over on Nameless diggin' 'sang."

"Why ain't you with 'em?"

"Same reason you're not. They didn' ask me."

He swaggers to the table, stands gripping it with both hands, stiff-armed above me. "No, you got to stay here an' sew a fine seam, ain't you, Miss Lacy Drawers? What you makin' 'em for—to git married in?"

He is drunk. He is mean. I don't know anything in the mountains meaner'n he is when he's like this! For a minute I see the rattlesnake on the wall at the Old House Place. But I feel a special veenom in him now. The one eye is blood-shot.

"Who you makin' them pants for?"

"It's not pants. Just a waist—a shirtwaist." Everything was nice before he busted in—just me an' my sewin' an' the sparks poppin' lazy in the fire that I made against the dampness. He don't even seem to hear what I say.

"*Who's gonna take 'em off you?*"

My face flourishes. I get weak all over from such talk. I lay a

« 237 »

tuck an' crease it in with my thumb-nail the way Aunt Chaney showed me. You *know* what a rattlesnake is. Fear was at the bottom of that. That's natural—it's even in the Bible. For the thousandth time, I try to figure what makes Heese like he is. He would have harmed Lewises if they hadn't shot him. Who was afraid there? *Lewises* weren't afraid. They just did what they had to do same as Tom stoned the rattler. But a man is not a snake. What did Heese have ag'inst Lewises that he had to strike atall? What does he have ag'inst *me? Is it my fault?* Pa's death has just seemed to make him uneasier.

"What's the matter with you Heese?" I draw out my thread. "Besides bein' drunk?"

He jerks a chair to the table, flops down in it, pulls out that little stone on a thong that he always carries, twirls it 'round his fore-finger. A drop of water sprinkles on the muslin in my hand. I move it and the knife that is washed an' lyin' under it, the one I was parin' potatoes with.

He tilts his chair back, spins the whirligig the other way. When he speaks ag'in it's natural. Nice as passin' the time of day.

"Neil McCurry's back home."

"So?" I tighten my arms ag'inst my sides to check a shiver—somebody walkin' over my grave.

"Neil's been all over the world. Englund, France, even Chiney, I guess—got paid for it, too."

I put all my strength into givin' no sign of my feelin' though my lips tingle at mention of him. The man I want is one you'd put out your arms toward—whether here or far away—not one you'd have to start by pushin' away.

Heese lets his play-pretty reel off the end of his finger. It flies across the table, nests against my cloth.

Lightning! I start. Heese don't budge. On it comes the sound of some old hemlock bein' split to the heart back up on a crag. Thunder rolls over us.

"I hope Ma and the boys are safe." I have come to the end of my seam, misplaced the needle. We have only two left. I run my fingers over my waist, search in my apern. Heese sits watchin' me an' grinnin' kind of eerie. Even his lost eye is like it's back ag'in speculatin' what he's goin' to say next. I get up and crack the shutter for light. Rain floods from the eaves in sheets. I prop the bar in the shutter for air—I didn' really need the fire only for comp'ny and the dampness.

"We been thinkin' 'bout havin' a little hoe-down over at our house," Heese shoves his hands deep down in his pockets stretchin' his pants too tight over his man's self, even with that fine cloth. "We thought we'd have a little celebration for Neil gittin' home."

I'm down on the floor now feelin' for the needle. Ma has every right to scold me if it's lost, we have just two left and a bodkin.

I come up by the table. "No thanks."

He brings the front legs of his chair down with a plop that shakes the house.

"*Why not?*" His face is flourished so red it makes his hair white.

My fingers move over my breasts seekin' the prick of a needle. I move the cloth—you know how you keep lookin' the same place twice when you have lost somethin'. I pick up the knife.

"Why not?" he says again.

"Well, it don't seem seemly—Pa and Wash dead such a short time and the church not yet had the public funerals." I've wondered sometimes if one way to purge Heese wouldn't be just to let him get as mad as he could—put all his hate feelin's like in a pan— Flash! Whoosh!! the way Samantha said he did the mosquitoes at Kinston. "Besides," I say, "I don't want to go!"

"Oh, you *don't!!*" he has got up, towers over me. I wouldn' be supprised to see him lift his arms swayin' like one o' those outlandish stick-like insects that lands in the spring house and gets its prey by scarin' it to death. But he can't scare *me*! If he wants to have it out once an' for all, it seems this is as good a time as any.

"*No I don't want to go!* Who'd there be to come? Little boys an' old men! Maybe a cripple or two, God help us! I'd rather stay here an' be lonely." Be as hard as it is! Rub your nose in it like you liked it! And don't be afraid! Aunt Chaney says sooner or later everybody has to make his peace with loneliness. I begin now to see what she means!

The one blue eye in his leathery face bores into me. "You're gonna be lonely all right, Miss Banty Feathers! Miss High Sights! Miss Parky Pine! An' for the rest o' your life! Unless you bring your sights out o' the valley an' rest 'em here on the mountain 'mongst livin' folks around you!" He lets out a string o' words I can't say. "James Lewis, your little round-faced tow-headed knee baby, is leavin' here. He is goin' away. To Kansas. He aims to find hisself a wife. He told me so not more'n two hours ago!"

"*I know that!*"

"*You seen him then!!*"

"No!!" I'm gripping the knife so tight it cuts my fist. Lightning ag'in! I wait 'till thunder has shaken the house. "Heese! What is the matter with you?! Why must you always be hurting something or somebody? You set fire to your own woods 'just to see the wild horses run!' you said. Oh I know! Samantha bragged about it, an' about a lot else. You attacked a poor Irish Peddlar with a stave and you got the worst of it—Hah! I saw you tease a poor half wit on Muster Day!" Now I'm bawling out loud! If only Ma would only come! "*Why do you hate me so!!*"

"You sly little sunburnt sneak! I'll dribble your feathers in the dust an' make you squirm!"

I have taken my distance to the door. I could always out-think him and I can out-run him too. He has reached for his rifle, draws on his cap slow but has not moved toward me.

"I'll tell you who you hate! *You! You! YOU!!* Now Pa's gone you're scareder an' lonesomer than anybody! *Yet there's good in you, too, Heese!* I don't know anybody could do some of the things you've done!" I'm pleadin'—I don't care if he does shoot me! "Why don't you start respectin' yourself? And bein' worthy of it! Then you'll get respect from other people!"

I drop the crumpled muslin from my hand. "Who's the little scared tow-headed knee baby? *You! You! YOU!!*"

To give me time to run, I grab the bloodstone on its thong from off the table an' throw it with all my strength into the fire.

"I'll attend to my own affairs, Heath Garvy! You'll never be the guardeen of me!!"

Mud weighs my flying feet, rain chokes my sobs as I wait to die, wait for the shot that will loose my insides on the ground the way Tom did the snake's! Rain streams down my face 'til I feel I'm part of all the agony ever was in the world. Rain cools the ache in my breast until I fall stumblin' an' whimperin' into Aunt Chaney's door!

JAMES LEWIS

AND that's where I found her.

"Margaret, I've come to ask you to marry me and don't stop me 'til you've heard me out, or start lookin' at all the reasons why we shouldn't because there's a hundred of 'em, an' I'll mention three an' I don't want you to mention any.

I'm not handsome.

I don't have a thing to offer you but my grandfather's old peach orchard and I don't even have it yet.

And Heath Garvy is your step-brother.

I believe all but the first can be overcome.

If you want to go to school, maybe we can fix it for you to go to one, Davenport College, they've just started in Lenoir. But I already asked and they don't take boys unless they can sing or paint pictures, an' I don't think I would like bein' away from you.

I've never seen any girl could come up to you, and *if you'll have me*, I'll thank you to say so with one of those not-gram'paw's kisses you gave me that evening on the cliff. *If you wont have me*, just don't say anything and I'll go on to Kansas."

There's no gram'paw's business in it but holdin' her I remember how the first Lewis cut all around his fields, got back to where he started from, and called it the Globe.

SAMANTHA

"Well, go on an' open it!"

"I'd druther for you to."

We set down at the table an' Heath takes out his knife to cut the string.

"Save the string! We'll need it packin'." We've made up our minds for Heese to run for the legislatur' on the Republican ticket so we're goin' to move down on Linville River—there's more votes in the precints than what there is up here on the Grandfather, and more goin' on—a reg'lar ron-dee-voo of mountain sassiety—that's what Shep' Dugger calls it, anyway.

Heese unwinds the string, hands me the box to take off the paper. "What does this writin' say?"

"Le's see—" The farther off I hold things these days the better I can read. Damned if I ain't too young to have my eyesight failin'. I turn my head on one side. "It reads—here, gimme your finger. You can learn to spell as good as I can. You *got* to if we're goin' to Raleigh. It says

>'Mr. and Mrs. William Angel Garvy
>Haw Branch
>Grandfather Mountain
>Watauga County
>North Carolina v-i-a Globe P. O.'"

He scowls. "What does that mean, *v-i-a* the Globe?"

"I dunno—mebbe somebody didn' know how to spell u.s.a. or somep'n. Damned if I've not got to try me on a pair o' glasses next time I go to Lenoir. Here—there's some more writin' up here in the corner. It reads

>'From William E. Davis, Jr.
>Cincinnati Gazette
>Cincinnati, Ohio.'

That's them, all right!"

"He's got me to thank the cam'ra never got wet."

We unwrap the box, rollin' the paper out careful on the table. What's inside is a little box itself. Or a little book—dark leather decorated pretty on the outside, fastened with the teeniest little gold hook I ever saw! Inside on the left, it's fancy red velvet—just beautiful! And on the inside is *us!*—Heese an' Sam an' me settin' ag'inst the wall . . .

Well, I don't know what we been expectin', anyway not anything like what it is. After I get over my first disappointment, I take another long look, an' say

"*You got both eyes!*"

He takes the pitchur from me an' looks at it so long I haf' to stand up an' peer over his shoulder.

After a while he says "You're a better lookin' woman than that, Samantha."

"Well—" I smooth my hair back that's growed out thick from bein' cut when I went off to the war, "it ain't like we'd had time to fix for it. I wisht you'd a-had on your Union uniform—Ain't Sam *little!* All eyes! Here, Sam! Quit pullin' the dog's tail an' come here an' look at your pitchur!"

He trots over, takes one passin' look, goes back to tormentin' the dog. He does love to pester our new young Plott hound.

"Gimme! I want to see it better!" I hold it further off. "There's not a p'izen spot on it—you know, like Davis said there might be? William Angel Garvy! I always did say you are the handsomest man in the world!"

He kinda stretches his arms up like he's goin' to yawn, pleased-like, an' then brings 'em down around me like a vize. "Wait for gosh sake! Gimme time to lay the pitchur down!"

We rassle around on the floor a while makin' love an' I do say he ain't only the handsomest man in the world but the most satisfyin'est! Sam gets in it too t'ords the last, an' it ends like usual with each tryin' to give the other a bop on the bottom without gettin' bopped hisself.

I get up then red an' flourished, outa breath an' I smooth down

« 243 »

my clo'es. I been tryin' to get ust to skirts ag'in. I doubt if ladies in Raleigh wear pants, they didn' at Kinston, anyway.

"Whur's the pitchur? My God, we done lost the pitchur!" We all scramble around on our hands an' knees lookin' for it, under the paper an' everywhur, an' Sam gets in it too, without knowin' what it's all about, only it's some kinda fam'ly calamity!

"There it is—mashed down in the trap door!" I open it careful. "It ain't hurt."

"We got to find a safe place for it."

"How 'bout up on the mantel by the Hamby clock?" We call it the Hamby clock because it come outa the Hamby house.

"Wait a minute!" I say, "Give it here."

I lay the pitchur on the table flat, with its back up, the part that's plain bronzy gold, an' I go find me a nail. I seat myself down at the table.

"Samantha! What are you goin' to do! You'll *ruin* the pitchur, scratchin' on it thataway!"

But I keep on scratchin' 'til I have spelt it out across the back. I hold it out at arm's len'th an' look at it. Then I reach for Heese's big pole of a finger an' guide it along the letters.

They say
        ALWAYS TOGETHER

BIBLIOGRAPHY

WHILE I know a bibliography is not customary with a work of fiction, I think some readers (especially those who have helped me,) may be interested in the reading I've done to authenticate this story. Sources preceded with an asterisk * are out of print, though I own most of them.

IN A CLASS BY THEMSELVES FOR MY PURPOSE ARE THESE FOUR:

*Arthur, John Preston. *History of Watauga County, N. C.* Richmond, Everett Waddey Co., 1915.
   A rare old gold mine of material. Copies almost unobtainable now. I used my grandfather's copy.
———. *History of Western North Carolina.* Raleigh, Edwards & Broughton, 1914.
*Clark, Walter, ed. (Lt. Col. 70th Regt. N.C.T.) Histories of the several Regiments and Battalions from North Carolina in the Great War 1861–'65; Written by members of their respective commands. Goldsboro, 1901. (5 volumes).
*War Records Office. *The War of the Rebellion: A Compilation of the Official Records of the Union and Confederate Armies.* Washington, D.C., Government Printing Office, 1880–1901 (70 volumes in 127 books, Atlas, Index).
   This is indispensable to anyone trying to write about the Civil War. It is well-indexed and fascinating in its whole sweep of the Civil War. I used it hundreds of times.

HISTORIES AND GUIDES TO STUDY

Alderson and White. *Guide to the Study and Reading of Tennessee History.* Tennessee Historical Commission, 1959.
Alexander, Thomas B. *T.A.R. Nelson of East Tennessee.* Nashville, Tennessee Historical Commission, 1956.
*Ashe, Samuel A'Court. *History of North Carolina, Vol. II.* Greensboro, 1908–1925.
Barrett, John Gilchrist. *North Carolina as a Civil War Battleground.* Raleigh, State Department of Archives and History.

Boykin, James H. *North Carolina in 1861*. New York, Bookman Associates, 1961.
*Connor, R.D.W. *Rebuilding an Ancient Commonwealth*. 1584–1925 (Vol. II). Chicago, American Historical Society, Inc.
Creekmore, Betsy. *Arrows to Atoms*. Knoxville, University of Tennessee, 1959.
Folmsbee and Parks. *Story of Tennessee*.
*Goodspeed Publishing Co. *History of Tennessee* from Earliest Time to the Present Together with Historical and Biographical Skech of from Twenty Five to Thirty Counties of East Tennessee. Nashville, Goodspeed Publishing Co., 1887.
*Henry, Robert Selph. *Story of the Confederacy*. New York, Bobbs Merrill, 1931 and 1943. Written with clarity, grace and force. Chronology chart in back. I used it a lot for that.
*Humes, Thomas William. *The Loyal Mountaineers of Tennessee*. Knoxville, Ogden Bros. Co., 1888.
Johnson, Guion G. *Ante-Bellum North Carolina, A Social History*. Chapel Hill, 1950.
Lefler, Hugh Talmadge. *Guide to the Study and Reading of N. C. History*. Chapel Hill. University of North Carolina, 1955.
———. *North Carolina as Told by Contemporaries*. 1524–1956. Chapel Hill, University of North Carolina Press.
Lefler, Hugh T. and Newsom. *North Carolina*. Chapel Hill, University of North Carolina Press, 1954. Good Appendices: Lists of principal events, governors, dates of founding and naming of counties, etc.
*Lenoir, W. B. *History of Sweewater Valley, Tennessee*. Richmond, Richmond Press and Presbyterian Committee of Pub., 1916.
Mebane, John. *Books Relating to the Civil War—A Priced Check List*. New York, London, Toronto, Thomas Yoseloff, 1963.
*Merritt, Frank. *Early History of Carter County, Tennessee 1760–1861*. Master's Thesis, University of Tennessee Graduate School. Knoxville, Arthur & Smith Printing Co., 1950.
Owsley, Frank L. *Plain Folk of the Old South*. Baton Rouge, 1949.
*Preston, Thomas W. *Historical Sketches of the Holston Valleys*. Kingsport, Kingsport Press, 1926.
Ramsey, J.G.M. *Annals of Tennessee*. Kingsport, 1926.
*Railroad. *Western North Carolina Railroad Company*. Proceedings of the General Meeting of the Western North Carolina Rail Road Company at Salisbury August 30, 1855, with the Charter and By-Laws of the Company. Salisbury, N.C., Banner Office, 1855–1862. Loaned to the author by Mr. C. V. Walton of Morganton, N. C.

Randall, J. G. *Civil War and Reconstruction.* Boston, D. C. Heath & Co., 1935-1953. Good bibliography.
*Roosevelt, Theodore. *The Winning of the West.* New York, G. P. Putnam's, 1889. (4 volumes).
*Scott, W. W. *Annals of Caldwell County.* Lenoir, N.C., News Topic Printers, 1924, Johnston Avery, editor.
*Smith, Frank Piogmore. *Military History of East Tennessee 1861-1865.* Unpublished Master's thesis. Knoxville, University of Tennessee, 1936.
Sharpe, Bill. *A New Geography of North Carolina, Vols. I and II.* Raleigh, Sharp Publishing Co., 1962.
*Temple, Oliver Perry. *East Tennessee and the Civil War.* Cincinnati, Robert Clark Co., 1899.
Tennessee Historical Commission. *Tennessee Historical Markers.* Fifth Edition. Nashville, 1962.
Tennessee Historical Commission. *Tennessee Old and New, 1796-1946.* Sesquicentennial Edition, Nashville (2 volumes).
U.S. Government. General Services Administration. Information concerning veterans of the Confederate and Union Armies.
U.S. Government Printing Office. *Heads of Families at the First Census of the U. S. in the Year 1790.* 1908. (Reprinted.)
Virginia, Department of Conservation and Development. *State Historical Markers.* Sixth edition. 1948.
*Whitener, D. J. *Local History and How to Find It.* Asheville, Western N.C. Historical Association.
———. *History of Watauga County, A Souvenir.* Watauga Centennial, Boone, July 5-10, 1949.

BOOKS RELATING MORE PARTICULARLY TO THE CIVIL WAR

Barrett, John Gilchrist. (Dept. of History, V.M.I.) *North Carolina as a Civil War Battleground.* Raleigh, State Dept. of Archives and History, 1960.
Yoseloff, Editor. *Battles and Leaders of the Civil War.* New York, 1887. (4 volumes).
*Billings, John D. *Hard-Tack and Coffee,* the Unwritten Story of Army Life. Illustrated by Charles W. Reed. Boston, George M. Smith Co., 1887.
Boatnor, Mark Mayo, III. *Civil War Dictionary.* New York, David McKay, 1959.
*Browne, Junius Henry. *Four Years in Secessia.* Hartford, O. D. Case & Co., 1865.
*Clark, Walter, ed. Histories of N.C. Regts. (See above, p. I).
Catton, Bruce. *The Coming Fury.* New York, Doubleday, 1961.

———. *Stillness at Appomattox.* New York, Doubleday, 1953.
———. *U. S. Grant and the American Military Tradition.* New York, Grosset & Dunlap, 1954. Universal Library Edition.
Cochran, Hamilton. *Blockade Runners of the Confederacy.* New York, Bobbs-Merrill Co., Inc., 1958.
Commager, Henry Steele, ed. *The Blue and the Gray*, The Civil War as Told by Participants. New York and Indianapolis, Bobbs-Merrill Co., 1950.
*Derby, W. P. *Bearing Arms in the Twenty-Seventh Massachusetts Regiment of Volunteer Infantry, 1861–1865.* Boston, Wright and Potter Printing Co., 18 P.O. Square, 1883.
   Contains material on N.C. coast, New Berne, Tarboro, Kinston, Whitehall, Goldsboro, etc.
Freeman, Douglas Southall. *Lee's Lieutenants.* 3 vols. New York, Scribners, 1942.
*Gilham, William. *Manual of Instruction for Volunteers and Militia.* Richmond, West & Johnson, 1861.
Grant, U. S. *Personal Memoirs.* Introduction by E. B. Long. New York, Grosset & Dunlap, Universal Library Edition of earlier one by World Pubs. Co.
*Holden, W. W. *Memoirs.* John Lawson Monograph of Trinity College Historical Society. Durham, Seeman Printery, 1911.
*Humphreys, David. *Heroes and Spies of the Civil War.* New York and Washington, D.C., Neale Publishing Co., 1903.
*Greenville, S.C. Ladies Association. *Proceedings and Minutes, in the Aid of the Volunteers of the Confederate Army.* Durham, Duke University Press, No. XXI of Historical Papers of the Trinity College Historical Association.
*Hardee, William J. *Rifle and Infantry Tactics.* 1862.
*Haskell, Frank Aretas. *The Battle of Gettysburg.* Wisconsin History Commission, 1908.
Jones, Virgil Carrington. *Gray Ghosts and Rebel Raiders.* New York, Henry Holt, 1956.
   Guerrilla warfare, 1861–1865.
Keene, Jesse L. *The Peace Conventions of 1861.* No. 18, Confederate Centennial Studies, Tuscaloosa, Confederate Publishing Co., 1961.
*Kirke, Edmund. *Adrift in Dixie* or A Yankee officer Among the Rebels. New York, Carleton, Publisher, 1966.
*Kirk, Charles H. *History of the Fifteenth Pennsylvania Volunteer Cavalry, 1861–'65.* Philadelphia, 1906. Contains Weand, H. K. "Our Last Campaign," on Stoneman's Last Raid in Western North Carolina.
Long, E. B., ed. *U. S. Grant, Personal Memoirs.* Cleveland, 1952.

*Lonn, Ella. *Desertion during the Civil War*. New York, Century Co., 1928.
———. *Salt as a Factor in the Confederacy*. New York, Walter Neale, 1933.
    Both of the above well written by a scrupulous scholar.
*Mann, Albert W. *History of the Forty-Fifth Regiment of the Massachusetts Volunteer Militia*. Boston, 1908.
    Valuable material on New Berne (each one spells it differently!), Fort Macon, and Army life.
*Moore, A. B. *Conscription and Conflict in the Confederacy*. New York, 1924.
*Moore, John W. Roster of N.C. Troops in the War between the States. Raleigh, Edwards & Broughton, 1882. (4 volumes).
*Morton, Joseph W. *Sparks from the Camp Fire*. Philadelphia, Keystone Publishing Co., 1890.
    One hundred and fifty comrades contributed. Funny old pictures.
Poe, Clarence. *True Tales of the South at War*, How Soldiers Fought and Families Lived. Chapel Hill, University of North Carolina Press, 1961.
*Ramsdell, Charles W. *Behind the Lines in the Southern Confederacy*. Baton Rouge, Louisiana State University, 1944.
Russell, Phillips. *The Woman Who Rang the Bell*. Chapel Hill, University of North Carolina Press, 1949.
*Robertson, George F. *A Small Boy's Recollections of the Civil War*. Clover, George F. Robertson, 1932.
    The Rev. Mr. Robertson was raised on a farm near Greeneville, Tennessee, home of the Governor (later President of U.S.), Andrew Jackson.
*Roe, Alfred Seelye. *The Fifth Massachusetts Volunteer Infantry*. Boston, 1911.
    Regimental history containing material on Newbern, Kinston, Goldsboro, Tarboro and (24 years after!) a nostalgic return to these old battlegrounds.
———. *Twenty Fourth Regiment Massachusetts Volunteers*. Worcester, Mass., 1907.
    Material on Roanoke; Newbern; Washington, N.C.; Kinston; Hilton Head; Seabrook Island; Charleston; St. Augustine and Virginia during the final months of the war.
*Scott and Angel. *History of the 13th Tennessee Volunteer Cavalry, USA*. Philadelphia, P. W. Zeigler & Co., 1903.
    I wish I could buy one! Two, in fact—one for Dan Ellis' granddaughter near Elizabethton, Tenn. It has material on Ellis.

Simpkins, Francis Butler and Patton, James W. *Women of the Confederacy*. Richmond and New York, Garrett & Massie, 1936.
*Sorrel, G. Moxley. *Recollections of a Confederate Staff Officer*. New York and Washington, Neale Pubs. Co., 1905.
   Contains material on First and Second Manassas, Seven Pines, Sharpsburg, Fredericksburg, Gettysburg, the Tennessee campaigns, the Wilderness, to Appomattox.
*Spencer, Cornelia Phillips. *Last Ninety Days of the War in N.C.* New York, Watchman Publishing Co., 1866.
Street, James. *The Civil War*. New York, Dial Press, 1953.
*Tatum, Georgia Lee. *Disloyalty in the Confederacy*. Chapel Hill, University of North Carolina Press, 1934.
Tucker, Glenn. *Front Rank, the Story of North Carolina in the Civil War*. Raleigh, Confederate Centennial Commission, 1962.
Van Noppen, Ina Woestmeyer. *Stoneman's Last Raid*. Raleigh, North Carolina State College Print Shop, 1961.
Velasquez, Madame Loreta Janeta. Otherwise known as Lt. Harry T. Buford, C.S.A. Hartfort, T. Belknap, 1876.
   A woman's adventures, not always entirely credible, as soldier, spy, and secret service agent.
*Watson, William. *Life in the Confederate Army*, being the Observations and Experiences of an Alien in the South during the Civil War. London, Chapman & Hall, Ltd., 1887.
Wellman, Manly Wade. *They Took Their Stand*—Founders of the Confederacy. New York, G. P. Putnam's Sons, 1959.
———. *Rebel Boast*. New York, Henry Holt & Co., 1956.
Wiley, Bell I. *Life of Johnny Reb*. New York, Bobbs-Merrill, 1943.
———. *Life of Billy Yank*. New York, Bobbs-Merrill, 1951, 1952.
———. *The Plain People of the Confederacy*, New York, Macmillan, 1959; Baton Rouge, 1943.
Wiley, Bell I. and Milhollen, Hirst D. *They Who Fought Here*. New York, Macmillan, 1959. (See under Pictures.)
*Wright, Gen. Marcus J. *Tennessee in the War 1861–1865*. Military Organizations and Officers in both the Union and Confederate Armies.
Yates, Richard E. *The Confederacy and Zeb. Vance*. Tuscaloosa, 1958. Confederate Centennial Studies.

ORIGINAL SOURCES, UNPUBLISHED LETTERS, DIARIES

Adams, Alfred. Papers. Letter from Hazelwood, Va., Dec. 22, 1862, Duke University Library Manuscript Division.

Ardrey, William E. War Diary, 1863–1864. Microfilm. Ardrey was from Mecklenburg County. Diary contains Mine Run and Bristoe Station campaigns, Winter of 1863–'64. Duke University Manuscripts.

Battle, Cullen A. Papers. Southern Historical, University of North Carolina. Battle served with the 3rd Alabama. Excellent letter on Gettysburg.

Belcher, Granville W. Letters 1861–65, Henry County, Va. On camp near Kinston 12/23/63; Bunkers Hill, Va., July 16, 1863. Duke University Manuscripts.

Benson, Berry Greenwood. Letter on Gettysburg, July, 1863. #2636 Southern Historical, University of North Carolina.

Brown, Campbell. Letters. Vol. II, pp. 59–85 on Gettysburg. Southern Historical, University of North Carolina. Brown was AAG to Gen. Joseph E. Johnston until 1863, then Ewell. Photostats hard to read but interesting.

Byrnes, William. Diary. 1 Vol. Letters, 7/5/63, Gettysburg. Duke University Manuscripts.

Cain, Patrick, H. Papers, 1783–1940. Duke University Manuscripts.

Campbell, Colston. Papers. #135 on Gettysburg and Chancellorsville. Southern Historical, University of North Carolina.

Chunn, Willie. Papers, 1861–1884. Cab. 2, 75 items. Duke University Manuscripts. Excellent letter from Maryland right after battle of Gettysburg, July 7, 1863.

Cleek, John. Papers, 1829–1863. Cab. 2, 15 items. Cleek was in Smith's Brigade, Early's Division, Ewell's Corps. Letter July 19, 1863 from Cleek's Mills, Bath Co., Va., on Gettysburg. Duke University Library, Manuscript Division.

Click, Jacob B. Letters, 1861–'67. Cab. 2, 30 items. Mostly to girls and rather silly, but good contemporary feeling. Small amount on Gettysburg. Duke University Manuscripts.

Confederate Papers. Miscellaneous collection. Southern Historical, University of North Carolina. #172 is fragment on Gettysburg, unsigned but eloquent.

Day, W. A. Memories of the Old Days, Iredell County, Back Creek, 1844. Excerpt copies by Raymond L. Hefner 9/12/50, inserted in Western N.C. Railroad Proceedings lent me by C. V. Walton, Morganton, N.C. (See above.)

Dandridge, Carolina Danske (Redinger). Papers. Southern Historical, University of North Carolina. On affairs at Gettysburg June–July, 1863.

Deaderick, Adeline McDowell. "Facts transpiring within my knowledge during the war in 1863 or '64." Concerns depredations of bushwhackers and other afflictions at her home on Nola Chucky, Tennessee. Typed copy given me by Mrs. Mary Hardin McCown, Johnson City, Tenn.

Embree, Elihu. Daybooks of the Pactolus Iron Works, 1811–1828. #2620 Southern Historical, University of North Carolina.

Erwin, George Phifer. Letter about Gettysburg casualties. #246 Southern Historical, University of North Carolina.

Espey, Joseph. Papers. #3349 Southern Historical, University of North Carolina. Concerns Clinton, Tenn., also Loudon and Lenoir's Station.

Furebaugh, Sam A. Diary. #3109 Southern Historical, University of North Carolina. On battle of Gettysburg.

Gooding, Zephaniah W. Papers, 1832–1872. Duke University Manuscripts.

Grimes, Bryan. Papers. #292 Southern Historical, University of North Carolina. Relates particularly to the battle of Gettysburg.

Harper, George W. F. Diaries, 1838–1921, Lenoir, N.C. These are my grandfather's diaries. Originals in Southern Historical, University of North Carolina. We have copies. Major Harper served in the 58th N.C. Regt. in Tennessee and Georgia, 1863–1865.

Holland, Martha. Letters. #3324 Southern Historical, University of North Carolina. The Hollands were from McDowell County. Husband served with Confederate army (Col. Patmer) in Kentucky and East Tennessee.

Holley, Tyrner W. Papers, 1784–1885. Cab. 33, 165 items. Duke University Manuscripts. On Gettysburg battle, letter July 10, 1863, very vivid. Holley was from Chester, S.C., Hampton's Legion.

Holden Papers. N.C. State Department of Archives and History. Raleigh, N.C., 1862–1865. I looked carefully here for listings of pardons, and anything letters might reveal about this reconstruction governor's relations with Col. George W. Kirk. Such letters were indexed, but missing from folder!

Jones, Edmund Walter. (26th N.C. Regt. C.S.V.) Letters from July 17–August 17, 1863 relate to Gettysburg. April 26, 1864. #3543 Southern Historical, University of North Carolina. Jones lived in the Yadkin Valley.

Loftin, William F. Collection 1834–1863. Duke University Manuscripts. Fascinating material on military and camp life near Kinston, N.C. March–June 1862.

Kennedy, Francis Milton. Microfilm #M–3008. Southern Historical, University of North Carolina (70 frames). Kennedy was a Methodist chaplain in the 28th N.C. Regt.

Lenoir family papers. 1753–1929. 10,000 items, 48 volumes. Southern Historical, University of North Carolina. I used particularly Vol. 124: 1862–63 for material on Kinston, western N.C. farming, etc., and Gettysburg, 1863.

Moore family history. Loaned to me by Mrs. Carroll Moore, Lenoir, N.C. Included: *Sketches of Globe Valley* by W. B. Moore, R. L. Moore and H. C. Moore, Lenoir, N.C., 1887. *In Memoriam, James Daniel Moore, 1846–1905*, privately printed by wife, Martha J. Moore, Raleigh, Edwards & Broughton, 1907. *The Moores of Globe Valley* compiled by Maude Estes Moore and Mary Estes Triplette. Privately printed, Tarpon Springs, Florida, 1951 (pamphlet). *Last Will and Testament of Jesse Moore, 1826* (1 page). "The Big Poplar" by Rev. Hight C. Moore, *Progressive Farmer*, Raleigh, N.C., 8/16/04. Includes two letters of Mrs. Lula Moore and an exchange of correspondence between Finley P. Moore and my father, J. M. Bernhardt, 9/23/27 on raids on Moore homestead, 1863–1865.

Moore, Harriett Ellen. Tennessee War Diary, 1861–65. #M-2485, Southern Historical, University of North Carolina. Rather level tone of a lady's diary, inveighing against Negro troops, Lincoln etc. Nice bit about preparing mourning clothes for funeral of Negro mammy's mother.

Moore, Martin V. (Captain, C.S.A.) Papers, 1873–1901. Box 1, Item #520. Relating to organization of first company of volunteers from Watauga County, N.C. Southern Historical, University of North Carolina.

Nelson, T.A.R. Papers, 1863–1864. McClung Collection, Knoxville Public Library, Knoxville, Tenn.

Orr, Mrs. Robert Frank. Experiences of a Soldier's Wife. ms. 937.7814, Pamphlet, Box 8. McClung Collection, Knoxville Public Library, Knoxville, Tenn. The amazing story of a mother and daughter (married daughter) and their flock of children *walking* from near Hendersonville, N.C. over the mountains to Knoxville, Tenn. in Aug.–Sept., 1864 to find their husbands who had joined up with the Union.

Overcash, Joseph. Letters and Papers, 1848–1865. Cab. 5, Duke University Manuscripts. Overcash was from Deep Well, N.C. Letter May 14, 1860, discontented with CSA Army. April 15, 1863 from Fredericksburg.

Palot, Lalla. Papers, 1852–1887. Laurens, S.C. Duke University Manuscripts.

Ramsey Papers. University of Tennessee, Special Collections Room. 1859–1874.

Reynolds, Isaac V. Papers, 1862–1865. Cab. 6, 38 items. Duke University Manuscripts. Reynolds was in 16th Va. Cavalry, CSA, Col. Ferguson's command. Letter from Gettysburg, July 20, 1863.

Reynolds, Mary Jane. Letters. University of Tennessee, Special Collections Room. A wonderful collection of sprightly letters written by Mrs. Reynolds to her husband, Simeon D. Reynolds, January, 1864–June, 1864.

Shell, Helen L. and Mary Virginia. 23 letters from Yankee soldiers, some concerning Gettysburg. XVIII E, 80 items. Shepardstown, W. Va., Duke University Manuscripts.

Soldiers Letters. Miscellany. XVI-A, 577 items. Duke University Manuscripts.

Tillinghast, W. N. Papers. XVI-F, Duke University Manuscripts. Miss Tillinghast was a relative of the Lenoirs in Happy Valley and a visitor there at the time Tom Norwood was given up for lost at Gettysburg. Two letters, July 21 and 27, 1863 tell of his getting out of danger. This is further confirmed in a letter of General R. E. Lee to Gen. J. E. B. Stuart 7/10/63 in Official Records of War of Rebellion, Series I, Part XXVII, Part III, p. 991.

Vance, Zebulon Baird. Papers. Raleigh, State Dept. of Archives and History.

Wilfong, John. Papers, 1809–1903. Letters. Lincolnton, N.C. Duke University Manuscripts.

Williams, Mrs. Georgia Burdett. (of Lenoir City, Tenn.) *General William Lenoir*. Paper prepared for the D.A.R. by Mrs. Williams. She is a member of the Lenoir family.

PUBLISHED LETTERS, DIARIES, REMINISCENCES

Chestnut, Mary Boykin. *Diary from Dixie*. Boston, Houghton Mifflin, 1949.

*Creecy, Richard Benbury. *Grandfather's Tales of North Carolina History*. Raleigh, Edwards & Broughton, 1901.

Dawson, Sarah Morgan. *A Confederate Girl's Diary*. Bloomington, Indiana University Press, 1960. Civil War Centennial Series.

*Ellis, Daniel. *Thrilling Adventures of Daniel Ellis, the Great Union Guide of East Tennessee, written by Himself*. New York, 1867.

This is considered to have been ghost written and I think due to classical allusions, etc., undoubtedly is. Copies are impossible to get so I had a typist copy the book for me. Robey Barton Brown, CSA, bought up all copies he could find and destroyed them because one illustration showed him doing a dance around the hanging bodies of Union men.

Freemantle, Lt. Col. James A. *The Freemantle Diary*. Boston (reprint 1954).
———. *Three Months in the Southern States*. Edinburgh & London, 1863.
Hamilton, J. G. de Roulhac. *Correspondence of Jonathan Worth*, Vols. I & II. Raleigh, Edwards & Broughton, 1909.
*Harris, Nathaniel E. *Autobiography*—The Story of an Old Man's Life with Reminiscences of Seventy Five Years. Macon, J. W. Burke Co., 1925.
   By a former governor of Georgia who grew up in East Tennessee.
*Harper, G. W. F. and Clark, Walter. *Reminiscences of Caldwell County, N.C. in the Great War of 1861–1865*. Lenoir, 1913.
*Harper, G. W. F. *In Memoriam of E.L.R.* Lenoir, 1908. (privately printed). The author's grandfather had this 40 page booklet printed in memory of our great aunt, Emma Lydia Rankin, a schoolteacher. At the time of Stoneman's raid, she was governess in the family of Col. Logan Carson, Pleasant Gardens (near Marion, N.C.) and the booklet includes her account of the raid there. She was a fine Latin student (her father, a Presbyterian minister, taught his daughters Latin as he drove them around on his calls), and this shows in her clear style.
Hesseltine, William B. *Dr. J. G. M. Ramsey, Autobiography and Letters*. Nashville, Tennessee Historical Commission, 1954.
Johnston, Frontis W. *The Papers of Zebulon Baird Vance, Vol. I, 1843–1862*. Raleigh, State Dept. of Archives and History.
Malone, Yancey Bartlett. *Whipt 'em Every Time*. Jackson, McCowat-Mercer Press, 1960 (reprint).
   Very human and vivid soldier's style.
*Post, Lydia Minturn. *Soldiers' Letters*. New York, 1865.
*Ragan, Captain R. A. *Escape from Tennessee to the Federal Lines*. Washington, D.C., James H. Dony, 1910.
   Ragan was one of the pilots who conveyed men to Kentucky 1861–65. McClung Collection, Knoxville Public Library, Knoxville, Tenn.
*Whitaker, Rev. R. H. *Incidents and Anecdotes*. Raleigh, Edwards & Broughton, 1905.
   A very human and funny series of stories with funny line drawings, about old times in N.C. Rare book.

BIOGRAPHIES

Camp, Cordelia. *Governor Vance, A Life for Young People*. Asheville, Stephens Press, Inc., 1961.

Cleves, Freeman. *Rock of Chickamauga*, The Life of Gen. George H. Thomas. Norman, University of Oklahoma Press, 1948.
*Dannett, Sylvia G. L. *She Rode with the Generals*, the True and Incredible Story of Sarah Emma Seelye. New York, Thomas Nelson and Sons, 1960.
   Another woman who impersonated a man in the Civil War.
*Dowd, Clement. *Life of Zebulon B. Vance*. Charlotte, N.C. Observer, Observer Printing House, 1897.
Dupree, A. Hunter, *Asa Gray*. Cambridge, Belknap Press of Harvard University, 1959.
   Beautifully made and beautifully printed biography of the naturalist who made a collecting trip into the N.C. mountains in 1843.
Freeman, Douglas. *R. E. Lee*. 2 vols. New York, Scribners, 1934-35.
*Lytle, Andrew Nelson. *Bedford Forrest and His Critter Company*. New York, 1931.

JOURNALS, MAGAZINES AND PAMPHLETS

*American Bemberg Corporation; Beauknit Fibres; N. American Rayon Corp.; Elizabethton, Tenn. "The Watauga Spinnerette," XXIV, iii, April, 1949, 10-39 to 41 contain article on Daniel Ellis, Union pilot, whose home was near Elizabethton, Tenn.
   Pamphlet given to me by Mr. Lewis Taylor, Industrial Relations Director, Beauknit Fibres.
Deyton, John Basil. *The Toe River Valley in 1865*. N.C. Historical Review, XXIV, iv (October, 1947).
Johnston, Frontis W. *Zebulon Baird Vance, A Personality Sketch*. N.C. Historical Review, XXX, ii (April, 1953).
*Lenoir City, Tenn. *Golden Jubilee Souvenir Program*. 1907-1957.
   Contains pictures of home of William Ballard Lenoir (1821 and *still standing and should be preserved*) and cotton mill (pretty as Williamsburg!) 1837. Booklet presented to me by a Lenoir descendant, Mrs. Georgia Burdett Williams and Mr. Clarence Burdett.
Brown, Louis A. *Correspondence of David Orlando Nantz and Amanda Nantz*. N.C. Historical Review, XXVI, i (January, 1949), 41.
   Nantz was a guard at Salisbury prison during part of his CSA service. Letters deal with scarcities of commodities etc.
New Bern. *Confederate Centennial Committee*. Battle of New Bern, 1862-1962 & other programs.
Newsome, A. R. *John Brown's Journal of Western Travel in Western N.C. in 1795*. N.C. Historical Review, IX, iv (October, 1934).
Phifer, Edward W., M.D. *Slavery in Microcosm*. Burke County,

North Carolina, Journal of Southern History, XXVIII, ii (May, 1962).

———. *Certain Aspects of Medical Practice in Ante-Bellum Burke County.* N.C. Historical Review, XXXVI, i (January, 1959).

Raper, Horace W. *William W. Holden and the Peace Movement in North Carolina.* N.C. Historical Review, XXXI, iv, 479, October, 1954.

Rights, Douglas Le Tell. *Salem in the War between the States.* N.C. Historical Review, XXVII, iii (July, 1950), 277.

Torrence, Leonidas. *Letters.* N.C. Historical Review, XXXVI, iv (October, 1959).

ECONOMICS, COMMUNICATIONS, SHORTAGES

Carolina Watchman. Salisbury, N.C. February–October, 1866. Mail Routes and P.O. conditions in western N.C.

Cunningham, H. H. *Doctors in Gray.* Baton Rouge, Louisiana State University Press, 1950, 1960.

Jones, John B. *A Rebel War Clerk's Diary.* Philadelphia, 1866.

Klingberg, Frank W. *The Southern Claims Commission, Vol. I.* Ed. Galbraith, Burr, Brainerd, Dyer. Berkeley and Los Angeles, University of California Press, 1955.

Lonn, Ella. *Salt as a Factor in the Confederacy.* N.Y., Walter Neale, 1933.

Massey, Mary Elizabeth. *Ersatz in the Confederacy.* Columbia, University of South Carolina Press, 1952.

Jordan, Weymouth T. *Herbs, Hoecakes and Husbandry.* Tallahassee, Florida State University, 1960.

Porcher, Francis Peyre. *Resources of the Southern Fields and Forests, Medical, Economical and Agricultural.* Charleston, Walker, Evans and Cogswell, 1869.

Post Routes in N.C. 1883. C-912, North Carolina Room, University of North Carolina Library.

Toombs, H. Y. "*The Postmaster at Bile Hill.*" Call #Cp 813 T672 p 1890. North Carolina Room, University of North Carolina Library.

NEWSPAPERS

Asheville, N.C. Citizen Times 8/9/53

Caldwell Messenger, Lenoir, N.C. (first issue), later the *Lenoir News Topic* (#261, July 27, 1957), 1875–1876 (earlier issues burned out).

Carolina Watchman, Salisbury, N.C., 1860–1866.

Raleigh N.C. News and Observer, March 20, 1849 and June 12, 1855.

Charlotte N.C. Observer, Gillet, Rupert, "Old Timers Love to Tell of Watauga Bushwhacking Hero." September 18, 1927.
Holston Journal, Knoxville, Tenn., Vol. I, #10. "A Religious Family Newspaper," 1861–1864; also 1863–64.
Knoxville Register, 1861–63.
Raleigh Standard, 1860–1866.

LOCAL HISTORY

Alexander, Nancy Thompson. *Here Will I Dwell*, The Story of Caldwell County, N.C., 1956.
Arnow, Harriette Simpson. *Seedtime on the Cumberland*. New York, Macmillan, 1960.
*Bowman, Elizabeth Skaggs. *Land of High Horizons*. Kingsport, Southern Publishers, Inc., 1938.
Burnett, Fred M. *This Was My Valley*. Privately printed, Ridgecrest, N.C., 1960. Illustrated.
   The Swannanoa valley, Asheville region and their history. A labor of love.
*Campbell, John C. *The Southern Highlander and His Homeland*. New York, Russell Sage Foundation, 1921.
*Carter, Mary Nelson. *North Carolina Sketches*. Chicago, A. C. McClung, 1900.
Caruso, John A. *The Appalachian Frontier*, America's First Surge Westward. New York and Indianapolis, Bobbs-Merrill Co., Inc., 1959.
*Clewell, Henry. *History of Wachovia in North Carolina*. New York, Doubleday & Page Co., 1902.
*Craddock, Charles Egbert. *In the Tennessee Mountains*. Boston, Houghton Mifflin, 1887. Short Stories.
Dargan, Olive Tilford. *From My Highest Hill*. New York and Philadelphia, J. B. Lippincott Co., 1925 and 1941.
Dugger, Shepherd M. *Balsam Groves of the Grandfather Mountain*. Banner Elk, Philadelphia, John C. Winston Co., 1907.
   There is an earlier edition but I can't find my family's copy.
———. *War Trails of the Blue Ridge*. Charlotte, Observer Printing House, 1932.
Dykeman, Wilma. *The French Broad*. New York, Rinehart & Co., 1955. American Rivers Series.
Fries, Adelaide T. et al. *Forsythe, A County on the March*. Chapel Hill, University of North Carolina Press, 1949.
Guerrant, Edward O. *The Galax Gatherers*. Richmond, Onward Press, 1910.

Hickerson, Thomas Felix. *Happy Valley* (Upper Yadkin Valley of N.C. in Wilkes, later in Caldwell County). Durham, Seeman Printery, 1940.

———. *Echoes of Happy Valley*. Durham, Seeman Printery, 1962.

*Isbell, R. L. (D.D.) *The World of My Childhood*. Lenoir, Lenoir News Topic Press, 1955.

Dr. Isbell, formerly pastor and pastor emeritus of the Tabernacle Advent Christian Church of Lenoir, N.C., grew up in a prosperous section of Caldwell county lying between the Yadkin river, the hamlet of Grandin, and Kings Creek on the east. It is a "time-binding" book, containing much he remembers hearing of earliest pioneer days as well as what he lived through himself from the 1880's on. It is a little sketchy on dates and rather rambling, but like the Burnett book, above, brings back much of the tender atmosphere of times before and after the Civil War.

Johnson and Holloman. *The Story of Kinston and Lenoir County*. Raleigh, Edwards & Broughton, 1954.

*Kephart, Horace. *Our Southern Highlanders*. New York, Macmillan, 1949.

This valuable book by another who wrote and thought well is now reprinted.

Kieran, John. *Treasury of Great Nature Writing*. New York and Garden City, Hanover House, 1957.

*Mason, Robert Lindsay. *Lure of the Great Smokies*. Boston and New York, Houghton Mifflin, 1927.

*Morley, Margaret W. *The Carolina Mountains*, Boston, Houghton Mifflin, 1913.

*Neve, Archdeacon, et al. *The Church's Mission to the Mountaineers of the South*. Hartford, Church Missions Publishing Co., 1908.

Particularly good for its pictures (photographs).

*Olmstead, Frederick Law. *A Journey to the Back Country*. New York, Mason Brothers, 1860.

Peattie, Roderick W., ed. *The Great Smokies and the Blue Ridge*. New York, Vanguard Press, 1943.

Prescott, Orville. *The Undying Past*. New York, Doubleday & Co., 1961.

A collection of the world's finest historical fiction by my favorite book reviewer. The offerings have been valuable in study of detail and techniques as well as content. "The Historical novel," Prescott says, "is any novel in which the action takes place before the author's birth so that he must inform himself about its period ... men and women who lived and loved and died in a world completely different from his own." While decrying what he calls "sub-literary atrocities—cheap, clumsy, superficial and sensational historical novels," he says, "A better way to re-create the past is to write from the point of view of the people themselves who took their world for granted. What seems strange to us was only natural for them, familiar to them. By artfully casual indications of what his characters believe, what customs and conventions they follow, how they fight or worship, the novelist can make them and their age seem as understandable and vitally alive as our own."

*Raine, James Watt. *The Land of the Saddle Bags.* New York, The Council of Women for Home Missions and Missionary Education Movement, 1924.

The appearance and manner of the Margaret in *The Grandfather and the Globe* was inspired by the photograph of a mountain girl on horseback, facing page 165 of Raine's book.

*Sheppard, Muriel Early. *Cabins in the Laurel.* Chapel Hill, University of North Carolina Press, 1935. Illustrated with the beautiful photographs by Bayard Wooten.

*Skiles, William West. *Missionary Life at Valle Crucis*, in Western North Carolina. New York, James Pott & Co., 1890.

*Warner, Charles Dudley. *On Horseback, A Tour in Virginia, North Carolina and Tennessee.* Boston, Houghton Mifflin Co., 1889.

*Wilson, Charles Morrow. *Backwoods America.* Chapel Hill, University of North Carolina Press, 1935. Also illustrated with Bayard Wooten's lovely photographs.

ARTS, CRAFTS, MUSIC, FOLKLORE

Botkin, B. A. *A Civil War Treasury of Tales, Legends and Folklore.* New York, Random House, 1960.

———. *A Treasury of Southern Folklore.* New York, Crown Publishers, 1962.

Brown, Frank C. *North Carolina Folklore*, Vols. I–VI. Durham, Duke University Press, 1952. Engravings by Claire Leighton.

Hall, Eliza Calvert. *A Book of Hand Woven Coverlets.* Boston, Little, Brown and Company. 1931.

Hall, Harry H. *A Johnny Reb Band from Salem, the Pride of Tarheelia.* Raleigh, Centennial Commission, 1963.

A fascinating little book about the Moravian band of the 26th North Carolina Regiment CSV—Captain Mickey's Band.

Harwell, Richard B. *Confederate Music.* Chapel Hill, University of North Carolina Press, 1950.

Henry, Mellinger Edward. *Folk Songs of the Southern Highlands.* New York, J. J. Augustin, Publisher, 1938.

Sharp, Cecil and Olive D. Campbell. *English Folk Songs from the Southern Appalachians*. New York, London, Oxford University Press, 2 vols., 1952.
Scarborough, Dorothy. *A Song Catcher in the Southern Mountains*. New York, Columbia University Press, 1937.
Wellman, Manly Wade and Frances. *The Rebel Songster*. Charlotte, Heritage House, 1959.

PICTURES

Ketchum, Catton and American Heritage Magazine of History. *Picture History of the Civil War*. New York, American Heritage Publishing Co., 1960.
*A. M. Waddell Chapter of the United Daughters of the Confederacy, Kinston, N.C. and Kinston Chamber of Commerce. *History of Kinston*. (Folder.) Photographs of old houses still standing that were used during the Civil War, with accompanying map and key. Presented to the author by Mrs. J. A. Jones of Kinston.
*Brown, S. S. "Album of Watauga County Views and Other Scenes in the 'Land of the Sky.' " Matney, N.C., 1911.

Rare pictures of the East Tenn. and Western N.C. Railway, the old iron mines at Cranberry, Beech Mountain, Sugar Mountain, Hanging Rock, and Banner Elk scenes. Matney then (and maybe now) has a population of less than 100. How this got printed over there, I don't know. But Mr. Earl Tester of Banner Elk lent it to me and allowed me to reproduce the pictures.

Buchanan, Lamont. *Pictorial History of the Confederacy*. New York, Crown Publishers, 1951.
Corbitt, D. L. and Elizabeth Wilborn. *Civil War Pictures*. Raleigh, State Dept. of Archives and History, 1961.
*Elson, Henry W. *The Civil War through the Camera*. New York, McKinlay, Stone & Mackenzie, 1912.
Gettysburg battlefield and region. Pamphlets, pictures etc., too numerous to catalog. Anybody can get them by going up there and it is worthwhile to go.
*Horan, James D. *Matthew Brady, Historian with a Camera*. New York, Crown Publishers, 1955.

This one should have gone up there under Biography, maybe. Anyway, it's been indispensable not only to learning about Brady, but early techniques of photography. 500 photographs.

*Scenes of Lenoir, N.C. and Caldwell County. From old stereoscope slides lent me for enlarging by the late Andrew S. Nelson of Lenoir, and Mrs. Nelson. First courthouse with street scenes, first train with Zeb. Vance arriving, Episcopal church (used as a prison during Stoneman's raid), etc., etc.

Porte Crayon (David Hunter Strother) Cecil D. Eby, Jr., Editor. *The Old South Illustrated*. Chapel Hill, University of North Carolina Press.

    Reprints of the amusing pencil & pen sketches of Old South and Civil War times by a writer-artist for Harper's Magazine. No one could take The War with whole seriousness who ever once studied this book.

*Waldron & Chisholm. *With Pen and Camera thro' the 'Land of the Sky.'* Portland, Maine, 1907.

    Ninety-two 8" x 6" photographs of Western North Carolina mountains, streets, resorts. Shows Biltmore House without a tree in sight. Shows the falls Elisha Mitchell fell over and Big Tom Wilson, white bearded, sitting by the falls. He found Mitchell's body.

Werstein, Irving. The Adventure of the Civil War, 1861–1865. Paterson, N.J., Pageant Books, 1969.

Wiley, Bell I. and Milhollen, Wirst D. *They Who Fought Here*. New York, Macmillan, 1959.

    Handsome pictures with text.

*Wilson, John Laird. *A Pictorial History of the Great Civil War*. Philadelphia, National Publishing Co., 1878 and 1881.

    Large book, large print, engravings.

MAPS

Atlas. To accompany the Official Records of the War of the Rebellion. Published by Yoseloff, New York and London, reprint, 1958. 175 pages, 14" x 17".

    Indispensable. I used it over and over.

Colton's Map. Of North Carolina in 1862. 14" x 17". New York Johnson and Browning.

    Shows Virginia, East Tennessee, and South Carolina.

Hazzard, J. A. A New Map of the State of North Carolina, 1860. North Carolina Room, University of North Carolina Library.

Johnson, Betty. Map of North Carolina, 1861–1865. Locates principal forts, towns, railroads and engagements fought in the State during the Civil War. N.C. State Dept. of Archives and History (I think!).

Keith, Arthur. Cranberry Folio. North Carolina-Tennessee, 1903; North Carolina-Tennessee border, 1903.

U.S. Department of the Interior. Geological Survey, Silver Spring, Maryland.

The following Quadrangles:
 Blowing Rock, N.C. (includes Boone, Caldwell, Globe)
 Chestnut Mt. (Wilson Creek, Upper Creek)
 Cranberry (Tennessee-North Carolina boundary)
 Drexel (Gamewell through Drexel)
 Linville (Grandfather Mountain to the Beech in the West, Globe in the East)
 Linville Falls (Linville River)
 Morganton (Yadkin in northeast to "Marion Station")
 Pisgah National Forest
Hammond, C. S. Commemorative Map, Campaigns of the Civil War, Centennial Edition. (Pictures of Generals, Flags, and a text accompanying). Color.

MUSEUMS, BATTLEFIELDS VISITED

The half of the New Bern battlefield that is left is on the land of Mr. Lester Bray of New Bern, along the Neuse river. It should be preserved. It is in pretty good condition.

Gettysburg, Fredericksburg, Harper's Ferry, Lexington, Winchester, Richmond: Confederate Museum; Valentine Museum, Civil War Centennial Building.

Kinston.

PEOPLE WHO HELPED ME

I wish I had time to make this the full list—there would be many names, some of men and women aged 70 to 94 with long memories and time to talk. A few have already died.

I cannot close though without expressing my gratitude to libraries and librarians who were so kind and helpful to me during my four years of writing *The Grandfather and the Globe*:

Miss Pollyanna Creekmore, McClung Collection of Lawson McGhee Library, Knoxville Public Library, Market Street.

Mr. John Dobson, Librarian, Special Collections Room, University of Tennessee Library.

Mrs. M. R. McVey, Librarian (now emeritus) of Morganton Public Library.

North Carolina State Department of Archives and History.

Mr. William Powell, Librarian, North Carolina Room, University of North Carolina Library and assistants, particularly Dr. Noble J. Tolbert.

Miss Mattie Russell, Curator and Mrs. Irving E. Gray, Assistant Curator, Duke University Library, Manuscript Division.

All librarians and the curator of the Southern Historical Collection, University of North Carolina Library.
New York Public Library, 42nd Street Branch.

WITH ALL THIS
    you'd think
        The Grandfather and the Globe
            should have been a better book!

And it should've!